***Steve Wilson** – Director of De...*
Langley, BC, Canada

"Men need help!" That's the ... Family. For the past years ... to me. I have seen his heart's passion for ...ping men in all cultures be a biblical man. It is a treat to see an older brother take time to share biblical insights gained from his 50-year marriage to Rita, lessons gained as a lifelong learner and disciple of Jesus Christ.

***Paul Estabrooks** MA – Senior Communications Officer, Open Doors International*
London, Ontario, Canada

Dr. Cunningham and I have shared a 60-year+ friendship. As best man at his wedding to Rita (July 1, 1967), I can attest that Jim has spent his lifetime gaining insights on the 12 Primary Roles of a Man. What he shares in this text is from his heart. I have witnessed his lifelong goal to "be conformed to the image of Jesus Christ." This has happened through good times and difficult personal defeats. He speaks from his heart. I recommend this text for any man wanting to fulfill his biblical roles as a man.

***John H. Redekop** Ph.D. – Professor of Political Science*
Wilfrid Laurier University (1968-1994) Professor Emeritus, Wilfrid Laurier University
Abbotsford, BC, Canada

I have followed Jim's career here in Canada and his numerous travels overseas to teach adults as a Christian Adult Educator. Jim has a proven vision to teach adults across cultures to model their teaching after the character and methods of our Lord Jesus Christ. He has done this with personal warmth and academic proficiency. His current text is evidence of Jim's ongoing contribution to his discipline of Adult Education to fulfill his 2 Timothy 2:2 discipling vision of training others to teach others.

Eitan Israeli Ph.D. *– Professor of Adult Education*
The Hebrew University of Jerusalem,
Rehovot, Israel

Jim and I share divergent views from our religious heritage, he as a practicing Christian, and I as a semi-religious Israeli Jew. Jim has been a gracious international adult educator in his dialogues, respecting other learners' worldviews and cultures. I regard him to be a gifted thinker, communicator and facilitator in the field of adult education.

Peter Mathenge *– Pastor*
Nairobi, Kenya

Men are missing in leadership in our culture. Women – wives, mothers and daughters – are giving the predominant leadership role in the home and church. Men need practical help and courage to graciously accept and lovingly fulfill their biblical roles. Dr. Jim's book has given us biblical insights and an understandable framework for this to begin.

MEN ALIVE

MEN ALIVE

Conforming to the Image of Jesus Christ

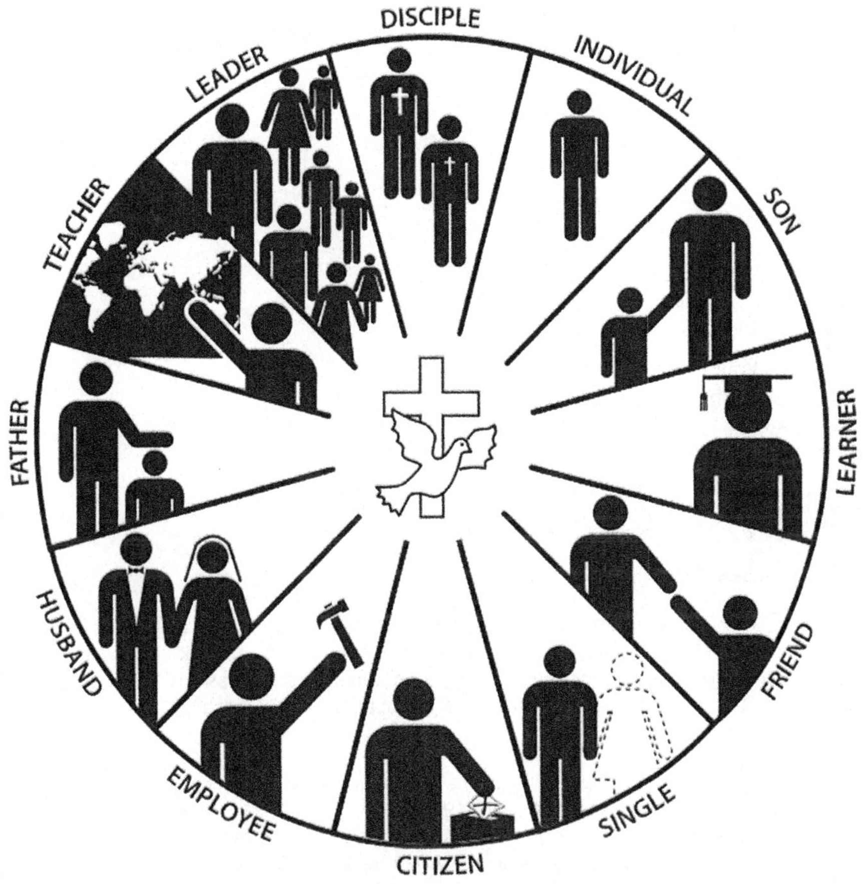

James D. (Jim) Cunningham, Ed.D.

XULON PRESS

Xulon Press
2301 Lucien Way #415
Maitland, FL 32751
407.339.4217
www.xulonpress.com

Printed in the United States of America.

ISBN-13: 978-1-54561-551-5

Primary Roles of Men

CONTENTS

Bio-Data of James D. (Jim) Cunningham Ed.D.

International Consultant in Adult Education
GO TEACH GLOBAL SOCIETY

Dr. Jim Cunningham is a *lifelong learner* with a passion – and training – to help adult learners teach adults across cultures. He has written curriculum and conducted seminars for encouraging Christians and training-trainers in numerous countries as a Consultant in Adult Education. Cunningham co-authored **Education In Christian Schools: *A Perspective and Training Model*** with Anthony Fortosis for the **Association of Christian Schools International** (ACSI). He helped compile **Standing Strong Through The Storm *(SSTS)*** for Open Doors International (ODI) with his lifelong friend Paul Estabrooks. Together they wrote the **SSTS Study Guide** and **Teacher's Guide**. Jim also gave oversight to the development of a Seminary Course for Bible Colleges in Sri Lanka entitled: **A Theology of Persecution and Discipleship.** His recent publication **The Art of Education: *A Biblical approach to Training – Teaching - Discipling Adults*,** is used in East Africa to cover a wide range of education topics from a Christian worldview.

Jim graduated from **Lakeshore Teachers College** (Toronto, ON) in 1963. After committing his life to Jesus Christ in 1964, he finished teaching Elementary School and pursued a ministry career at **Tyndale University College** (formerly London College of Bible and Missions - London, Ontario). He graduated in 1968 with a BRE (Bachelor of Religious Education) degree. While training leaders for ten years in the ministry of **Christian Service Brigade**, he received his Master of Science (M.Sc.) degree in Adult Education from **Northern Illinois University** – DeKalb, IL, in 1976. In 1979-80 Cunningham completed a year of doctoral research in Jerusalem prior to receiving his Doctorate (Ed.D.) in Adult Education from the **University of Toronto** in 1981.

In 1982 "Dr. Jim" joined the faculty of **Trinity Western University** www.twu.ca a private Christian university – in Langley, British Columbia where he taught **Philosophical Foundations in Education** until 1990 (part-time till 2002). He serves as a Consultant to **Open Doors**

International www.od.org in developing field-training models for teaching SSTS. His travels include diverse regions such as **Algeria,** Australia (2x), **Azerbaijan, Bangladesh (2x),** Belgium, **Bhutan (2x),** China (5x), **Colombia,** Cuba (3x), **Egypt, England** (3x), **Ethiopia (6x) France,** Germany (2x), Greece (2x), **Holland (4x),** Hong Kong (10x), Hungary, **India (3x), Indonesia (4x), Iraq (Kurdistan)**, Israel (1 year + 6xs), Jordan, **Kazakhstan (2x), Kenya (5x), Malaysia (4x),** Mexico, **Philippines (2x), Rwanda,** Russia (4x), Singapore (3x) Scotland, Slovakia, **South Sudan (2x), Sudan, Sri Lanka (9x), Tanzania, Tajikistan, Tibet, Turkey (2x), USA** (44 States + **Alaska (2x**) & Hawaii (6x), **Uganda,** Ukraine, Uzbekistan, Yemen, Zanzibar – and Canada (10 Provinces/2 Territories) - **(Bold = Teaching Adults**).

From 2007-2015 Jim served as a faculty member of **Wycliffe Bible Translators Canada** at the **Canada Institute of Linguistics (CanIL)** http://canil.ca/ on the campus of TWU, teaching **Training Adults Across Cultures.** He is currently the Executive-Director of **Go Teach Global Society, www.goteachglobal.com** a not-for-profit society that trains adult educators across the globe. He teaches **Theology of Persecution and Discipleship** at selected seminaries and "Trains Trainers" for **Trauma Healing Seminars** (in South Sudan/Ethiopia).

Jim and his wife, Rita married on Canada's Centennial Day, **July 1, 1967**. They attend Willingdon Church www.willingdon.org where Jim served many years as an Elder. They have two grown sons—and two gracious daughter-in-laws—who are mothers of the world's "five greatest grandchildren." Jim and Rita make their home in Langley, British Columbia, Canada. Jim's life verse is 2 Corinthians 3:5-6*"It is not that we think we are qualified to do anything on our own. Our qualification comes from God. 6 He has enabled us to be ministers of his new covenant…under the new covenant, the Spirit gives life."* (NLT).

www.goteachglobal.com

ILLUSTRATIONS AND CHARTS

INTRODUCTION

1. INDIVIDUAL

2. SON

3. LEARNER

4. FRIEND

5. SINGLE

6. CITIZEN

7. EMPLOYEE

8. HUSBAND

9. FATHER

10. TEACHER

11. LEADER

12. DISCIPLE

Introduction

As women become actively involved in the male arena men ask, "What's happening to my traditional roles?" Marshall McLuhan believed roles have become more important than goals. He stated it this way, "*The young today reject goals. They want roles.*" [1]Malcolm Knowles, a prolific writer in the field of adult education, developed his 'Taxonomy of Life Roles' with specific competencies needed to fulfill that role.[2]

Roby Kidd, my mentor at the University of Toronto, believed certain occasions in a person's life may necessitate a role change. For example: 1) reaching a peak in one's career, 2) setting adolescent children free and helping them, 3) working out a satisfactory relationship with aging parents, and 4) creating a home that has a new focus as the children leave. [3]Roby also noted, "people sometimes confuse roles with status (one's place in the order of things) or with social class (one's place on the socio-economic scale). Changes in one's role may be related to changes in personality and the growth of one's self. Each change in economic or social roles requires learning." [4]Roles can change or even overlap as one ages. One must identify their primary life roles; find appropriate role models, and learn the competencies required to fulfill these roles. This is a man's lifelong pursuit. The phrase "life roles" implies that roles are part of life but not always lifelong. Some roles may remain for life,

---

1 Marshall McLuhan, The medium is the message, accessed online 02 August 2017 at http://www.themediumisthemassage.com/the-young-today-reject-goals-they-want-roles/,

2 Malcolm Knowles, Toward a Model of Lifelong Education, August, 1972. Working paper for Consultative Group on "Concept of Lifelong Education and Its Implications for School Curriculum." UNESCO, Institute for Education, Hamburg, Oct. 9-12, 1972. ED 066 632 "For example, the abilities, skills, or attitudes a person needs to be a Friend would include such items as 'loving, empathizing, listening, collaborating, sharing, helping, giving feedback and support.'" Knowles further suggests that adults can learn life competencies: "at each developmental stage...the learning projects consultant exposes the learner to appropriate role competency models...the learner then selects a set of competencies for which learning projects would be developed."

3 J. R. Kidd, How Adults Learn. (Revised) New York Association Press, 1975, p.41.

4 ibid

but most are affected by aging or changes in relationships (e.g. the death of one's wife).

In my career, I've related to men in a variety of life roles. Many shared concerns, fears, frustrations and challenges at accepting the common changes imposed by aging and the confusing changes within one's culture. Some feel so exhausted by the changes they just want everything to stop – and return to normal. [5]The shifting roles in the traditional family make it problematic for young men to find competency models. Most, if not all, of men's life roles are learned from other males who become their model.[6] It is my thesis that the most significant male role model for any man is Jesus of Nazareth, Son of God. It is no secret that I am a Disciple of Jesus Christ. I also believe the Bible teaches principles a man might apply in fulfilling his primary life roles.

Words have power to change your thinking. Ideas can become catalysts to stimulate you towards wholesome thinking. It is my desire that this text will create a passion in you to become a *Man Alive Unto God.* My goal is to examine the competencies associated with each role. It is my prayer that you and I will become *"men alive unto God through Jesus Christ"*— (Romans 6:11) to *"build up one another"*— (1 Thessalonians 5:11) to fulfill our life roles by having *"life more abundantly"*— (John 17:6).

Life is fulfilling when we are under the control of the greatest role model possible, Jesus Christ.

---

5 http://earthquake.usgs.gov/learn/kids/eqscience.php

6 Some would argue even homosexuality is a learned behavior http://borngay.procon.org/view.answers.php?questionID=001335 Quote: "Homosexuality was once thought to be the result of troubled family dynamics or faulty psychological development…to date there are no replicated scientific studies supporting any specific biological etiology for homosexuality. Similarly, no specific psychosocial or family dynamic cause for homosexuality has been identified, including histories of childhood sexual abuse. Sexual abuse does not appear to be more prevalent in children who grow up to identify as gay, lesbian, or bisexual, than in children who identify as heterosexual." (American Psychiatric Association).

How To Use This Book

Each of the 12 Chapters describes a possible role in a man's life. Each chapter ends with a set of_competencies required to fulfill that role. The "Personal Checklist" allows the reader to choose his best answer to the question: "Do I have the competencies needed for this role?" Once completed, total your score, divide by the number of questions and give yourself a self-assessment score of your competency level for that role.

The next page outlines a number of evidences that the role is being fulfilled. Again this is a "Personal Checklist" where you circle the best answer for each to determine if you have demonstrated or evidenced this role is being fulfilled.

Then comes a page of "Projects for Investigation and Discussion." These can be worked on as an individual or with a group of men. Either way is possible with this text.

Throughout the text there are places where you can do a self-assessment as it relates to the role you are studying.

Since I'm a visual learner, the text has a number of charts and graphics. As an adult educator, I desire to receive your feedback and suggestions for how to improve this text for the future so we may continue to be *"conformed to the image of Jesus Christ."*

Thanks.
Your fellow lifelong learner,
James D. (Jim) Cunningham

1 July 2017 – the 50th Wedding Anniversary with Rita – *"the wife of my youth"*
Langley, British Columbia, Canada
www.goteachglobal.com

Chapter 1

Individual • Relationship With His Inner Self

Love your neighbor as yourself • Mark 12:30-31
(Repeated 9x's in the Bible)

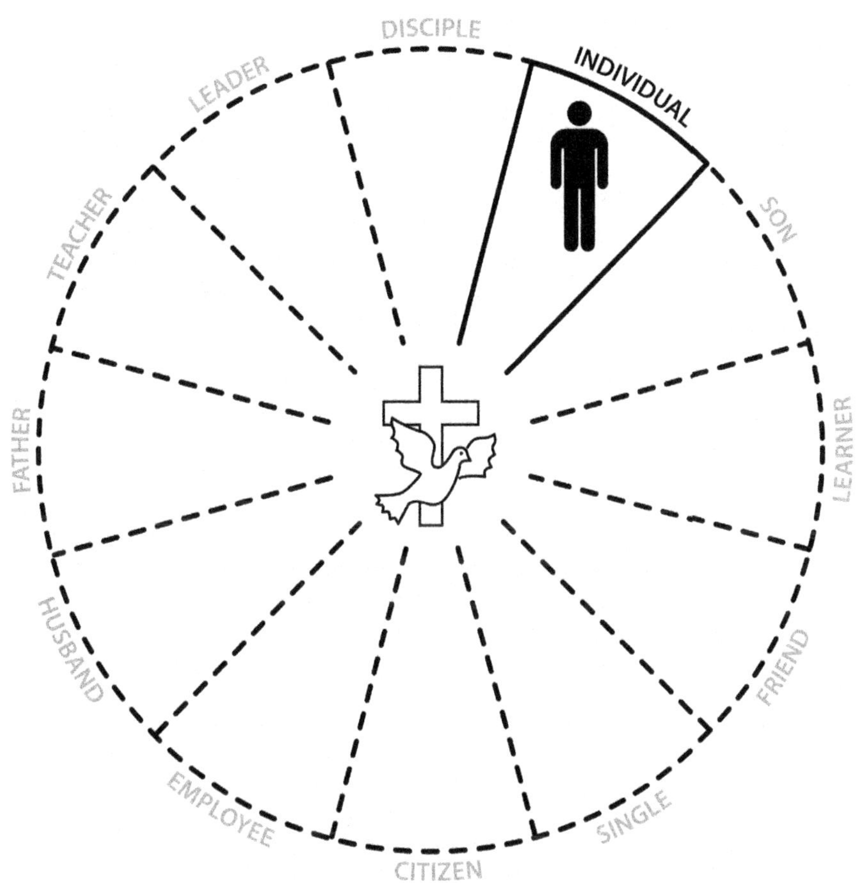

There's Only One Like Me Model

I AM UNIQUE – Self-Acceptance – The Key to Successful Service

You and I are unique: matchless and irreplaceable!

No other person on the planet is like us. Even identical twins acknowledge being different. We are recipients of a custom-design by God our Creator. In the book written by Jeremiah the prophet, God says:

> *"Before I formed you in the womb I knew you.*
>
> *And before you were born I consecrated you.*
>
> *I have appointed you a prophet to the nations."*[7]

In essence, God is saying: I made you. I know you intimately. I understand how you work. And I have a plan for your life that is *"good, acceptable and perfect…"* [8] Trust me.

Consider what makes us unique:

Father and Mother – Our father and mother shared a unique combination of DNAs that make us truly unique. Out of billions of people on Earth, only one is exactly like us.

Genetics – Our new DNA contains virtually unalterable genes and chromosomes that identify us by the color of our skin, eyes, hair (or lack thereof), body build, health factors and height.

History and Heritage – Without prior approval our lineage, mother-tongue-language, ancestry, even some foods we like were pre-arranged for us. As one born in Canada, I must still enter on my passport application the nationality of parents. It matters not

---

7 Jeremiah 1:5

8 Romans 12:1-2

how many generations they have lived in Canada. To some, I am not a Canadian; I am a Scottish-Irish-Welsh-English-Man whatever that creature may be!

People love to play Name Games. They hear your last name ends in "ski." "Oh, you must be Polish." If it ends in "sen," "You're a Swede. And an "Ng" has to be born in China, right? Maybe. You cannot do much about your heritage – or your history. It's yours. Some will shorten or alter or "Anglicize" their name but cannot change their history or heritage, culture or relatives by changing Olichny to Olsen.

God's master plan made us fulfill a particular role in history. Look at the redemptive lineage of Jesus Christ of Nazareth. Our Lord's history and heritage included the great, the godly, the least and the lowly. Tucked into the branches with Abraham, David and Hezekiah, are Rahab (a prostitute), Ruth (a Moabite), plus a Boaz and a Bathsheba. Never despise a heritage. Look for the qualities of character, strength and opportunities God can and will develop in our lives based on the unique blend of two lineages.

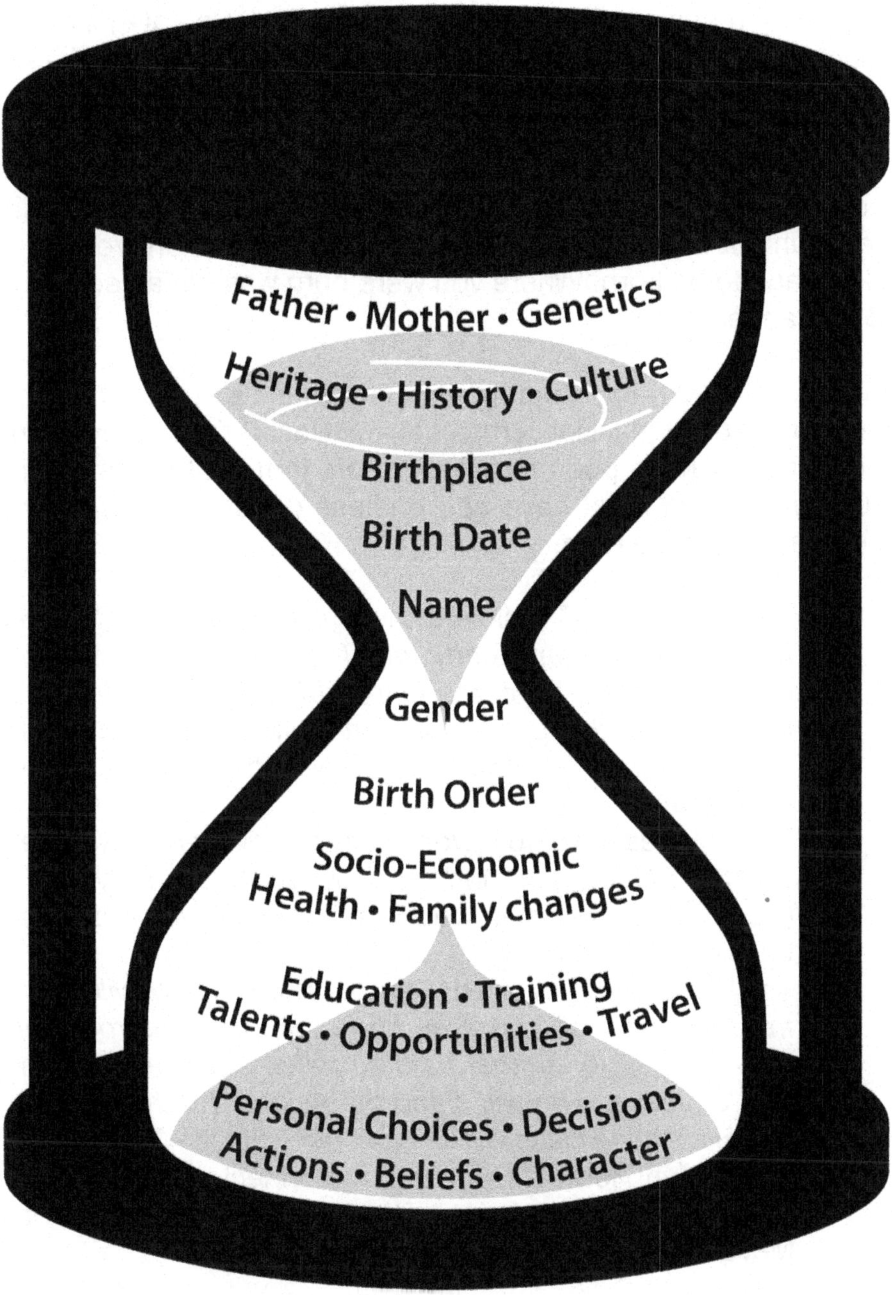

Father • Mother • Genetics

Heritage • History • Culture

Birthplace

Birth Date

Name

Gender

Birth Order

Socio-Economic

Health • Family changes

Education • Training

Talents • Opportunities • Travel

Personal Choices • Decisions

Actions • Beliefs • Character

Place of Birth – I was born in Hamilton, Ontario, Canada.

That simple statement just reduced the 50% male category to a much smaller percentage. How many men reading this book can write Hamilton, Ontario, Canada as their place of birth? Hamilton used to have large steel mills belching stinky smoke across Lake Ontario. So some may be asking: "Who would want to be born there?" That is the point. I didn't choose it. God planned it. Jehovah knows exactly where He wants every human created in His image to be born. Where you were born was not an accident. God planned it!

God wanted Jesus, Immanuel, God with us, to be born in Bethlehem of Judea. Not Jerusalem, not Nazareth, nor Egypt, but Bethlehem. Those poor Jewish scholars in the inter-Testament 400-year period must have had endless debates about where Messiah had to be born.

- The "Micah-ites" believed the prophet Micah – *"But as for you, Bethlehem Ephrathah, Too little to be among the clans of Judah, from you One will go forth for Me to be ruler in Israel. His goings forth are from long ago, From the days of eternity"* – (Micah 5:2). Messiah had to be born in Bethlehem.
- The "Hosea-ites" followed Hosea – *"When Israel was a youth I loved him, and out of Egypt I called My son"* – (Hosea 11:1). Messiah would be born in Egypt and called out like another Joseph.
- The "Isaiah-ites" followed Isaiah – *"Then a shoot will spring from the stem of Jesse, and a branch from his roots will bear fruit...Then in that day the nations will resort to the root of Jesse, who will stand as a signal for the peoples; and His resting place will be glorious"* – (Isaiah 11:1 and 10). "*Branch*" in Hebrew (*ah-Nahf*) is connected to the name of the town where Jesse's descendants lived: *Nazareth*. Messiah had to be born in Nazareth.

Three irreconcilable verses of scripture were fulfilled within a few short years. Mary and Joseph apparently planned to remain in

Nazareth and have their son born there. No effort was made in nine months to move to Bethlehem or Egypt. Perhaps they were Isaiah-ites. Mary was now a few days away from her due-date and counting. Something had to happen quickly. Caesar Augustus decreed a census that all had to return to their hometown. So Joseph loaded up the donkey. Off they went, some 100 km for Mary's divine appointment in Bethlehem. The angels in Heaven must have held their breath in hope and anticipation of their every step.

Listen. A child is born – in Bethlehem. They made it! *"Glory to God in the highest, And on earth peace among men with whom He is pleased"* – (Luke 2:14). The Micah-ites were right. Messiah was born in Bethlehem. But wait, Joseph. Herod is killing all children under the age of two in Bethlehem. Joseph obediently flees to Egypt and waits some three-and-a-half years till it is safe to return to Bethlehem. The Hosea-ites were also right. God called His Messiah out of Egypt. Joseph returns to Bethlehem. But look who is ruling in Bethlehem. Archelaus was that ungodly, unmerciful pagan who killed his brothers to secure access to his father's throne. Life would not be safe for Joseph in Bethlehem. So an angel instructs them to move back to Nazareth. The Isaiah-ites were now correct: Messiah would be called a Nazarene. All three prophecies fulfilled within (by my estimation) a brief seven-year span – after some 400 years of God appearing silent!

Your place of birth is not an accident. Our first son was born during a brief five-month stopover for staff orientation in Winnipeg, Manitoba. Twelve days later we moved to Richmond, British Columbia, some 2,400 km west, and over 5000 km from our family homes in Ontario. Why Winnipeg? I do not know. But God does. There are no mistakes on His timetable. The place you were born, both the city and the country, was the beginning of a great plan God has for your life. You had no control over it. Accept it and praise God that He loved you enough to design a perfect plan for you.

Date of Birth – Your birth-altered history! Your birth date continues to influence history to this day. It determined when you would be old enough to drive a car, vote, and become a legal adult. The people you meet, the people you influence by your arrival at a divinely appointed time in history the day of your birth or as Scripture says: *"In the fullness of time…"* [9] I was born during the 2nd World War. Why would anyone have a baby during a war, some may ask? Thousands did, and most of the babies survived. Jesus was born during the reign of the most despicable leader at that time, King Herod. *"In the fullness of time."* What a great marker for our tombstone.

HAPPY BIRTHDAY – Celebrate! Mark Twain said, *"There are only two important days in your life. The first is the day you were born. The second is the day you discover why!"* [10]

Gender– You were born a MAN! Wow! Who made that decision? God did. Before sex-selective abortions, the ratio of males to females was fairly even and sustained the survival of the species. Men, you are Men. Learn your roles, enjoy your roles, but above all learn to be *"men alive unto God."* [11]

Birth Order – First-born, and Baby of the family are two phrases identifying one's placement in the family. This becomes our 7th independent factor that each man must accept. It's apparent that we begin life with these choices made for us. We are unique. I recall one evening on a canoe trip in Tweedsmuir Park in Northern BC. Eight men sat around the campfire and the topic of birth order started. We went back and forth, expressing consensus or disagreement with the traditional studies and broad generalizations:

a) Frist-born tend to have leadership qualities.
- Was to be dedicated to the Lord
- Accustomed to being *put in charge.*

---

[9] Galatians 4:4 - *"But when the fullness of the time came, God sent forth His Son, born of a woman, born under the Law…"*

[10] https://www.goodreads.com/quotes/505050-the-two-most-important-days-in-your-life-are-the - Accessed 02 August, 2017.

[11] Romans 6:11 – *"Even so consider yourselves to be dead to sin, but alive to God in Christ Jesus."*

- High percentages of leaders are first-born (i.e. many initial astronauts etc.)

b) Second-born tend to be more competitive.

- Had to carve out a *notch of recognition* from beneath the first-born's branch.
- Sports figures and military officers rate higher in the second-born category (Supposedly many of 2nd WW tank commanders were second-born).

c) Third-born tend to be more easy going.

- These are the diplomats with people-oriented skills in their worldview.

We each identified our position and shared stories and humor about how our birth order had affected our identity. Finally, we came to the camp comedian. This guy was the most effervescent one in the group. His mischievous manner, contagious smile, and razor-quick wit, kept the crowd entertained and relaxed. When asked, "Where did you fit in Dan?" he replied, "I was number 10 in a family of 10. I had to learn to get along with everyone 'cause I was outnumbered!'"

Being #10 was every bit as unique as being the first-born. Your placement in the family order has given you insights, rights, privileges, responsibilities and opportunities that have been the proving grounds for developing character qualities God can use today, to His glory. Character counts more than birth order or credentials. Check out the story of ruddy little David, the 8th of eight boys. He became King of Israel and *"a man after God's heart."* [12]

One of the few in scripture who made it to the final bell with virtually no character flaws recorded against him was Joseph. While born #11 of 12 sons at home, by God's plan Joseph rose to be the 2nd-in-command in all of Egypt. In the birth order game Jacob was number two and Jesus was number one, but notice the absence of family placement for Abraham and the Apostle Paul. It encourages us to note that the man who is *alive unto God* can be filled with the

---

[12] I Samuel 16:1-13 and verse 7b: *"But the Lord said to Samuel, 'Do not look at his appearance or at the height of his stature, because I have rejected him; for God sees not as man sees, for man looks at the outward appearance, but the Lord looks at the heart.'"*

Holy Spirit and used in a mighty way by God, regardless of his position in the family.

Name – The angel instructed Mary, "*(You) will bear a Son; and you shall call His name Jesus, for He will save His people from their sins." Now all this took place to fulfill what the Lord through the prophet spoke: "Behold, the virgin shall be with child and shall bear a Son, and they shall call His name Immanuel," which translated means, "God with us."* [13]

What's in a name? Is it possible that your name has a greater influence on your character than most of the factors considered thus far?

I once introduced myself to a man by saying my name, "Hi, I'm Jim Cunningham…" He immediately replied: "You have a good name, a strong name. I hate mine. I would give anything to be called something else. You're so lucky." *Oi, voi vey!* How can a man hate his name? But some do. We program a person with the names we call them. The positive or negative names are like caresses or claws on the psychological back of a man's personality.

> "Hey, Stupid." (-)
> "You're the kind guy who helped me…" (+)
> "That was a wise decision." (+)
> "Why, you clumsy jerk." (-)

To rephrase an old children's nursery rhyme: "Sticks and stones may break my bones, but names can make or break me." What's in your name? Plenty! Like many parents, we chose names for our sons because we liked them. But these names accompany them, into eternity.

Jesus looked at Simon (meaning *little stone*) His disciple and said, "You shall be called Cephas" (or Peter – meaning *rock*).[14] And God

---

[13] Matthew 1:21-23

[14] John 1:42 "Jesus looked at him and said, *"You are Simon the son of John; you shall be called Cephas"* (Peter).

told Abram (meaning *exalted father*) that his name was now Abraham (*father of a multitude of nations*). [15]

When we named our first-born son David, we were aware that it means *beloved of God.* Giving him a middle name of James was in honor of yours truly. His mom and I wanted him to know he was loved by God, his Heavenly FATHER, and by me, his earthly Father. We fully anticipated seeing a son who was able to love people and communicate the love of Christ to others because of the love received while he was growing into manhood.

Michael, the name of our second son, means *the messenger of God.* A Michael fully surrendered and obedient to the indwelling power of the Holy Spirit can, by faith, be a mighty and loving messenger of God in his lifetime.

What's in your name? Do you know what it means? Do you think it matters? Perhaps it is time to consider the historical meaning of your name and the scripture verses that may relate to your name. Why was this name given to you? How might God use the qualities of your name to work His will in your life? You are unique. Your name is part of the eternal brand God has placed on you. Genesis 2:19 says: "*... and whatever the man called a living creature, that was its name.*"

Environment-Socio-Economic Background, Health and Family: The 4th dimension we call Time (Length, Width, Height, *Time*). Time is that brief line of History flowing from Eternity-Past to Eternity-Future. It goes from the Garden of Eden through the Garden of Gethsemane to the Eternal Garden by the River of Life in Revelation. [16]

---

[15] Genesis 17:5 - *"No longer shall your name be called Abram, but your name shall be Abraham; for I have made you the father of a multitude of nations."*

[16] A most helpful book to explain Time and Eternity is Journey out of Time by Arthur C. Custance. Based on a series of lectures at the Ray Stedman Foundation in Palo Alto CA in 1981. The Foreword acknowledges: "It begins with familiar concepts of space and time, which may even seem a bit dull and prosaic. But as one reads on, the walls silently move back; the commonplace begins to glow and soon one is aware of a new dimension of thought that startles and captivates the fancy." Self-published, Doorway Papers.

The events of history in process at your birth, adolescence and adult life affect your actions, beliefs and character. Some experience war, famine, prosperity, depression, peace, ideologies, government decisions, religious conflicts, and natural disasters. Two individuals born on the same day in history may respond to life circumstances the different ways. To quote an adage "the same sun that hardens the clay, will also melt the butter."

Story: Rita had two 90-year-old patients in the same room when she worked at the hospital. Both were born in the same town, raised in the same socio-economic-environment. As she picked up the food trays after lunch, the one lady said calmly, "Thank you, dearie, I haven't had raspberry Jell-O ® for years. It was delicious." Rita asked the other patient "And how did you enjoy your meal?" expecting a similar gentle response. Instead, the other 90-year-old woman pointed to her uneaten food and loudly exclaimed: "I wouldn't feed that slop to my pigs!" We may be similar in age and environment but different in reactions, prejudices, fears, goals, and beliefs.

> *"I again saw under the sun that the race is not to the swift and the battle is not to the warriors, and neither is bread to the wise nor wealth to the discerning nor favor to men of ability; for time and chance overtake them all"* – (Ecclesiastes 9:11).

Every man has what we can call: *His Past.* Life dealt you a deck of circumstances over which you had no control. Some came from a wealthy family and lived in prosperity. Some had a heritage of poverty. Some lived during a war. Some never met their father. Realize how these past factors affected you. Filter the painful memories through God's filter of Grace. Collect the distilled, pure results in the vessel uniquely designed by God, called 'You.' Become what God intended you to be. He has a unique plan that is beyond our comprehension.

"And we know that God causes all things to work together for good to those who love God, to those who are called according to His purpose" – (Romans 8:28).

What about a man's physical defects? We all have them. There is no perfect body. Ask a group, "If you could change one thing about your body, what would it be?" Each will likely name their desired change.

Story: Nick Vujicic has proven that a man's physical condition never limits what God can do.[17] Nick was born in 1982 in Melbourne, Australia, without arms and legs. "Nick has traveled around the world, sharing his story with millions, sometimes in stadiums filled, speaking to a range of diverse groups such as students, teachers, young people, business professionals and church congregations of all sizes... Nick says, 'If God can use a man without arms and legs to be His hands and feet, then He will certainly use any willing heart!'" [18]

In 1 Corinthians 6:19-20 the Apostle Paul says: *"...do you not know that your body is a temple of the Holy Spirit who is in you, whom you have from God, and that you are not your own? For you have been bought with a price: therefore glorify God in your body."*

---

17 Nick Vujicic's (pronounced VOO-yee-cheech) website http://www.lifewithoutlimbs.org/about-nick/bio/ says: "Picture your life without the ability to walk, care for your basic needs, or even embrace those you love...The early days were difficult. Throughout his childhood, Nick not only dealt with the typical challenges of school and adolescence, but he also struggled with depression and loneliness. Nick constantly wondered why he was different than all the other kids. He questioned the purpose of life, or if he even had a purpose.... his strength and passion for life today, can be credited to his faith in God... Today this dynamic young evangelist has accomplished more than most people achieve in a lifetime. He's an author, musician, actor, and his hobbies include fishing, painting, and swimming. In 2007, Nick made the long journey from Australia to southern California where he is the president of the international non-profit ministry, Life Without Limbs, which began in 2005.

18 Ibid

We praise God for what He has done for us. Everything we do – *Whether, then, you eat or drink* – or whatever you do, including the air we inhale – *do all to the glory of God.* [19]

Education-Skills-Training-Natural Abilities-Hobbies – The uniqueness of a man shows in this area more than most. First, we see his *vocational ability* – the thing he does to support himself financially (a dentist). Second, we note his *personal ability* – what he does for recreation and personal satisfaction (a mechanic). And third, we sometimes see his *interest ability* – with peripheral involvement and perhaps some ability (a writer). Each of these abilities contributes to his uniqueness as an individual. Each man is an Individual gifted by God, *one-of-a-kind* loved by God, and bestowed with abilities to be used to the glory of God.

Experiences-Cultural Influences-Travel – Two months after Rita and I married, we had nine children! We became house parents at a Salvation Army Children's Village for my final year of undergraduate studies in London, Ontario. Each child had a story as to why they were unable to live with their natural parents. I have no comprehension of what it means to be an orphan, a refugee or a battered child. I have never been institutionalized, hospitalized or served meals on a 24K gold plate! My experiences are uniquely mine. Yours are yours. *"For through the grace given to me I say to everyone among you not to think more highly of himself than he ought to think; but to think so as to have sound judgment, as God has allotted to each a measure of faith"* – (Romans 12:3).

"Blessed be the God and Father of our Lord Jesus Christ, the Father of mercies and God of all comfort, who comforts us in all our affliction so that we will be able to comfort those who are in any affliction with the comfort with which we ourselves are comforted by God" – (1 Corinthians 10:3-4). You and I bring our life experiences, both positive and painful, to serve the people God brings into our lives.

---

[19] 1 Corinthians 10:31

Life Decisions-Values-Beliefs – Will I stay single, or marry? Will we have children? How many? Do I go to grad school? What do I want to do with my life? Life is a continual flow of decisions – reactions – circumstances and timing! Each becomes part of our *Uniquization* (my word for becoming a man alive unto God through Jesus Christ).

Few live under the daily, sovereign control of the indwelling Holy Spirit. Therefore, the more decisions we make by the will and word of God the more we are guaranteed uniqueness with this *'modus operandi'* (lifestyle).

Take a moment and fill in the following chart to see how unique you are!

MY "ONE OF A KIND" UNIQUENESS CHART

1. FATHER AND MOTHER

Father: ________________ born _________ in: __________

Mother: _______________ born _________ in: __________

2. GENETICS

Father's Height: ___ Color of Skin: ___ eyes: ___ hair: _____

Mother's Height: ___ Color of Skin: ___ eyes: __ hair: _____

3. HISTORY AND HERITAGE

Father: Languages spoken _____________________________

Religious Heritage: ___________________________________

Mother: Languages spoken_____________________________

Religious Heritage: ___________________________________

4. PLACE OF BIRTH

City: _______________Province/State: ____ Country: ______

5. DATE OF BIRTH: HAPPY BIRTHDAY

Day: _________________ Month: __________ Year: ______

6. SEX

Male [___________________] Female [__________________]

7. BIRTH ORDER

I am # _____________ of ___________ siblings in my family.

8. NAME: Meaning and why chosen:

First: ____

Middle: ____

Last: ____

9. SOCIO-ECONOMIC-FAMILY

My environment while growing up (Family changes, Moves, Deaths, Adjustments)

01-06 ____

07-12 ____

13-19 ____

20-30 ____

10. SKILLS-EDUCATION-TRAINING

Elementary Schools: ______________________________

Secondary Schools ________________________________

Colleges / Universities ___________________________

Vocational Abilities ______________________________

Personal Abilities ________________________________

Interest Abilities _________________________________

11. TRAVEL-CULTURE-EXPERIENCES

Friends in the following countries/cultures: ___________________

____

12. LIFE DECISIONS-VALUES-BELIEFS

Major Life-Decisions that brought me to where I am now: _____

____

Ways God could use my unique life to bring glory to Jesus Christ.

____

____

____

____

____

Signed _________________________________ Date ____________

What Makes Him That Way?

Ever wonder why a man behaves the way he does? Let's look at Romans 6:16-23.

"Do you not know that when you present yourselves to someone as slaves for obedience, you are slaves of the one whom you obey, either of sin resulting in death, or of obedience resulting in righteousness? But thanks be to God that though you were slaves of sin, you became obedient from the heart to that form of teaching to which you were committed, and having been freed from sin, you became slaves of righteousness. I am speaking in human terms because of the weakness of your flesh. For just as you presented your members as slaves to impurity and to lawlessness, resulting in further lawlessness, so now present your members as slaves to righteousness, resulting in sanctification. For when you were slaves of sin, you were free in regard to righteousness. Therefore what benefits were you then deriving from the things of which you are now ashamed? For the outcome of those things is death. But now having been freed from sin and enslaved to God, you derive your benefit, resulting in sanctification, and the outcome, eternal life. For the wages of sin is death, but the free gift of God is eternal life in Christ Jesus our Lord."

In essence, there are only two Masters a man may serve. He is either the servant of sin (disobedience) or obedience. When a man becomes a *"follower-servant-disciple-obeyer"* of Jesus Christ, he stays on Earth. No immediate transfer to Heaven. He is still in a world where the forces of sin are in control. But now a change takes place.

The new Christian man enters what the Bible calls *Spiritual Warfare.* Satan (the Deceiver), our Enemy, has been given control of the world outside of man. After a man turns the controls of his life over to Christ, the Holy Spirit takes up residency in his heart. [20] So the

---

20 1 Corinthians 6:19-20 says: *"Or do you not know that your body is a temple of the Holy Spirit who is in you, whom you have from God, and that you are not your own? For you have been bought with a price: therefore glorify God in your body."*

battle lines are now drawn up. The Holy Spirit is within (inside). Our Adversary is without (outside). But tucked into this picture is a little force called *sinful nature* that remains inside us until we die and meet Jesus in Heaven in our transformed-sinless resurrected body. Our sinful nature remains inside us like our Enemy's 5th column [21] – *defeated but not eliminated.* At best our sinful nature can only be leashed and controlled by the Holy Spirit.

Before going further, let's clear up some items.

Our Mind is our assigned domain. [22] God controls all of Creation and the Universe. Satan, a fallen, disobedient Archangel (equal in power and authority only to Michael the Archangel), has been given limited authority over Earth, *defeated but not eliminated.* As men, we have responsibility for controlling our minds! "*Have this attitude in yourselves which was also in Christ Jesus, who, although He existed in the form of God, did not regard equality with God a thing to be grasped, but emptied Himself, taking the form of a bond-servant, and being made in the likeness of men. Being found in appearance as a man, He humbled Himself by becoming obedient to the point of death, even death on a cross"* – (Philippians 2:5-8). This *man-mind-attitude* is one of obedience and submission to the will of the Father. We are to keep our minds thinking about things that are true and honorable and right and pure and lovely and of good repute, excellent and worthy of praise.

---

21 https://en.wikipedia.org/wiki/Fifth_column A fifth column is any group of people who undermine a larger group—such as a nation or a besieged city—from within, usually to aid an enemy. The activities of a fifth column can be overt or clandestine. Forces gathered in secret can mobilize openly to assist an external attack. Military personnel also extend this term to organized actions. Fifth column activities can involve acts of sabotage, disinformation, or espionage executed within defense lines by secret sympathizers with an external force. (Accessed 20 April 2016).

22 *"For those who are according to the flesh set their minds on the things of the flesh, but those who are according to the Spirit, the things of the Spirit. For the mind set on the flesh is death, but the mind set on the Spirit is life and peace…"* – (Romans 8:5-6).

[23]Proverbs 23:7 teaches a clear principle: *"As he thinks within himself, so is he."* Our responsibility as men is to let the Holy Spirit control our minds and tell us what to think in agreement with the will and Word of God.

Our Adversary is limited in his power. He is not omnipresent, nor is he able to live in us, like the Holy Spirit can. Satan is real – but external. Eve saw him in the Garden of Eden in the form of a serpent. [24] James tells us to resist him. And when resisted he will flee. [25] Peter tells us, that Satan goes about like a roaring lion seeking whom he may devour. [26] The Allied forces landed in France on D-Day, June 6, 1944. However, the war did not end until VE-Day, May 9th, 1945 after Hitler committed suicide. Three key things to remember: Satan is alive. Satan is powerful. But Satan is defeated. Jesus' death at Calvary became D-Day for Satan when Jesus rose from the dead. Satan knew he was Defeated. But Satan will not be destroyed until Christ returns at the end of this age. That will be our Lord's VE-Day over Satan. [27]

Our struggles begin in our mind. James says, "*Let no one say when he is tempted, "I am being tempted by God"; for God cannot be tempted by evil, and He Himself does not tempt anyone. But each one is tempted when he is carried away and enticed by his*

---

[23] The full verse says: *"Finally, brethren, whatever is true, whatever is honorable, whatever is right, whatever is pure, whatever is lovely, whatever is of good repute if there is any excellence and if anything worthy of praise, dwell on these things"* – (Philippians 4:8)

[24] See Genesis 3:1-4

[25] James 4:7

[26] 1 Peter 5:8

[27] On a personal note, I have a 1st Cousin buried in a Canadian Military Cemetery in Holden, Holland (The last cemetery before the war ended May 9th 1945). He died April 29, 1945 – ten days before Germany officially surrendered. Spiritually speaking we will have "casualties" up to the last moment before the Lord returns. Stay on guard my brothers. As the old song says, *"It's a battlefield brother, not a recreation room. It's a fight and not a game. Run if you want to, flee if you must, but I came here to stay!"*

own lust." [28] Our warfare is not physical. This spiritual battle is in our mind.

Satan cannot have direct control of our mind. Satan can only try to influence our mind by seducing our sinful nature through external forces to think of things that are

a) Not *true*, false, misleading, rumors, fake, deceptive;
b) And not *honorable*, immoral, wicked, dishonest, unkind, gossip, slander;
c) And not *right*, incorrect, erroneous teachings contrary to scripture;
d) And not *pure*, rude, crude, corrupt, filthy, sensual, seductive, deceitful;
e) And not *lovely*, unpleasant, evil, diabolical, obscene, lewd, indecent, horrible, unattractive, violent;
f) And not *of good repute*, shady, deceitful, manipulative, untrustworthy;
g) Not *excellent*, shabby, poor quality, rubbish;
h) And not *worthy of praise*, critical, cynical, mocking.

Satan can manipulate and even possess the forces of evil under his control to be *a servant of sin.* These pawns (a.k.a. minions, gofers) under his control try to discourage or influence any man seeking to be obedient to God and His Word.

Satan knows in every man there's a *starving dog* called *carnal nature* begging us to feed him. Satan's goal: feed the dog! He has two main gates of access to the dog (our pride): the eye gate and the ear gate. Whatever contrary data he can get through the gate is bound to produce havoc, conflict, and disruption for the indwelling Holy Spirit. Whether it's a plunging neckline on the secretary, a juicy piece of gossip, song lyrics that would make grandma *roll over in her grave,* a hurt ego or a shot of pride, there are uncountable ways to *feed the dog.* Rita and I have often said, as we changed channels or even turned off the television, "Would we let a houseguest sit in our living room and say (do) what we

[28] James 1:13-14

just heard that person say (do) on TV?" If the answer is "No" then the program is *turned off.*

Satan likes to receive *Progress Reports* of how things are going on the Inside. We give him these reports every day by our words, actions, and appearance.

a) Words – The greatest barometer of the spiritual climate in a man's heart are words, spoken and written. Satan's minions can read and listen! Jesus said: "*For each tree is known by its own fruit. For men do not gather figs from thorns, nor do they pick grapes from a briar bush. The good man out of the good treasure of his heart brings forth what is good, and the evil man out of the evil treasure brings forth what is evil; for his mouth speaks from that which fills his heart*" – (Luke 6:44-46).

Words tell our Adversary exactly what is going on inside our mind. James says: "*For we all stumble in many ways. If anyone does not stumble in what he says, he is a perfect man, able to bridle the whole body as well*" – (James 3:2). Our Lord told his disciples who were concerned about the Pharisaical legalism of what to eat and drink: "*...Do you not understand that whatever goes into the man from outside cannot defile him, because it does not go into his heart, but into his stomach, and is eliminated?*" (Thus He declared all foods clean.) And He was saying, "*That which proceeds out of the man, that is what defiles the man. For from within, out of the heart of men, proceed the evil thoughts, fornications, thefts, murders, adulteries, deeds of coveting and wickedness, as well as deceit, sensuality, envy, slander, pride and foolishness. All these evil things proceed from within and defile the man*" – (Mark 7:18b-22).

Even our salvation is revealed to Satan and the world by our words. "*...If you confess with your mouth Jesus as Lord, and believe in your heart that God raised Him from the dead, you will be saved; for with the heart a person believes, resulting in righteousness, and with the mouth, he confesses, resulting in salvation*" – (Romans 10:9-10). That could explain why interrogators of Christians, whether they be Communist atheists or fanatical

Islamic State (ISIS) will torture a Christian until he denies with his mouth that Jesus is Lord. Peter knew the Enemy psychologically beat him when he denied knowing Christ, three times. Then he saw Christ, the rooster crowed and Peter wept. [29]

Perhaps our greatest weapon against Satan is vocal praise! Paul Billheimer writes:

> "The missing element that is necessary to energize prevailing prayer that binds and casts out Satan is triumphant faith. And the missing element that is necessary to energize triumphant faith is praise—perpetual, purposeful, aggressive praise. Praise is the highest form of prayer because it combines petition with faith. Praise is the spark plug of faith...praise is the detergent that purifies faith...the secret of answered prayer is faith without doubt (Mark 11:23). And the secret of faith, without doubt, is praise, triumphant praise, continuous praise, praise that is a way of life. This is the solution to the problem of a living faith and successful prayer. The secret of success in overcoming Satan...is a massive program of effective prayer. The secret of effective prayer is a massive program of praise." [30]

Job refused to curse God or charge God foolishly with his lips, even when being tested by Satan. Whenever Satan deals us a blow, and a word of *Praise* comes from our mouth, that shows him who's *Boss*: The Holy Spirit living within us! It reminds our Adversary that he's defeated, so he leaves us alone.

b) Actions – Our behavior indicates who is in control for all to see, including our Adversary's minions. Notice three actions that we are taught to do *in secret*: giving, praying and fasting (See Matthew 6). And we are told that the God who sees what we do in secret

[29] See full story in Matthew 26

[30] Paul E. Billheimer, *Destined for the Throne*, Revised Edition, Christian Literature Crusade, Bethany House Publishers, Grand Rapids MI. 1996, pp.17-18.

will reward us openly before man – and our Adversary. Each time we successfully obey a biblical principle (i.e. show hospitality to strangers, [31] visit the fatherless and widows and remain unspotted, [32] forsake not meeting with other Christians, [33] encourage one another), [34] it tells our Enemy who's controlling our inner man.

c) Appearance – Proverbs says: *"A joyful heart makes a cheerful face, But when the heart is sad, the spirit is broken"* – (Proverbs 15:13). In essence, our daily countenance reveals who is winning the spiritual battle around us. Some men have convinced themselves they cannot smile – or show a pleasant face since "It's not my nature to be smiley." Or, "If you had gone through what I went through you would not be walking around with a smile..." Fair enough. We do not want artificial, pasted on smiles, but let's agree that our countenance needs to try and match the joyful heart promised in the Bible when the Holy Spirit is in control.

What makes us the way we are? Chuck Swindoll says:

> "The longer I live, the more I realize the impact of attitude on life. Attitude, to me, is more important than facts. It is more important than the past, than education, than money, than circumstances, than failures, than successes, than what other people think or do. It is more important than appearance, giftedness or skill. It will make or break a company...a church...a home. The remarkable thing is we have a choice every day regarding the attitude we will embrace for that day. We cannot change our past...we cannot change the inevitable. The only thing we can do is play on the one string we have, and that is our attitude. I am convinced that life is 10% what happens

---

31 Hebrews 13:2

32 James 1:27

33 Hebrews 10:25

34 1 Thessalonians 5:11

to me and 90% how I react to it. And so it is with you…we are in charge of our attitudes." [35]

In Everything – Give Thanks, Praise, Rejoice and Bless God Himself.

Doxology comes from *"doxa-ology"* meaning *"The making of Glory!"* To magnify His name is to make Him larger – expand His Glory – to make Him visible and known to everyone around us.

[35] Chuck Swindoll, quote from text Grace Awakening, https://www.goodreads.com/author/quotes/5139.Charles_R_Swindoll - Accessed 02 August 2017.

- **Thanks** – *giving appreciation for temporal blessings received by the mercy and power of God Himself.*

- **Praise** – *offering adoration of creation and worship of the sovereign power and beauty of God Himself.*

- **Rejoice** – *verbalizing expressions of gratitude for eternal blessings provided by God Himself.*

- **Bless** – *extending worship of character qualities possessed by God Himself.*

Let's go deeper into these four ways to *magnify the Lord* – to enlarge His Glory in the eyes of all who see us, His followers

First, **Thanks** – *giving appreciation for temporal blessings received by the mercy and power of God Himself.* One of the Bible's most challenging verses, for me, is 1 Thessalonians 5:18, "*...in everything give thanks; for this is God's will for you in Christ Jesus."* I've met people who can do this. Who winds them up each morning? They never appear to grumble. They rarely, almost never, gripe or complain. Impossible? I first thought it was a personality gene, but the command keeps popping up. *"...always giving thanks for all things in the name of our Lord Jesus Christ to God, even the Father..."* – (Ephesians 5:20). God tells us how to give thanks (Psalm 150) and why we're to give thanks (Psalm 146 and 147).

Thanks must be directed at someone. If we receive an apple we do not say, "Thank you, apple" (unless we have gone *bananas*).[36] Instead, we say "Thank you" to the person who gave us the apple. The Giver of every good and perfect gift is God, *"the Father of lights."*[37] God IS. God identifies Himself, as "I AM WHO I AM."[38] As the Psalmist says, *"The earth is the Lord's, and all it contains, the*

---

36 English slang meaning "gone crazy"

37 *"Every good thing given, and every perfect gift is from above, coming down from the Father of lights, with whom there is no variation or shifting shadow"* – (James 1:17).

38 *"God said to Moses, "I AM WHO I AM"; and He said, "Thus you shall say to the sons of Israel, 'I AM has sent me to you'"* – (Exodus 3:14).

world, and those who dwell in it" – (Psalm 24:1). God made every person on Earth.[39] Therefore, our highest expression of giving thanks would be to thank God for each person we meet who was made by God and retains some aspect of His image.

There's a huge difference between *being thankful* and *giving thanks.* Being thankful is at best a comparative evaluation that leads to the acceptance of an otherwise awkward or difficult situation. Giving thanks is the personal submission to God's plans being worked out by faith in our lives.

> One of my favorite stories is about an African King whose thankful servant always said: *"This is good!"* no matter what happened. One day the King was hunting with his servant. The King fired his gun at some birds, and the gun backfired and blew off the King's thumb. The servant looked at him and said, "O, King, this is good!" The King was writhing in pain, looked at the servant and said, "It hurts, you foolish servant. I am putting you in prison for always saying everything is good." A year later, the hand has healed, and the thumb-less King goes hunting by himself. He wanders into a region where cannibals live. They capture the King, tie him up and are going to eat him. The cannibals believe if they eat a person they get that person's spirit, then they have two spirits and are more powerful in battle. But before they eat a person they have to examine him to make sure his spirit is perfect. They examine the King and see he has no thumb. "We cannot eat him; he is not perfect. Get him out of here." So they release the King and send him home. As he is walking back he looks at his hand, sees where the thumb was blown off and says, "This is good—it saved my life!" Then he recalls that he placed his servant in prison for saying "This is good!" He rushes to the prison and says to his servant, "Please forgive me for putting you in my filthy prison with bad food for saying 'This is good' It was good. It saved my life." The servant responded and said, "Oh no King, this is

---

[39] *"Before I formed you in the womb I knew you, and before you were born I consecrated you; I have appointed you a prophet to the nations"* – (Jeremiah 1:5).

Good that I was in prison." The King was amazed. "How can you keep being thankful and saying 'This is good' even in my prison?" "Oh, my King, this is good that I was in prison. For you see, if I were not in prison, I would have been hunting with you. I would be the one captured. And I have a thumb!"

I must confess, years ago, when I was "*terminated without cause and in lieu of notice received a severance package*" my immediate response was not, *"This is good!"* But it proved to be good. I learned a lesson about forgiveness that has been used to help people in over 40 languages.[40] When I sought public office in a by-election, to become a member of the Canadian Federal Parliament, and was defeated by a narrow margin, my immediate response was not, *"This is good!"* But it was. Both incidents caused a humbling, inward look at my character, my abilities and where to use my gifts. It's a hard lesson to learn to *give thanks—in everything*, but I am learning how.

Six categories emerge that deserve our Thanks.

1. Material Items—Thank God for food, clothing, shelter which is all God promised in Matthew 6:33. [41] *"But seek first His kingdom and His righteousness, and all these things will be added to you."* The main thing that gets added to this attitude of gratitude is contentment. Paul told Timothy, *"If we have food and covering, with these we shall be content"* – (1 Timothy 6:8).

2. Conditional Things—Thank God for the sunshine, rain, mountains, flowers, health and the things we enjoy for the moment. They may change or be taken away but are things we thank God for while we have them.

---

[40] Standing Strong Through the Storm, Paul Estabrooks and Jim Cunningham, Open Doors International, 2nd ed. 2017. (See: Chapter 20 'Forgiveness and Grace' 'Figure 16', page 328 prepared by author based on lesson learned through being *"terminated without cause and in lieu of notice received a severance package"* – currently translated into 40+ languages. Praise God!

[41] Matthew 6:33

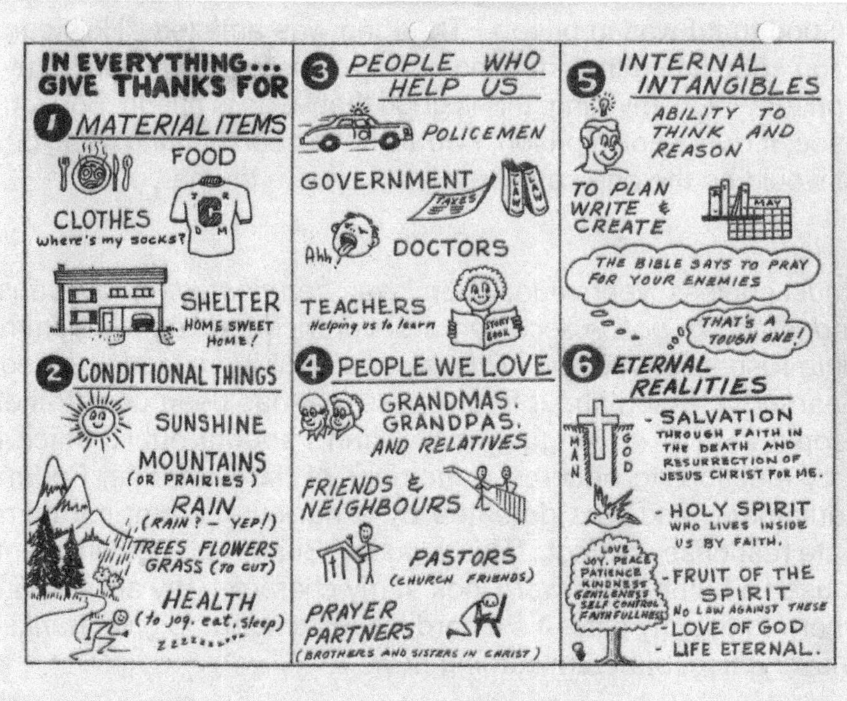

Artwork by Commissioned Artist - Reid Andrews - circa 1970's [42]

3. People Who Help Us—Thank God for police, government officials, doctors, teachers or anyone in the service industry who helps make our life more comfortable and safe. We pray for the ones in authority with thanksgiving! *"First of all, then, I urge that entreaties and prayers, petitions and thanksgivings, be made on behalf of all men, for kings and all who are in authority, so that we may lead a tranquil and quiet life in all godliness and dignity"* – 1 Timothy 2:1-2).

4. People We Love—Thank God for family, parents, grandparents, grandchildren, neighbors, church members, and work associates. God *gifted* them to us to be part of our life on Earth. Keep a

[42] The first draft of this book began in the 1970's! I commissioned Reid Andrews to draw (before computers!) the six categories for which we give "Thanks." His style was Classic-1960's graphics. Reid went to Heaven prematurely (in my eyes) at the age of 52 with an untreatable lung cancer. I included his artwork in this book as a tribute to a gifted brother, friend, artist and one amazing Scottish bagpipe player! ☺

journal entry of their names and what specifically you are thankful for about this person.

5. Internal Intangibles—Thank God for the ability to think, read, write, remember, plan, create, build and make. All are gifts from God to us.

6. Eternal Realities—Thank God for salvation, the Holy Spirit, the Fruit of the Spirit, the Love and Mercy of God and Eternal Life!

Wait, you are saying, "How can I give thanks for an abusive father, a drug abusing son, a murderous dictator, or a garbage man who smashes my garbage can?" I cannot explain why we are to do it, but I can assure you we are commanded to do it as in #3 above: "*thanksgivings, be made on behalf of all men…*"

Paul reinforces this by saying, *"Therefore as you have received Christ Jesus the Lord, so walk in Him, having been firmly rooted and now being built up in Him and established in your faith, just as you were instructed, and overflowing with gratitude"* – (Colossians 2:6-7).

Are you like me? When a verse of scripture appears in a book by a Christian author, I say to myself, "Oh, I know those verses," and skip over the verse without reading it in its entirety or without thinking about what I just read! Time to go back and read the verses. They contain essential insights.

Two thoughts. First, giving thanks is unrelated to the price tag. Men love to *give thanks* IF they get a bargain. Solomon understood: *"Bad, bad," says the buyer, but when he goes his way, then he boasts"* [and gives thanks for the bargain! – Proverbs 20:14]. It pays to put eternal price tags on all temporal values.

Second, thanks given voluntarily have more value than an artificially forced response.

Story: When our sons were younger, a friend used to knit each of them a wool sweater as a Christmas present. She lived some 5,000 km away from our home and did not always know their sizes, so she would tend to make the sweaters bigger thinking they could *grow into them.* Dave and Mike viewed the annual "Letter of Thanks to Mrs. L for the sweaters" as a less than desirable part of Christmas. Around age six, our youngest son wrote this famous short letter: *"Dear Mrs. L, Thanks for the nice sweater. I would write more, but the sleeves keep getting in the way. Love, Mike."*

Parents are more excited to provide for their children when they sense both appreciation and unsolicited thanks. Our Heavenly Father also appreciates our sincere, spontaneous thanks for the benefits He bestows on us daily.

Secondly, **Praise** – *offering adoration of creation and worship of the sovereign power and beauty of God Himself.*

Praise needs to be verbalized to both God and man to have significance. With our lips, we praise God for who He is—and the awareness of our recognition of His work in our lives each day.

Everything that has breath is to praise the Lord. *"Enter His gates with thanksgiving and His courts with praise."* (Psalm 11:4). The Psalmist writes, "*Praise the Lord, all nations; Laud Him, all peoples! For His loving kindness is great toward us, and the truth of the Lord is everlasting. Praise the Lord!"* – (Psalm 117:1-2). In Psalm 146:1-2 he exclaims, *"Praise the Lord! Praise the Lord, O my soul! I will praise the Lord while I live; I will sing praises to my God while I have my being."*

Psalm 148:1-6 rings out with
Praise the Lord!
Praise the Lord from the heavens;
Praise Him in the heights!
Praise Him, all His angels;
Praise Him, all His hosts!

Praise Him, sun and moon;
Praise Him, all stars of light!
Praise Him, highest heavens,
And the waters that are above the heavens!
Let them praise the name of the Lord,
For He commanded and they were created.
He has also established them forever and ever;
He has made a decree which will not pass away."

What a great challenge to *Praise the Lord* and not sound like it is an artificial tacked-on mantra such as, "Hi, Praise the Lord," "How are you today, Praise the Lord." "Well, I just lost my job, Praise the Lord, and my wife is sick, Praise the Lord." While having a heart overflowing with praise is good, praise can become a conditioned artificial response. However, we live in a world where more people respond with "*Oh, something else*" than "*Oh, Praise the Lord.*"

***Story: 'Te Deum Laudamus'* – "You Lord We Praise" The Buddha and the Bell** In 1716, a Jesuit priest named Father Desiden was sent by the Catholic Church to live in Lhasa, Tibet. He studied the Tibetan language for five years while earning the respect of the resident local monks. They consequently invited him to live at Sera Monastery, one of three great monasteries in Lhasa. The monk's appreciation of Father Desiden as a teacher of apologetics and inter-disciplinary dialogue, gained him invitations to conduct Mass and prepare a treatise comparing the Christian and the Buddhist faiths. Some years later, in 1721, the Vatican removed Father Desiden due to a territorial dispute between the Jesuits and Capuchins. The Capuchin order claimed Tibet as their territory. Soon new priests from the Capuchin order were sent to Lhasa to build a new Catholic church that was completed in 1726. The new church gradually gained converts until a congregation of some 60 baptized Tibetan believers and enquirers worshipped together. Feeling threatened, the local Buddhist monk-hood put pressure on the Dalai Lama to suppress the fledgling Church. As a result, in 1742 the Capuchin priests were expelled, the church building was torn down and its members persecuted.

The Buddhist monks took the bell from the steeple to the Jokhang Temple: the holiest site of the Buddhist faith. During a visit to Tibet in the summer of 1994, I heard about this 'captured bell' and desired to see it. Our tour included a visit to the Deprung Monastery – a holy site of training and worship for Monks, located some 10 km from the city of Lhasa, on a hillside facing the Lhasa River in the southern valley of Gengbuwuzi Mountain. Built in 1416 by Jiangyang Quije, a famous disciple of Zong Kaba, Deprung is the largest of six famous monasteries belonging to the Gelukpa Sect. It covers an area in excess of 20,000 square meters and houses numerous items of worship including gold-gilded statues of Buddha. At the highest level of the monastery is the room containing a statue of the most recent Buddha. In the doorway, facing the massive statue, hangs a bell to summon the monks to come for their times of prayer and devotion to the Buddha. You can imagine my excitement when I thought I had found 'the bell' inscribed with the Latin words: *'Te Deum Laudamus'* ("You Lord We Praise!")

I was struck by the irony. The Buddhist monks were ringing what I supposed to be the Capuchin's bell to worship, not my living Lord, but a dead Buddha. Buddha has:

- eyes, but cannot see his disciples;
- lips, but cannot speak to them;
- ears, but cannot hear their prayers; and
- a body, but no ability to meet their needs.

Buddha is dead! He has no power, no emotions, no life. In contrast, our God, the God and Father of our Lord Jesus Christ is alive. He has all power both in Heaven and on Earth. He has all authority. He sets up kings and puts down kings. He is Sovereign. He is called:

- Lord Jehovah;
- King of Kings and Lord of Lords;
- Almighty;
- The Wonderful Counselor;

- Prince of Peace; and
- Everlasting Father.

Tibetan Buddhists practice five different kinds of burial styles determined by the rank or status of the deceased during their earthly life:

- **Temple Burial** – first the Buddha gets buried in the Temple.
- **Cremation** – then the rich are cremated resulting in instant transfer to the next life.
- **Sky Burial** – ordinary folks have their bodies dismembered, stripped of all flesh and their bones crushed. The remains are spread out for the vultures. If the birds eat the remains, the person was 'OK' and will enter the next cycle of reincarnation at a higher level.
- **Water Burial** – as above, but the remains are deposited in the river for the fish to consume.
- **In a Cave** – Criminals – the lowest of all people in the eyes of Buddhists are buried in the earth thus taking the longest time to gain entry into the next life.

Jesus of Nazareth, our Messiah, the only begotten of the Father was crucified as a common criminal, between two thieves, buried in a tomb in a cave, and rose again from the dead on the third day! Galatians 3:13 says: *"Christ redeemed us from the curse of the law, having become a curse for us, for it is written, cursed is everyone who hangs on a tree"*. The death of our Lord – who paid the price for our sins – was the death of a criminal in the earth so to speak. This provides a powerful cultural key to reach Tibetan-Buddhists. Buddhism teaches world peace and universal brotherhood with harmony for all who pursue one source and one law. "All life is one", is the goal of modern Buddhism. In contrast, Christianity teaches that we are all equally loved in the eyes of God. Isamu Yamamoto, writing in the Christian Research Journal (Summer, 1994) says: "...there can be *no harmony* between the Buddhist doctrine and the Christian faith." (p.11). It is not up to the living to determine who is the most 'worthy' of eternal life. Jesus loves everyone equally, the rich, the ordinary folks and the criminals. Jesus taught that He alone is 'The Way, The Truth and The Life" and that "no one comes to the Father except through (Him)."

The song "Jesus loves me this I know, for the Bible tells me so..." came to my lips as I walked throughout the Deprung Monastery. When I saw that bell, my heart leaped for joy: "We Praise You Lord!" The high-water mark of the Christian faith is pure joyful Praise! Let everything that has breath praise the Lord. We are one, through faith in Jesus Christ as our personal Savior and Lord. As I went to take a picture of 'he Bell, a stern faced monk pointed to a sign indicating a photo could only be taken if I paid an amount in *Yuan* equal to about two and a half US dollars. I handed him the money and stepped back to frame the Buddha and the Bell within the doorway. I waited as a Tibetan devotee walked out of the holy site – and snapped the shutter. Flash! I got my picture of the Bell! "You Lord We Praise!" – or did I? From that moment on the flash in my new camera never worked again. On my return to Canada, I rushed the film in to be processed. All the pictures turned out with one exception: "The Buddha and the Bell!"

Years later, in telling my story to Tibetan Christians, I was told that what I saw at the Deprung Monastery was not "the Capuchin Bell." That Bell is supposedly in storage in the Jokhang Temple, right in the center of the old city of Lhasa, having sustained some damage during the Cultural Revolution. It is no longer in use! One Tibetan Christian believer I subsequently met (and there is a growing number of them) said: "Too long Tibetans have served dead gods. They need a living, loving Heavenly Father who loves them." When this happens *"Te Deum Laudamus"* will occur throughout Tibet. Pray that our brothers and sisters in Christ who live in Tibet may experience "the joy of the Lord as their strength" and exude "the fragrance of Christ's love" to each Buddhist they meet. They will know we are Disciples of Christ – by our love for one another. May God help true Christians ring that "Bell" of Praise, ***'Te Deum Laudamus'*** **– "You Lord We Praise"**

Third, **Rejoicing** – *verbalizing expressions of gratitude for eternal blessings provided by God Himself.*

Rejoicing is a higher level of praise beyond thanksgiving related to eternal benefits. These eternal values cannot be removed or altered. They are secure. God has guaranteed them to us and for these things we can Rejoice. Look at the things for which scripture tells me to Rejoice.

1. Rejoice when persecution comes. What? Luke 6:23 says, *"Be glad (**rejoice**) in that day and leap for joy, for behold, your reward is great in heaven. For in the same way their fathers used to treat the prophets."* Jesus taught, *"Blessed are you when people insult you and persecute you, and falsely say all kinds of evil against you because of Me. Rejoice and be glad, for your reward in heaven is great; for, in the same way, they persecuted the prophets who were before you" – (Matthew 5:11-12).*

2. Rejoice in my salvation. Luke 10:20 – *"Nevertheless do not rejoice in this, that the spirits are subject to you, but rejoice that your names are recorded in heaven."*

3. Rejoice for the future. 1 Peter 1:8-9 – *"...and though you have not seen Him, you love Him, and though you do not see Him now, believe in Him, you greatly rejoice with joy inexpressible and full of glory, obtaining as the outcome of your faith the salvation of your souls."*

4. Rejoice in the Lord. Philippians 4:4 – *"Rejoice in the Lord always; again I will say, rejoice!*

5. Rejoice forever and always. 1 Thessalonians 5:16 – *"Rejoice always."*

6. Rejoice in the wife of my youth. Proverbs 5:18 – *"And rejoice in the wife of your youth. As a loving hind and a graceful doe, let her breasts satisfy you at all times; be exhilarated always with her love."* What a list, and there are close to 200 verses in the Bible that tell us to Rejoice, even when things appear to be going contrary to our plans. Giving thanks, offering praise and taking time to rejoice are likely the healthiest force in my body, affecting my energy, my moods, and my wellbeing. The more we change into the image of Christ now, the less culture shock when we get to Heaven and begin Praising God and Rejoicing in His goodness.

In Ephesians 1:3-14 there is a list of 15 things eternally set aside for which we can Rejoice. Check ones you've experienced.

Blessed be the God and Father of our Lord Jesus Christ,

(__) *Who has blessed us with every spiritual blessing in the heavenly places in Christ,*
(__) *Just as He chose us in Him before the foundation of the world,*
(__) *That we would be holy and blameless before Him. In love*
(__) *He predestined us to adoption as sons through Jesus Christ to Himself, according to the kind intention of His will,*
(__) *To the praise of the glory of His grace, which He freely bestowed on us in the Beloved.*
(__) *In Him, we have redemption through His blood,*
(__) *The forgiveness of our trespasses, according to*
(__) *The riches of His grace, which He lavished on us. In all wisdom and insight*
(__) *He made known to us the mystery of His will, according to His kind intention which He purposed in Him with a view to an administration suitable to the fullness of the times, that is, the summing up of all things in Christ, things in the heavens and things on the earth.*
(__) *In Him also we have obtained an inheritance,*
(__) *Having been predestined according to His purpose*
(__) *Who works all things after the counsel of His will, to the end that*
(__) *We who were the first to hope in Christ would be to the praise of His glory.*
(__) *In Him, you also, after listening to the message of truth, the gospel of your salvation—having also believed, you were sealed in Him with the Holy Spirit of promise,*
(__) *Who is given as a pledge of our inheritance, with a view to the redemption of God's own possession, to the praise of His glory.*

And fourth, **Bless** *– extending worship of character qualities possessed by God Himself.*

The first person I ever heard *Bless the Lord* in a prayer was David Bell, my Professor at Bible College, just before our choir sang in a church service. As a relatively new disciple of Jesus Christ, I was amazed. My concept of a *Blessing* was that the greater blessed the lesser. How then could we as created beings ever bless our Creator? It was then I discovered that the one who blesses is acknowledging what the other person rightfully deserves. When King David, blessed the Lord he was acknowledging God's character as a higher form of Praise.

> *"Bless the Lord, O my soul,*
> *And all that is within me bless His holy name.*
> *Bless the Lord, O my soul,*
> *And forget none of His benefits;*
> *Who pardons all your iniquities,*
> *Who heals all your diseases;*
> *Who redeems your life from the pit,*
> *Who crowns you with loving kindness and compassion;*
> *Who satisfies your years with good things,*
> *So that your youth is renewed like the eagle"* – (Psalm 103:1-5)

And in Psalm 34:1-3 David passionately writes, "*I will bless the Lord at all times; His praise shall continually be in my mouth. My soul will make its boast in the Lord; the humble will hear it and rejoice. O magnify the Lord with me, and let us exalt His name together."* Wait, did David say the humble will *"hear it"*? The "it" David is referring to is his Praise of God spoken audibly to others about our God.

"So David ***blessed the Lord*** *in the sight of all the assembly; and David said, "****Blessed*** *are You, O Lord God of Israel our father, forever and ever. Yours, O Lord, is the greatness and the power and the glory and the victory and the majesty, indeed everything that is in the heavens and the earth; Yours is the dominion, O Lord, and*

You exalt Yourself as head over all. Both riches and honor come from You, and You rule over all, and in Your hand is power and might, and it lies in Your hand to make great and to strengthen everyone. Now, therefore, our God, we ***thank*** *You and* ***praise*** *Your glorious name"* – (1 Chronicles 29:10-13).

I like David's prayer. He is blessing the Lord and thanking Him and praising Him while rejoicing in Him all at the same time. David is called *"a man after God's own heart."* [43] What a testimony.

In the New Testament, we are told that God chose us *"to be conformed to the image of Jesus Christ."* (See Romans 8). That's our goal men, *"to magnify the Lord" and to "Bless the Lord, O my soul, and all that is within me, bless his holy name"* at every age and stage of our Christian life. When we do, it enables others to look at us and see the character of Jesus Christ increased or enlarged through us.

THY WILL BE DONE

According to Thy will O Lord,
Be it unto me.
It's easy for me to say it,
But harder for me to see.

I keep on making daily plans,
In my own sweet human way,
Saying "maybe, just maybe,"
You'll let me do them—some day.

I need the inner patience Lord,
To walk instead of run,
So you will have the glory,
When all is said and done.

---

43 *(God) raised up David to be their king, concerning whom He also testified and said, "I have found David the son of Jesse, a man after My heart, who will do all My will"* – (Acts 13:22).

Your way is good and perfect,
And very well thought through,
So keep me in the center of it,
When I have doubt or two.

And help me to delight each day,
In doing "Your Will" O Lord,
For walking in the Spirit.
Sure keeps me from being bored.

By faith, I know that You will give,
The desires of my heart.
Just help me to be honest enough,
To keep "My Will" apart!

James D. (Jim) Cunningham
29 October 1976

Composed in 1976 on sabbatical-education leave for Master's degree in DeKalb, Illinois. Deciding whether to return to Christian Service Brigade and serve in the Canadian National Office or apply for Doctoral Studies in Adult Education at the University of Toronto.

Answer? I did both. I served at the Christian Service Brigade office till September 1978, then headed to OISE (Ontario Institute for Studies in Education) at the University of Toronto including a year of doctoral research in Jerusalem, Israel 1979-80. Graduated with Doctorate in Adult Education in 1981.

Competencies Required to Fulfill the Role of INDIVIDUAL.

Personal Checklist – (Circle the best answer for each to determine score)

Do I have…

1. A personal conviction that God has a plan being worked out in my life that is *"good, acceptable and perfect"?* [Romans 12:1-2; 8:28; Philippians 2:13; Ephesians 1:11]

1	2	3	4	5
Not at all	A little bit	Usually	Most of the time	Always

2. A good awareness of my abilities (gifts) and an appreciation of my limitations (needs)? [Philippians 4:13; 1 Peter 4:10-11; 2 Corinthians 12:9-10]

1	2	3	4	5
Not at all	A little bit	Usually	Most of the time	Always

3. The realization that I am on Earth as a unique individual with eternal value and purpose as part of God's Master Plan, made in His image? [Jeremiah 1:5; Psalm 139:13-16]

1	2	3	4	5
Not at all	A little bit	Usually	Most of the time	Always

4. A right relationship with God through faith in Jesus Christ, to assure that God's best for my life will be available for me as an Individual? [Hebrews 11:6; Ephesians 2:8-9; John 1:12]

1	2	3	4	5
Not at all	A little bit	Usually	Most of the time	Always

5. A desire for personal growth, whatever the cost? [Philippians 3:10; Luke 6:22; 2 Peter 3:18]

1	2	3	4	5
Not at all	A little bit	Usually	Most of the time	Always

6. The ability to accept responsibility for my actions and be held accountable for my decisions? [1 Corinthians 10:12-13; James 1:12-14]

1	2	3	4	5
Not at all	A little bit	Usually	Most of the time	Always

7. An acceptance of the unalterable factors that have shaped my heritage and development to this point in my life, as part of God's design for me as an individual (parents, birth order, sex, environment, etc.).

1	2	3	4	5
Not at all	A little bit	Usually	Most of the time	Always

Total divided by 7 =

Evidences that the Role of Individual is Being Fulfilled

Personal Checklist – (Circle the best answer for each to determine score)

Have I demonstrated…

1. A healthy, positive, balanced self-image with a realistic growing awareness of the strengths and weaknesses I possess as an Individual? [Psalm 139:14, Philippians 2:13]

1	2	3	4	5
Not at all	A little bit	Usually	Most of the time	Always

2. A personal inner peace that allows me "*If possible, so far as it depends on (me), to be at peace with all men*"? [Romans 12:18; James 3:17-18]

1	2	3	4	5
Not at all	A little bit	Usually	Most of the time	Always

3. Godliness, combined with inner contentment apart from the selfish pursuit of possessions, power, and prestige? [1 Timothy 6:6-10]

1	2	3	4	5
Not at all	A little bit	Usually	Most of the time	Always

4. Increasing freedom from prejudice, partiality and intolerance towards people who are different while "loving my neighbor as myself"? [James 2:8-9; 1 Timothy 5:21]

1	2	3	4	5
Not at all	A little bit	Usually	Most of the time	Always

5. The ability to readily and sincerely give thanks to God for all things, to praise Him with my lips, to rejoice always and bless His Holy Name at all times?

1	2	3	4	5
Not at all	A little bit	Usually	Most of the time	Always

6. Acceptance of life changes that are part of my maturing as an individual, by evidencing a contentment and inner peace without bitterness or regret?

1	2	3	4	5
Not at all	A little bit	Usually	Most of the time	Always

7. A balanced variety of personal life interests that provide growth, enjoyment, and satisfaction at all age levels?

1	2	3	4	5
Not at all	A little bit	Usually	Most of the time	Always

8. Personal convictions based on strong principles of scripture that permit me to dialogue with and respect the ideas, opinions of others who do not share my faith in Christ?

1	2	3	4	5
Not at all	A little bit	Usually	Most of the time	Always

Total divided by 8 =

Projects for Investigation and Discussion

[__] **Define Masculinity.** What would be the scripture verses you would use to support your definition?

[__] **List ten words that contain the word *self*.** How do these words relate to helping a man understand the expectations society places on him as an Individual. Are they valid?

1 ____________________ 6 ____________________

2 ____________________ 7 ____________________

3 ____________________ 8 ____________________

4 ____________________ 9 ____________________

5 ____________________ 10 ____________________

[__] **Identify *masculine/machismo cultural expectations*** you see portrayed in the media (sports, Hollywood/Bollywood, TV, music, news). Which of these do you regard as scripturally valid? Reasons?

[__] **Complete "My Uniqueness Chart."** Share with one other person your answer to "Ways I see God using my unique life to do things that perhaps no one else could do to the Glory of Jesus Christ."

[__] **List the two things for which you find it easiest to** a) Give Thanks; 2) Praise God; 3) Rejoice Evermore; 4) Bless God. Then list one thing you find a challenge to do in each area.

[__] **Think of a Man you know who *is not making it as an individual.*** What might be your approach to encourage him?

[__] **Life changes are normal and should be accepted by each man.** – Is there a truth or a danger attached to this statement?

Chapter 2

Son • Relationship With His Parents

Honor your Father and Mother… • Ephesians 6:2-3

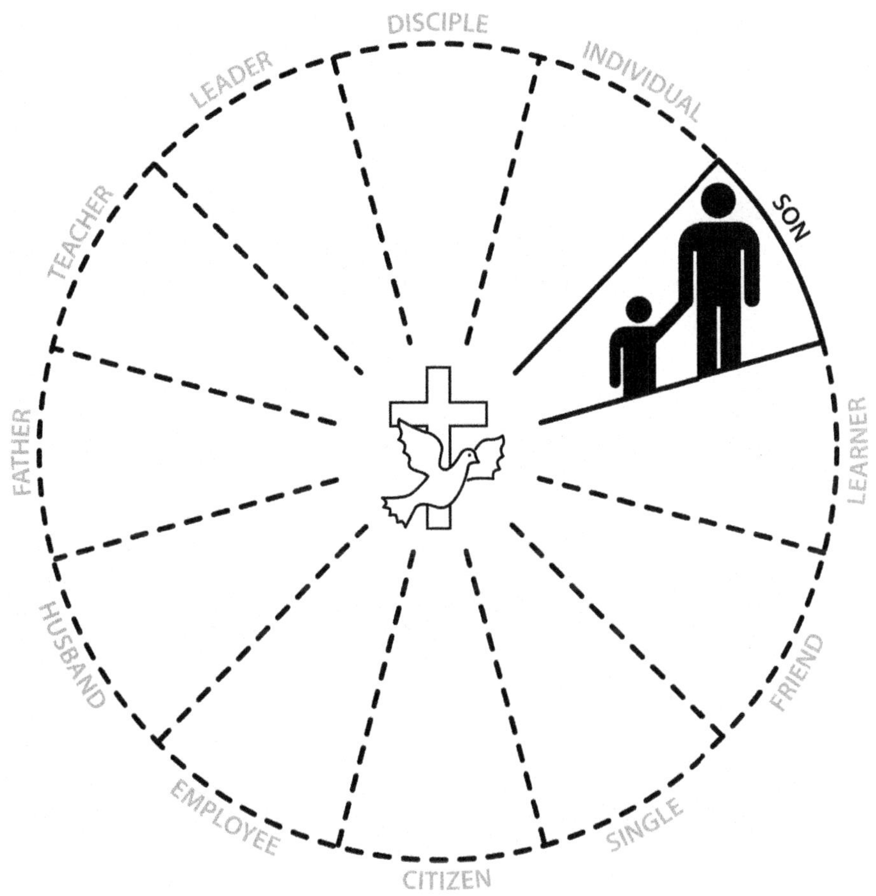

Children Obey Your Parents

The Serpent planted seeds of rebellion against God's plan in the Garden of Eden. Today, the crop of personal rebellion is ripe as every man does *"what is right in his own eyes…"* [44]

The relationship between a son and his father influences the son's relationship to God. If a son rebels against his father and mother, it is unlikely he will honor or submit to the authority of God or accept God's will for his life. Relationships in the home affect relationships with our Heavenly Father!

Proverbs are very clear. *"The eye that mocks a father and scorns (refuses to honor) a mother, the ravens of the valley will pick it out and the young eagles will eat it."* [45] Ouch. I have been in three different towns in Canada when news came of a young teenage son whose life ended in tragedy. Two were motor vehicle accidents. One was a suicide. All three were in an apparent state of rebellion against their parents.

Nowhere does Scripture say we have to understand our parents or even enjoy what they tell us. But the Bible does teach: *"Children, obey your parents in the Lord, for this is right."* [46] At what age does *son-child-obey* change to *son-adult-honor*? Each country and culture has different ages for when individual choices become legal (to drive a car, to drink alcohol, to vote, to fight in the army). In reality, some sons mature more quickly than others. The transition is not so much a matter of a calendar date as it is a maturation process.

Each son must grow into adulthood by evidencing an acceptance of self-responsibility. First, comes parental protection, then wise counsel. A wise father trains up a child in the way he should go and leaves the results to God.

---

[44] *"In those days there was no king in Israel, but every man did that which was right in his own eyes."* (Judges 17:6)

[45] Proverbs 30:17

[46] Ephesians 6:1

Honor Your Father and Mother

To date, as I write these words, every man alive on Earth had a Father and a Mother. Perhaps, soon, we may land on the *Biological Moon* and create something called *Life* without a male sperm and a female ovum! Some men have never met their biological Father. Let's look at the options.

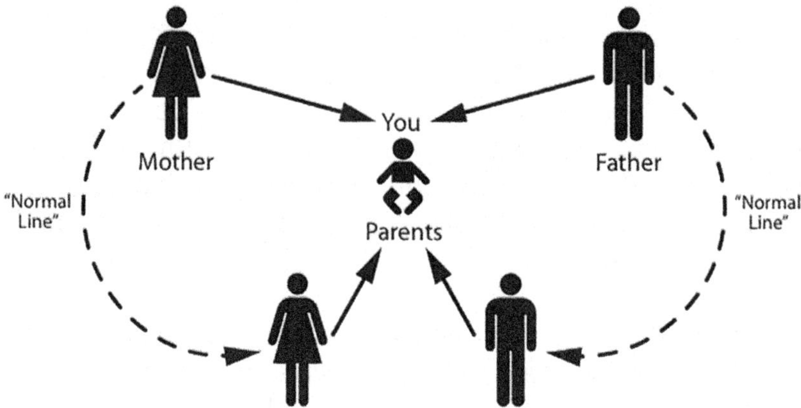

Possible Changes in Relationships

(woman ╲ man)	**"Gone"** (may still be alive)	**Dead**	**Alive**
"Gone" (may still be alive)	**Adopted** or Ward of Society	**Adopted** "new parents"	**Divorced or Separated** • with dad • no mom • maybe "new mom"
Dead	**Adopted** "new parents"	**Orphan** Raised by: • relatives • instution or adopted	**Widower** • with dad • may marry "new mom"
Alive	**Divorced or Separated** • with mom • no dad • maybe "new father"	**Widow** • with mom • may marry "new dad"	**"Normal"** child lives with bio father & bio mother

If you never met your biological father and mother, and you are still alive, then someone fed you, clothed you, changed your diaper, protected you and helped you survive to today. Let's call these particular people your *Parents.* In many, perhaps most cases your Parents are also your Father and Mother. Notice the scriptures tell us to *Obey* our Parents, the ones who kept you alive and *Honor* your Father and Mother, the two who made you who you are. Does that help to see the difference?

Obey Parents – "*Children be obedient to your* ***parents*** *in all things for this is well pleasing to the Lord" – (Colossians 3:20). "Children, obey your* ***parents*** *in the Lord for this is right" – (Ephesians 6:1).*

Honor Father and Mother – *"Honor your **father and mother** (which is the first commandment with a promise) that it may be well with you and that you may live long on the earth"* – (Ephesians 6:2).

Obey Parents. Honor Father and Mother. We are back to the Ravens picking eyeballs again. *"The eye that mocks a father and scorns (refuses to acknowledge) a mother, the ravens of the valley will pick it out, and the young eagles will eat it."* [47]

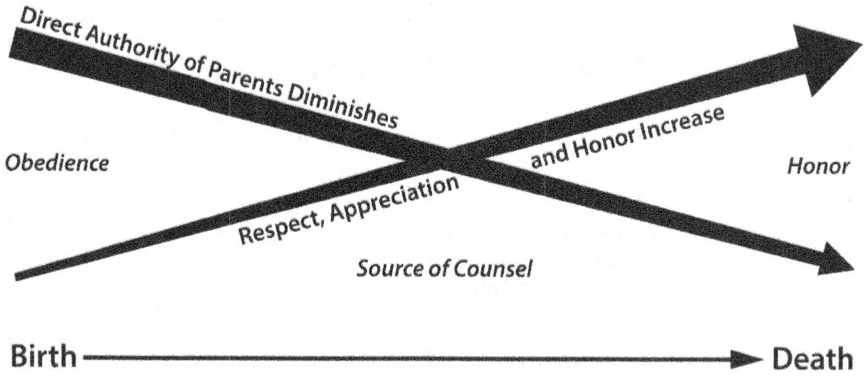

What is involved in the command to *"honor our father and mother"*?

- Granting them the minimum of *Universal Responsibilities* owed to all men and women on earth (see Appendix A).
- One has a genuine appreciation and thanksgiving for whomever the persons were who caused you to be born at this time in history. All men are born in sin. Some appear to have been born in more sin than others. Accepting your father and mother first as sinners, second as human beings made in the image of God, and third as divine timekeepers in causing your birth *"in the fullness of time"* [48] in God's meticulous sovereign plan!

---

[47] Proverbs 30:17

[48] Galatians 4:4 and Ephesians 1: 3-10

- Finding creative ways of providing for their needs if known and alive. It may involve appreciating his or her memory in the way King David did when he said, *"Is there anyone left of the house of Saul, that I may show him kindness for Jonathan's sake."* [49]
- Planning carefully to be assured your response is appropriate to their need and their personality.
- Beginning, if needed, a new relationship of love towards them that may grow to include letters, calls, visits, gifts, assistance, prayer or counsel.

Every son at some point fights the *battle of wills.* And every parent is on the *front line* of testing and learning for the child. If a man learns to obey his parents, society wins. If he fails to obey his parents and transfers that disobedience to other authorities, society loses. He becomes a rebel. And the rest of us in society have to pay for his rebellion, disobedience, lawlessness, incarceration, and rehabilitation. Disobedience is costly. It leads to the destruction of property, loss of life and loss of personal inner peace.

There is a story that begs inclusion at this point! It took place in Nashville Tennessee in the first week of January 1996 at the Opryland Hotel. Bill Baker, Mobile Operations Manager at Sightpath Medical, wrote the article.

> In Nashville, Tennessee, during the first week of January 1996, more than 4,000 baseball coaches descended upon the Opryland Hotel for the 52nd annual ABCA convention.
>
> While I waited in line to register with the hotel staff, I heard other more veteran coaches rumbling about the lineup of speakers scheduled to present during the weekend. One name, in particular, kept resurfacing, always with the same sentiment — "John Scolinos is here? Oh man, worth every penny of my airfare."

---

[49] 2 Samuel 9:1

Who, is John Scolinos, I wondered. No matter, I was just happy to be there. In 1996, Coach Scolinos was 78 years old and five years retired from a college coaching career that began in 1948. He shuffled to the stage to an impressive standing ovation, wearing dark polyester pants, a light blue shirt, and a string around his neck from which home plate hung — a full-sized, stark-white home plate. Seriously, I wondered, who in the world is this guy?

After speaking for twenty-five minutes, not once mentioning the prop hanging around his neck, Coach Scolinos appeared to notice the snickering among some of the coaches. Even those who knew Coach Scolinos had to wonder exactly where he was going with this, or if he had simply forgotten about home plate since he'd gotten on stage. Then, finally ...

"You're probably all wondering why I'm wearing home plate around my neck. Or maybe you think I escaped from Camarillo State Hospital," he said, his voice growing irascible. I laughed along with the others, acknowledging the possibility. "No," he continued, "I may be old, but I›m not crazy. The reason I stand before you today is to share with you baseball people what I›ve learned in my life, what I›ve learned about the home plate in my 78 years."

Several hands went up when Scolinos asked how many Little League coaches were in the room. "Do you know how wide home plate is in Little League?"

After a pause, someone offered, "Seventeen inches?" more of a question than the answer.

"That's right," he said. "How about in Babe Ruth's day? Any Babe Ruth coaches in the house?"

Another long pause.

"Seventeen inches?" came a guess from another reluctant coach.

"That's right," said Scolinos. "Now, how many high school coaches do we have in the room?" Hundreds of hands shot up, as the pattern began to appear.

"How wide is home plate in high school baseball?"

"Seventeen inches," they said, sounding more confident.

"You're right!" Scolinos barked. "And you college coaches, how wide is home plate in college?"

"Seventeen inches!" we said, in unison.

"Any Minor League coaches here? How wide is home plate in pro ball?"

"Seventeen inches!"

"RIGHT! And in the Major Leagues, how wide is home plate in the Major Leagues?"

"Seventeen inches!"

"SEV-EN-TEEN INCHES!" he confirmed, his voice bellowing off the walls. "And what do they do with a Big League pitcher who can't throw the ball over seventeen inches?" ...... "They send him to Pocatello!" he hollered, drawing raucous laughter.

"What they don't do is this: they don't say, 'Ah, that's okay, Jimmy. You can't hit a seventeen-inch target? We'll make it eighteen inches, or nineteen inches. We'll make it twenty inches, so you have a better chance of hitting it. If you can't hit that, let us know so we can make it wider still, say twenty-five inches.'"

"Coaches ... what do we do when our best player shows up late to practice? When our team rules forbid facial hair, and a guy shows up unshaven? What if he gets caught drinking?

Do we hold him accountable? Or do we change the rules to fit him. Do we widen home plate?"

The chuckles gradually faded, as four thousand coaches grew quiet, the fog lifting as the old coach's message began to unfold. He turned the plate toward himself and, using a Sharpie, began to draw something. When he turned it toward the crowd, point up; a house was revealed, complete with a freshly drawn door and two windows. "This is the problem in our homes today. With our marriages, with the way we parent our kids. With our discipline. We don't teach accountability to our kids, and there is no consequence for failing to meet standards. We simply, widen the plate!"

Then, to the point at the top of the house he added a small American flag.

"This is the problem in our schools today. The quality of our education is going downhill fast and teachers have been stripped of the tools they need to be successful and to educate and discipline our young people. We are allowing others to widen home plate! Where is that getting us?"

Silence.

He replaced the flag with a cross.

"And this is the problem in the Church, where powerful people in positions of authority have taken advantage of young children, only to have such an atrocity swept under the rug for years. Our church leaders are widening home plate for themselves! And we allow it."

"And the same is true with our government. Our so-called representatives make rules for us that don't apply to themselves. They take bribes from lobbyists and foreign countries. They no longer serve us. And we allow them to widen home plate and we see our country falling into a dark abyss while we watch."

I was amazed. At a baseball convention where I expected to learn something about curveballs and bunting and how to run better practices, I had learned something far more valuable. From an old man with home plate strung around his neck, I had learned something about life, about myself, about my weaknesses and my responsibilities as a leader. I had to hold myself and others accountable to that, which I knew to be right, lest our families, our faith, and our society continue down an undesirable path.

"If I am lucky," Coach Scolinos concluded, "you will remember one thing from this old coach today. It is this: if we fail to hold ourselves to a higher standard, a standard of what we know to be right; if we do not manage to hold our spouses and our children to the same standards, if we are unwilling or unable to provide a consequence when they do not meet the standard; and if our schools and churches and our government fail to hold themselves accountable to those they serve, there is but one thing to look forward to ..."

With that, he held home plate in front of his chest, turned it around, and revealed its dark black backside. "... dark days ahead."

Coach Scolinos died in 2009 at the age of 91, but not before touching the lives of hundreds of players and coaches, including mine. Meeting him at my first ABCA convention kept me returning year after year, looking for similar wisdom and inspiration from other coaches. He is the best clinic speaker the ABCA has ever known because he was so much more than a baseball coach.

His message was clear: "Coaches, keep your players—no matter how good they are—your own children, your churches, your government, and most of all, keep yourself, ALL, at seventeen inches."

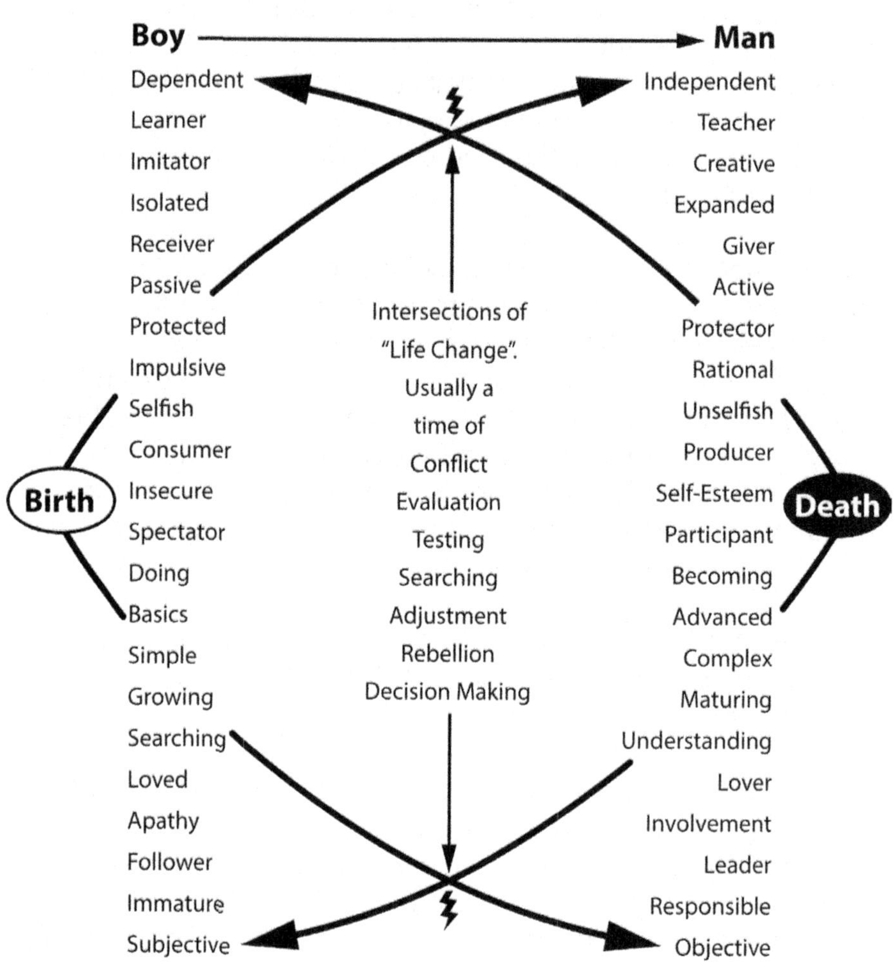

Eli was the spiritual leader of Israel in the book of 1 Samuel, yet it says in the second chapter, ***"the sons of Eli were…"***

- **Good-For-Nothing** – *"worthless men, (who) did not know the Lord"* – (v.12).
- **Bullies** – *"give it to me now, and if not I will take it by force"* – (v.16).

- **Arrogant** – *"despised the offering of the Lord"* – (v.17).
- **Promiscuous** – *"lay with the women who served at…the tent of meeting"* – (v.22)
- **Disobedient** – *"…would not listen to the voice of their father…"* – (v.25).

Then God told Samuel in a vision: *"I am about to judge his* (Eli's) *house forever for the iniquity which he knew because his sons brought a curse on themselves and he did not rebuke them.* [50] Each of us as a Son has a responsibility to *"obey our parents…"* It is for our good and their edification. Our obedience to our father permits him to extend spiritual leadership to others. Titus was told to appoint elders who have *"…children who believe, not accused of dissipation or rebellion…"* [51]

One author refused to write a book on raising children until he saw his grandchildren walking with the Lord. Then, he felt, he would have some insights to share with others.

Story: In 1989 I had the privilege of visiting a home in China of a couple we will call *"Fanny & Charlie"*. They had lived in the same tiny flat for 57 years. In this room, they raised four sons. During the Cultural Revolution, Fanny survived profound persecution for her faith in Jesus Christ. Chairman Mao received thanks for the daily food they ate, but Fanny hung a sign on their wall that said (in English!) – *"CHRIST is the HEAD of this HOUSE."* Eleven years later, in 2000, I took my wife to show her where they used to live. We met their youngest son Paul. He had inherited and upgraded his parent's flat with A/C, fridge, and a WC. I asked Paul's 21-year-old son Jimmy if he remembered the sign on his grandparent's wall. His response was polite but curt: *"I do not share my grandmother's faith!"* That's how fast we can lose our Christian heritage.

---

50 1 Samuel 3:13

51 Titus 1:6

Fanny and Charlie's Story

1st Generation – Parents: Committed Persecuted Christians;
2nd Generation – Children: Indifferent Secular Materialists;
3rd Generation – Grandchildren: Active Professing Agnostics

The framework of God's plan for the family, society, and the church requires each of us as sons to obey our parents and honor our father and mother.

"Yet Learned He Obedience"

It may seem strange to us as Christians to think that Jesus Christ, our Messiah, Emmanuel, God with us, in-the-flesh, would have to learn obedience to His Heavenly Father while He was here on Earth! That is what the Bible says:

> *"Although He was a Son, He learned obedience from the things which He suffered."* [52]

Jesus, God's *"only begotten Son,"* born among men as the *Son of Man* had to learn to submit His will to His Heavenly Father. In the Garden of Gethsemane, on the eve of His crucifixion, His prayer was, *"Father, if it be possible, let this cup pass from Me…"* Silence echoed back from Heaven. No other way. So Jesus adds these words which will some day earn Him the greatest honor ever bestowed on any man on Earth to the glory of God the Father: *"Yet not as I will but as Thou wilt."* [53]

Jesus obeyed, and our salvation was secured.

Luke records that Jesus, as a young (12-year-old) boy, was living with His earthly Father (Joseph) and Mother (Mary) in Nazareth. Jesus was taken to Jerusalem to the Temple for his induction ceremony as a Jewish man. He stayed behind with the leaders of the

---

52 Hebrew 5:8

53 Matthew 26:39

Temple asking them questions not knowing his parents had left for home. They assumed him to be with the relatives who were traveling together with them. When His parents found Him, His response proved He was aware that Mary and Joseph were only His earthly parents given to Him by God. *"Did you not know that I had to be in my Father's house?"* [54]

Small wonder Scripture records, *"they did not understand the statement which He made to them…"* But, Praise the Lord, Jesus, this same Jesus who made the Heavens and the Earth, the One who created the ones who were now His surrogate parents, *"went down with them and came to Nazareth; and He continued in subjection to them…"* [55] Jesus obeyed His earthly mother and father. Could that be why Jesus found it possible to obey His Heavenly Father as well – even when it led to His death!

In the countries I have visited, I have tried to establish a relationship between the families' culture, economics, education, even birth-order, and how the child turns out as an adult. As significant as these factors may be to a sociologist, there is no apparent correlation between these factors and an obedient son. I have met children in poor families and wealthy families who choose to obey their parents. I have met sons of illiterate fathers and sons of university graduates who both obey their parents. I have met first-born children and tenth-born sons who both know how to obey their parents and honor their father and mother.

Obedience is the responsibility of the father to teach. It is the role of the son to learn. A Son who learns to obey his Father reaps a lifetime of dividends from obeying and honoring his Heavenly Father.

---

[54] Luke 2:49

[55] Luke 2:50-51

Evidences, the Role of SON, Fulfilled

Personal Checklist

Circle the best answer for each to determine score.

Have I demonstrated…

1. A growing love and harmony in the relationships between my parents and me?

1	2	3	4	5
Not at all	A little bit	Usually	Most of the time	Always

2. The ability to complete the *Universal Requirements towards All Men* (see Appendix 'A') towards my parents?

1	2	3	4	5
Not at all	A little bit	Usually	Most of the time	Always

3. An increased sensitivity to the changing needs of aging parents?

1	2	3	4	5
Not at all	A little bit	Usually	Most of the time	Always

4. Finding practical ways of ministering to their needs (whether physical, mental, social or spiritual) in an accepted manner?

1	2	3	4	5
Not at all	A little bit	Usually	Most of the time	Always

5. Evidence of appreciation for the counsel and advice received from parents (after establishing my own home)?

1	2	3	4	5
Not at all	A little bit	Usually	Most of the time	Always

6. Discovering ways to 'honor my parents' on special occasions such as anniversaries, birthdays and holidays?

1	2	3	4	5
Not at all	A little bit	Usually	Most of the time	Always

7. Acting as a mutual friend and confidant to both parents without taking sides or seeking to be manipulative in their interpersonal relationships?

1	2	3	4	5
Not at all	A little bit	Usually	Most of the time	Always

8. Open communication (and availability where possible) with my parents?

1	2	3	4	5
Not at all	A little bit	Usually	Most of the time	Always

9. Assisting in practical ways to provide for the physical health and well being of my parents – without being asked?

1	2	3	4	5
Not at all	A little bit	Usually	Most of the time	Always

10. Providing counsel when appropriate to assist in their adjustments to life-changing styles and alterations?

1	2	3	4	5
Not at all	A little bit	Usually	Most of the time	Always

11. Evidence of respect for both parents at all times?

1	2	3	4	5
Not at all	A little bit	Usually	Most of the time	Always

Total divided by 11 =

Projects for Investigation and Discussion

[__] What responsibilities does a son have for his mother and father, if they are living, but are not his present *parents*? (i.e. due to divorce, separation, adoption, etc.)

[__] Find examples from the Scripture of sons who honored and obeyed their parents. List and discuss results.

[__] Find examples of sons in the Bible who failed to honor and obey their parents. List and discuss the results.

[__] *A rebellious son is a threat to society* – debate the validity of this statement.

[__] Proverbs 30:17 says, *"The eye that mocks a father and scorns a mother, the ravens of the valley will pick it out, and the young eagles will eat it."* What is the modern application of this truth?

[__] What are some practical ways in which a son may "honor his father and mother"?

[__] How can unresolved conflict with a parent be resolved if the parent has died?

[__] When does a son cease obeying his parents? Explain your answer.

Chapter 3

Learner • Relationship With His Teachers

But continue in the things you have learned and become convinced of, knowing from whom you have learned them • 2 Timothy 3:14

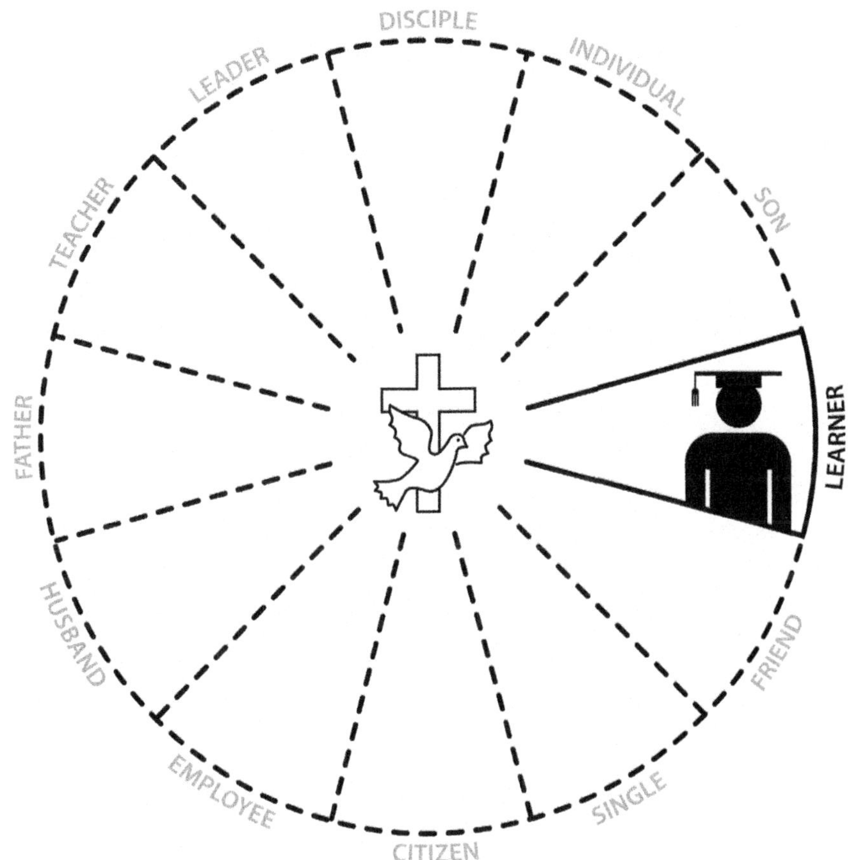

Self-Initiated Lifelong Learning

"North Americans, in general, are obsessed with finishing their education. We finish high school. We finish college. And we finish our doctorate. To suggest that learning is for life, is new territory. Learning is a process pursued by the individual learner by personal goals based on personal needs: a radical and challenging idea for many to grasp – and do!" [56]

Men love a challenge. And Men love to learn.

A friend who is a successful dairy farmer went for his first plane ride with a group of boys. Dave enjoyed the flight so much the pilot offered him an opportunity to take lessons on his own. He did. Today he has his private pilot's license.

Another friend discovered rock climbing at a men's retreat. His comment was, *"Rock climbing is for mountain goats. If God wanted me to climb mountains, He would have given me hoofs."* But after he bravely agreed to rappel down a rock face on a rope, he got so excited by the experience he signed up for a 28-day Mountain Course at Outward Bound in British Columbia.

The urge to know is a lifelong compulsion. Men are keen to pursue areas of personal interest. Night classes, weekend workshops, learning online are a sample of self-initiated learning project. Some learn to swim in their 70's. Others begin painting in their 80's. Men today are proving that *age is no barrier to learning.*

Lifelong learning helps men re-evaluate their ideas, ideals, and vision for the future. One 80-year-old man I read about still sets *10-year Goals*!

Colonel Sanders started his KFC business at age 65. Nine years and 600 franchises later he sold his shares for $2 million. Keep Learning. Keep Growing.

[56] Author's conversation with Professor John Niemi, Northern Illinois University, Dekalb, Illinois, Fall Semester, 1976.

"Be diligent to present yourself approved to God as a workman who does not need to be ashamed, handling accurately the Word of Truth." [57] Lifelong Learning is a synonym for Livelong Living.

How do we learn?

Jesus of Nazareth was a lifelong learner. "*Although He was a Son, He* <u>*learned*</u> *obedience from the things which He suffered."* [58] Men come to a Learning Task with three factors in their background:

1. Content—Adult learners have some experience or knowledge or skills related to the *Body of Truth* they are about to study. Learners enjoy hearing a Teacher say: "Let's find out what we already know about the subject and then learn together." There may be some re-learning for the Learner, but some content does come with them. They are adults.

2. Conditions—Each adult learner has been exposed to teaching methods and techniques in the past. This awareness of how to learn does exist in the adult's psyche. Adults know what they like and what they don't like about *How to Learn.*

> Story: I was sitting on the floor, leaning against the wall in a classroom back in my university grad school days. The professor turned out the lights, had us all close our eyes, as she guided us through a series of directives to understand our inner self and come to inner peace with ourselves. I think she called it *Guided Learning.* After class, the prof spoke to me and said, "I sense you were not 'getting-into' the guided learning experience..." I smiled and asked: "Was it that obvious?" Her answer was "You don't seem open to new learning techniques." My response was, "My faith in Jesus Christ achieves that inner peace..." Needless to say, she did not share my perspective.

---

[57] 2 Timothy 2:15

[58] Hebrews 5:8

3. Concern—Adult learners have sensitivities, attitudes, prejudices, values, beliefs and behaviors that will either be respected—or trampled—by the Teacher.

> Story: I remember another university class studying Adult Learning. At the time the Professor was 37 years old. I was 35. He was not warm towards me being in his class. Years later, after I graduated, I returned to my alma mater and had coffee with the prof. I asked: "You appeared to have some reservations about me in your class. Any clues why?" He openly admitted: "You were a Christian. I read your application. I was 37. You were 35. I was still trying to sort out my life, and I could tell you already *had your life together*. I didn't want you in my class."

The old Roman tutor, Seneca, told his students: "As long as you live, keep learning how to live." Good advice for his student Nero to follow, but he didn't!

Learning is a lifelong process. Every new day you breathe air when you awake is a new day for more living, more learning, and more loving the freedom we have in Jesus Christ to explore His created universe. Let me share a Learning process I use as an example. See if it sounds familiar to your learning style.

Each man is a collection of personal experiences, training, knowledge, faith, values, mistakes, biases, and motivations. These are all "*in there*" somewhere. There must emerge within us the conceptualization of a *need.* It may be a need to do something (skill) or to know something (knowledge) or to be something (an attitude). This *need* will emerge from an experience, a present reality or a future expectation. Mix with this the expectations of the *significant others* in one's life: spouse, children, peers, and authorities. Then add the extrinsic rewards offered by learning or doing this new thing to meet the *need.*

All of the above goes into some internal mental mixer of thinking and becomes what I call an *idea.* This idea starts in my mind (or wherever ideas start).

Some ideas start in my head and end in my head exactly as that: an idea.

Some ideas make it into my journal as a written idea.

Sometimes I even write it all out as a plan on how to implement the idea.

From here forward there are varying degrees of times before the idea becomes verbalized. Eventually, I take the big step and share the idea with someone I trust (usually Rita, my wife).

Scripture says, *"as a man thinks in his heart so is he…"* and every time a man opens his mouth he speaks out of the abundance of what is in his heart. If we listen to our words, we soon discover what is flowing out of our heart in abundance. Our need/idea becomes *verbalized.*

Once the idea is *out there in the public*, it is now subject to scrutiny. Questions begin. Immediately a man finds he is explaining his idea, defending his plans or promoting his project—that just a few moments ago was nothing more than an idea in his frontal lobe.

Assuming the reception is positive, a Man may get excited and proceed with further planning towards making a decision. If he gets a negative response, he may drop back, regroup his ideas and make some significant adjustments to the original thought.

Once verbalized it is now time for planning, listing objectives and doing a needs analysis to assess benefits and limitations. Pros and cons are listed and run through the final filter of scripture values and past experiences. It is now time for a decision for action.

Theologian Harvey Cox said: "*Not to decide is to decide!*" Decisions made are like wooden frames put together before pouring the concrete. Likewise, a decision, once made, releases energy to meet the needs related to the decision. Ways to address the need begin formulating. Counsel is sought. Goals are established.

Once one makes the decision, whether writing a book, training for a marathon or starting doctoral research, one's energy level increases. Priorities are re-arranged. Schedules are adapted. And the level of satisfaction increases as the goal is achieved.

The newly minted skill, knowledge or attitude is now ready to be integrated into one's daily routines. You have *finished the race* so to speak. Now comes a time of reflection and evaluation of the impact of the learning on your Lifestyle. The Learner in you feels good. Mission accomplished. Well done. The level of confidence has increased to tackle the next challenge.

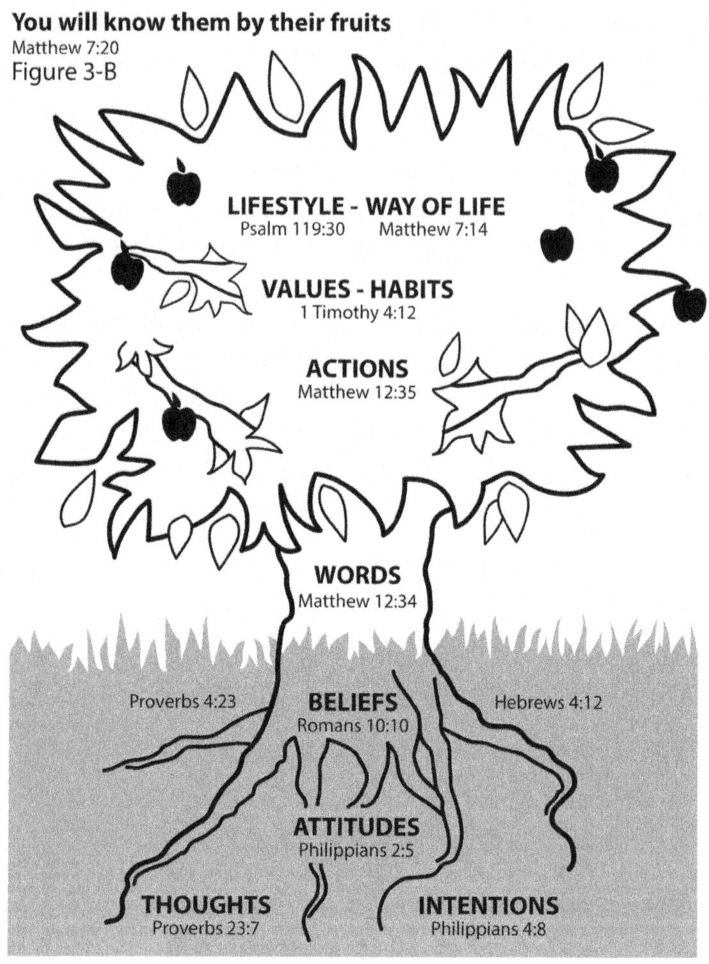

Consider the fruit tree image above. A healthy root system sustains the tree. Roots provide the strength to remain standing and the sustenance to stay healthy. Men, we are like trees. What people see is the visible exterior. But, inside is our invisible root system. Our thoughts, intents, attitudes, and beliefs are all kept deep within until we speak! Proverbs tell us: *"even a fool is regarded as a wise man—if he keeps his mouth shut"* [59]

[59] Proverbs 17:28 – Cunningham paraphrase.

Nutrition flows up the trunk from the roots. So our spoken words progress from the roots into actions. It is not possible to document each case in history, but there are numerous examples where a person preceded their actions with spoken words or written expressions before they ever did the action. Adolph Hitler wrote *Mein Kampf,* or *My Fight,* before he was leader of Germany. Criminals often voice their proposed plans before doing them.

And these repeated actions become habits that eventually bear the fruit of values and habits leading to one's lifestyle or way of life. Christians must remember: *"the heart is deceitfully wicked..."* Only God knows the *"thoughts and intents of the heart."* Paul warned: *"examine everything carefully* (and) *hold fast to that which is good;* (and) *abstain from every form* (or appearance) *of evil."*

Christ gave us universal, transcultural principles that all men, regardless of culture or heritage, must learn:

- **Learn to Love People**—for this is the way to prove we are His Disciple (John 13:35).
- **Learn to Bear Fruit**—(Matthew 7:20)—*"the fruit of the Spirit is love, joy, peace, patience, kindness, goodness, faithfulness, gentleness, self-control, against such there is no law."* [60]
- **Learn to Keep His Commandments**—(1 John 3:24).
- **Learn to Love God**—(1 John 4:20).

One wonders why Jesus did not make an extensive list of rules and regulations to be a child of God. Perhaps some people can keep standards and still be deceptive. Plus, legalism and rules tend to divide and make one judgmental. The goal of the Holy Spirit is Unity. The purpose of our Enemy (who could be called **The D-Man**) is to do things that start with the Letter D: Disappoint, Discourage, Destroy, Deny, Debate, Depress, Demolish, Disagree, and Dispute. One of his primary strategies is to Divide people so they cannot encourage one another. Two other methods are

[60] Galatians 5:22-23

Deceive (with false doctrines) and Intimidate with a fear of Death to keep us fearful and silent.

As Learners, our goal is to accept and love virtually every person who claims to be a follower of Jesus Christ until they reveal from their heart any errors in their beliefs or lifestyle. We are told not to Judge. God is the only Judge of mankind. He is in control. Our task is to be *Fruit Inspectors*.

Our goal is to *"know Christ..."* and keep learning more about His commands.

Lifelong Learning to *know* God will someday, become Eternal Learning *with* God!

Evidences, the Role of LEARNER, Fulfilled

Personal Checklist
Circle the best answer for each to determine score.

Have I demonstrated…

1. A *"hunger and thirst for righteousness?"* (Matthew 5:6).

1	2	3	4	5
Not at all	A little bit	Usually	Most of the time	Always

2. An increased desire to know God? *"that I might know Him and the power of His resurrection and the fellowship of His sufferings, being conformed to His death; in order that I might attain the resurrection from the dead"* (Philippians 3:10).

1	2	3	4	5
Not at all	A little bit	Usually	Most of the time	Always

3. An avoidance of time spent reading, listening, sharing and participating with those who *"walk in the counsel of the wicked, stand in the path of sinners, sit in the seat of the scoffers"* (Psalm 1:1)?

1	2	3	4	5
Not at all	A little bit	Usually	Most of the time	Always

4. A newfound appreciation for the book of the law? "*It shall not depart from your mouth, but you shall meditate on it day and night, so that you may be careful to do according to all that is written in it, for then you will make your way prosperous, and then you will have success"* (Joshua 1:8).

1	2	3	4	5
Not at all	A little bit	Usually	Most of the time	Always

5. The ability to apply the wisdom learned from the Scriptures to the needs of my life and those of people I meet? *"I will destroy the wisdom of the wise, and the cleverness of the wise will I set aside…has not God made foolish the wisdom of the world?... because the foolishness of God is wiser than men. Let him who boasts, boast in the Lord"* (See 1 Corinthians 1:18-31).

1	2	3	4	5
Not at all	A little bit	Usually	Most of the time	Always

Total divided by 5 =

Projects for Investigation and Discussion

[__] What is the difference between Knowledge and Wisdom? What is the relationship?

[__] James 3:13-18 and 4:1-10 suggest a difference between "*earthly, natural, demonic*" wisdom and "*wisdom from above.*" Compare the characteristics of these two kinds of wisdom.

[__] *"A Christian should avoid association with those who hold Divine Truth in somewhat less esteem."* - What would be your response to a man who shared this view with you?

[__] What might be done to assist the man who is genuinely handicapped by a low reading level, sight reduction or limited academic progress to learn the Word of God?

[__] In your community of friends, who buys and reads the most "self-help" books and magazines: men or women? Why?

[__] Identify five Learning Projects that you have participated in during the last two years.

1. ______________________________

2. ______________________________

3. ______________________________

4. ______________________________

5. ______________________________

What was your motivation to learn? How could you share the value of your learning experiences with another man in such a manner that he would be encouraged to become a 'lifelong learner' with Integrity.

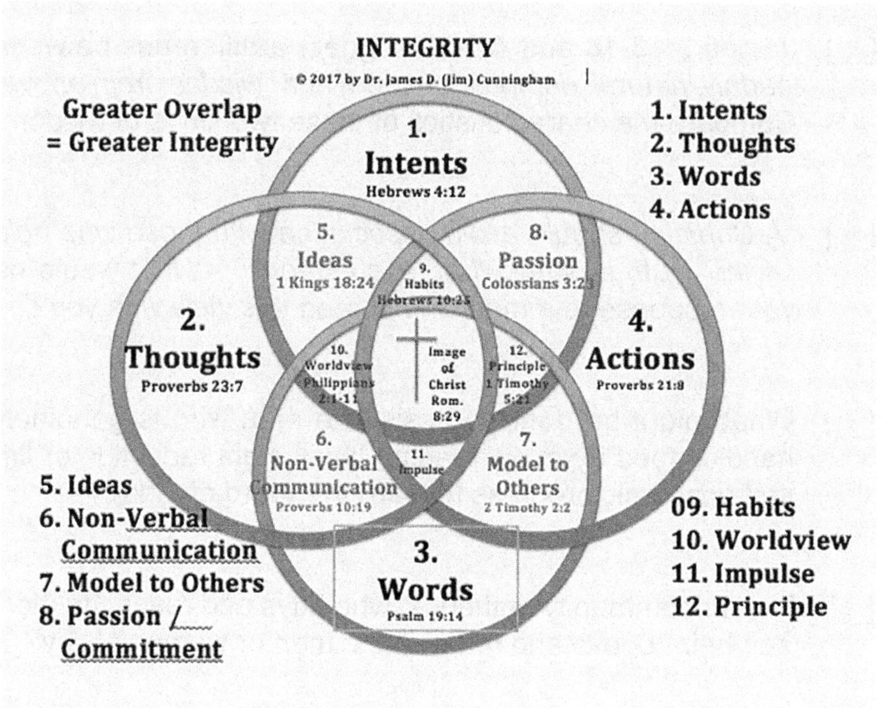

Chapter 4

Friend • Relationships With His Friends

A friend loveth at all times... • Proverbs 17:17

If we walk in the light as He Himself is in the light
we have fellowship with one another • 1 John 1:7

"Most men do not have one intimate male friend..."

I said that to a men's group in a seminar and almost before I could finish asking, "Do you agree?" three men simultaneously began to speak:

"I agree," offered the first.

"That's right on," confided the second, "In today's society, people consider you're either gay or weird if you have a close male friend."

The third added: "Believe it or not guys, my wife gets jealous if I spend time with another man!"

What a predicament. Today's men are busy working, doing, being, earning wages, but without close intimate male friends to share life's good, bad and ugly times.

Sidney Jourard said: "Every maladjusted person is a person who has not made himself known to another human being and in consequence does not know himself. Nor can he be himself. He struggles actively to avoid becoming known by another human being. He works at it ceaselessly, twenty-four hours a day and it is work!" [61]

Let's look at how we fulfill our role as a Friend.

Solomon, who happened to have an above average number of women in his life says: *"If a man would have friends, he must show himself to be friendly"* – (Proverbs 18:24, KJV). I was astounded to read the same verse in another translation (NASV): *"A man of too many friends comes to ruin..."* The implication appears to be that a man must have a right relationship with his friends or else the very ones he is calling his friends could become his ruin!

---

[61] Sidney Jourard, The Transparent Self. Princeton: D. Van Nostrand Co., 1964. P. 26

7 Levels of Friendship

Let's move through these seven levels starting at the bottom and working higher.

Level 1: The Masses

These are the people we *bump into as we live life.* We periodically, randomly meet or see each other at the grocery store, on an airplane or at a game. We see them once, perhaps we never see again.

Level 2: Body-Level Handshake Friendships

Let's call this the *Body-Level* Friendship. We now recognize their face having met them once or twice. Thus begins the possibility of friendship as three things silently happen:

- We recognize him (the body)
- We know certain visible physical characteristics of him: "The guy with the scar on his forehead..."
- We may know his name enough to identify him.

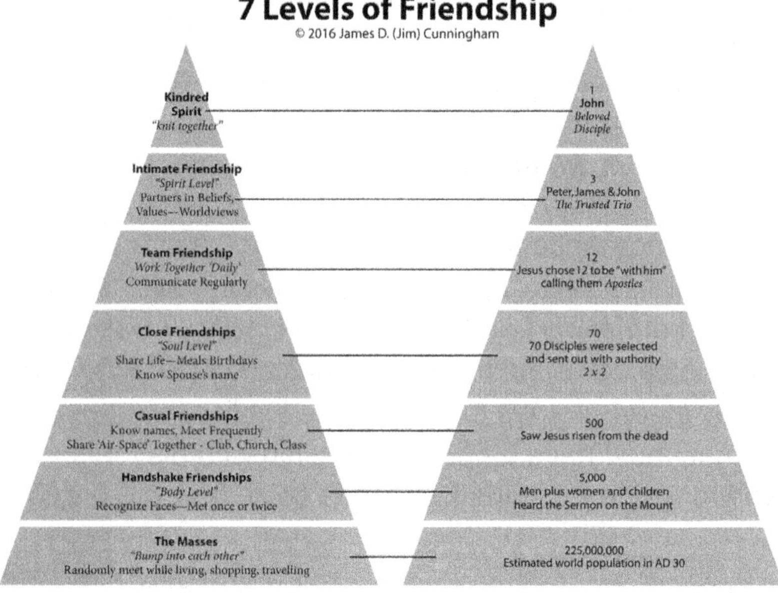

Our response to this *Handshake Friendship* can be one of the following:

- **Acceptance (based on biblical love)** – "I like that guy." "I enjoy meeting him." "I'd like to get to know him."
- **Neutrality (based on personal apathy)** – "Hi." "Nice day." "See you around."
- **Rejection (based on selfish indifference or prejudice)** – "He talks too much." "Can't stand fat guys like that." or rejection based on personal unbiblical attitudes.

The process has begun. Our short-term memory retains information about the person as long as we feel the need for it. Example: You're standing at the Rift Valley outside Nairobi, staring at the grandeur of God's Creation. The tourist beside you (from Sweden) says, "Hi." Unlikely a lifelong friendship will begin unless you happen to be going to Sweden and initiate a conversation beyond the handshake.

If that happens, we now have a name and perhaps his business card! [62] The relationship has a formal beginning. This Introductory *Handshake Friendship* may contain what could be considered public domain information: occupation, residence, family, etc. For many people, this is as far as the friendship goes. "Do you know (name)?" is answered with "Yeah, he's the mechanic at Ed's Garage." That's all it is men, just a handshake friendship.

Level 3 – Air-Space Casual Friendships

Things now progress further. We know his name and have met him more frequently. We may even be sharing air space in a club, church or classroom.

Eleanor Roosevelt was thought to be the originator of this insight: Great minds talk about ideas; average minds about things and small minds about people. A certain shift or segue takes place in

---

[62] I often thought a good name for a child would be *"There."* Then no matter where in the world he went people would remember his name. Even if they forgot, they could boldly walk up to him like they do when they forget a name and say: "Oh, hi *There!*" And they would have it!

a relationship once the conversation moves from things to ideas. So begins one of the greatest adventures on Earth: knowing the thoughts of another person. In the process one learns to accept him as a friend in spite of occasional disagreements.

A person's thought life is his own. We must learn how to enter this area with gentleness, honesty, respect and love. *"Speaking the truth in love"* is the secret to building a Casual (Sharing) Friendship – (See Ephesians 4:17). Many people carry bruises and scars from past friends who betrayed their trust by deceit, fraud or manipulation. They may be reluctant to start a deeper friendship with anyone for fear of a repeated betrayal.

Some live in what could be called a short-term community. They may refuse to consider a *Sharing Friendship* with anyone who has not been in the community for a pre-determined length of time. In Canada's northern Territory called the Yukon, one was considered an "Outsider" until they lived "North of 60 degrees" for 50 years!" Then they became an "Insider."

> Story: Our family spent a year living in Jerusalem. The first Sabbath we went to Narkis Street Southern Baptist Church. To begin making some new friends we picked a family standing in the foyer and boldly said: *"Would you like to come home with us for lunch?"* They agreed. It turned out they were visitors from Atlanta, Georgia. They only had one week in Israel, and they thought we were long-time Jerusalem resident's who could *"tell them all about Israel..."* We laughed until it happened again the next week with a second couple. They too were tourists! By week three we started to notice those who were regular attenders.

Confession time. Why can you *share air* with some people every day for years: the same office, same lunchroom, same Board Meetings, yet, as soon as you leave their presence (end of the day, week, job, or retirement) they disappear out of your mind. Let's call them *Close Strangers Who Share Air Space.* You have about as much in common with them as the guy in the next seat on a 10-hour flight to Frankfurt. Nice to talk to, perhaps, maybe shared a few personal details, but virtually no connection at the Soul Level. It remains just a Casual Friendship.

Level 4 – Soul-Level Close Friendships

This deeper, or higher depending on your perspective, Soul-Level Friendship is closely related to 1 John 1:7. *"If we walk in the light as He Himself is in the light, we have fellowship with one another and the blood of Jesus His Son cleanses us from all sin."*

This level requires two men *"walking in the light"* of God's Word before they can begin a Soul Level Close Friendship. More than sharing work together, this level includes meals, special occasions, and family events to help bond a Close Friendship. At this stage, you likely know, appreciate, and pray for his spouse, kids, and family. I must confess, it's either there, or it isn't. I had a friendship with one leader in another city for years. Then I discovered he had committed adultery with three different women, yet still said *Grace* at every meal we shared and never revealed any moral struggles when we met! Discernment is needed to avoid the *"wolf-in-sheep-clothing sociopath"* who seeks your close friendship to enhance his ego, status or reputation.

Level 5 – Team Friendships

David Bentall describes the Covenant Partnership he, Carson Pue and Bob Kuhn agreed to at the beginning of their friendship. I share this as an example of a *Team (Commitment) Friendship* that has stood the test of many, many years in what they call a "transformational friendship." They committed to eight promises: [63]

- To affirm one another
- To be available to one another (in proper relation to our commitments to marriage and family)
- To pray with and for one another

[63] I highly recommend their book, The Company You Keep: The Transforming Power of Male Friendship," Augsburg Books, Minneapolis, 2004.

- To be open with one another
- To be honest with one another
- To treat one another with sensitivity
- To keep our discussions confidential
- To be accountable to one another

Close working Team Friendships remind me of the Billy Graham Team of Cliff Barrows, Beverly Shea and Billy Graham, who after meeting and ministering together in 1949 continued to serve as a team until Bev Shea died in 2013, at the age of 102! Cliff Barrows died in 2016, at 93! And, at the time of writing this (August 24, 2017), Billy Graham (born November 7, 1918) is still alive at age 98! That's a high-level long-term Team Friendship. [64]

Level 6 – Intimate Friendship

Intimate Commitment-Level Friendships require reciprocal contributions ingredients from each participant. Early in my adult years I created a list of what I was looking for in a Friendship. It almost matched the list above by David Bentall, but I had two additional items:

- To lovingly accept each other *as we are* and let the Holy Spirit do the changing.
- To help each other improve character and grow the fruit of the Spirit.

Spirit Level Commitment Friendship is like good health, hard to define and describe but you know when you *don't* have it.

---

[64] In the Hebrew Scriptures Methuselah was the longest living man on earth (969 years old). His name means "after-his-death-comes-judgment." He died one week before The Flood (Genesis 5). Billy has preached salvation and repentance to over 200 million people worldwide. To me, Billy Graham may well be America's "Methuselah." Are you ready?

Level 7 – Kindred Spirit Friendship *"…their souls were knit together…"*

1 Samuel 18:1 tells us the soul of Jonathan was *knit* (united) to the soul of David *"and Jonathan loved him as himself…"* When David heard news of Jonathan's death he chanted his lament by saying in part… *"I am distressed for you, my brother Jonathan; you have been very pleasant to me. Your love to me was more wonderful than the love of women…"* – (2 Samuel 1:26).

Now, guys, this gets a little awkward. I am making no comment on what David might have meant. I only know what it says: *"their souls were knit together."* What a beautiful illustration of the intricacy and interlocking of two individual's lives. Kindred-spirit friendships remain elusive for many men. [65]

A married man learns how to be intimate (open, honest) with the one person with whom he is in a *Covenant Relationship*, his wife. He is more likely to find courage or faith to share at a *kindred spirit* level with another man if he is open with his wife. A single man can enjoy that same level of "kindred-spirit" friendship – if he is willing to be open and honest.

Friendships can rarely be superimposed or transplanted from one man to another. Because A is good friends with B and A is also good friends with C does not guarantee that B and C will automatically be friends. Each person must build his level of friendships.

Covenant Level Friendship

Look at a photo of an older couple married for 50+ years. Did you notice (or is it my imagination?) that often the husband and wife begin to look alike? Don't laugh. Virtually every time this is mentioned, someone says, "That's right."

---

[65] A "kindred spirit" usually refers to a bond between two men. Sometimes it may describe a bond between a team or the "esprit-des-corps" among a military unit. One rare example in my experience has been the "three-way-kindred-spirit" shared by David Bentall (a builder); Carson Pue (a pastor) and Bob Kuhn (a lawyer and president of Trinity Western University).

Let's consider why it could be possible:

- *The two have become one physically.* They share the most intimate possible physical relationship in a manner that no one else can (or should try to) replicate with either of them.
- *The two have shared their goals, aspirations, sorrows, tragedies, disagreements, and joys.* Their lifetime of experiences has bonded them together.
- *The two have committed themselves to help build character in each other.* The closest model for comparison has been their mate. If I like his smile, I smile like he does. If she is angry, I learn to look angry just like her. And so it goes.
- *The two have shared the most powerful emotional pressure mold ever known to man*, love through marriage.

A biblical marriage between a man and a woman is a Covenant Relationship! God and Israel had (and still have) a Covenant Relationship. God had an intimate relationship/friendship with Adam and Eve in the Garden of Eden before The Fall. God speaks to Amos about His relationship to the nation of Israel and says: "*You only have I chosen among all the families of the earth…*" – (Amos 3:2). God's relationship with Israel is an unbroken, eternal covenant relationship.

Covenant relationships cause us to be committed, try harder, and never give up! As a result, they evolve into something beautiful. David and Jonathan had both: a covenant relationship as well as a kindred spirit – (See 1 Samuel 18:3 and 20:42). Did their kindred spirit come first? Probably.

At the time of this writing I share a 60-year friendship with my kindred spirit friend: Paul Estabrooks. Does a BFF (Best Friend Forever) just develop with lots of input and time – or is there something there from the initial meeting? Probably both.

Salvation brings us into a new covenant relationship with God through faith in Jesus Christ. God chose us (See Ephesians 1:3-14] and gave us both the grace and the faith to receive His gift of salvation and friendship. "*For by grace, you have been saved through faith; and that not of yourselves, it is the gift of God; not as a result of works, so that no one may boast. For we are His workmanship, created in Christ Jesus for good works, which God prepared beforehand so that we would walk in them"*—(Ephesians 2:8-10). We are God's friends and co-heirs (Romans 8:17) based on the covenant friendship He established with us forever!

My Kindred Spirit Club

Some Friends **Move**—Out-of-Touch—**Gone**
Some Friends
Change—Roles-Relationships-Spouse—**Gone**
Some Friends **Disappear**—What-ever-happened to good ol' [whatshisname]?—**Gone**
Some Friends **Share Air**—After Meeting-end of day—**Gone**
Some Friends **"Facebook"** ®—Turn off computer—**Gone**
Some Friends **Die**—*Cross-over-the-river*—**Gone**
But some Friendships are **Alive and Healthy**—True Friends are hard to come by!
Alive and Healthy Friendships Remain—Neither Time, Distance, Age, Mobility, Health
Nor Disagreements affect this Friendship.
They are **More-Than-A-Friend**—They are **Kindred Spirits.**

How do we achieve Intimacy in a Friendship?

One of life's greatest pleasures is to have a friend. A person with whom there is no agenda, no pretense, with whom you can be yourself. A person willing to be bold and wisely correct you in love for doing, thinking or saying something unbiblical.

1955 < Jim Cunningham and Paul Estabrooks > 2015

The friends with whom I have the most intimate friendships are ones with whom I can pray one-on-one. Watch out for attention-seekers who only pray in public or a group to impress you with their spirituality.

Friendship to Discipleship
A Model Demonstrated by Jesus

- may hear about a person
- meet for first time
- introduced, learn each other's name
- John 1:29 "Behold the Lamb of God"

- want to meet again
- think of each other when not together
- meet again planned or unplanned
- time spent speaking to each other
- John 1:39 "They stayed that day"

- appreciation develops for the ideas, values, and beliefs of each other
- Matt 4:21 "Come follow me"

- ways to share time—meals
- relaxing visits are sought and arranged
- Luke 6:13 "chose 12 to be the apostles"

- some source of irritation such as a manner, habit, value , attitude begins to emerge
- John 6:6 "This is hard saying"

- pros and cons of continued involvement are weighed against the replacement effort and cost

- decision made to resolve "conflict"
- reconfirmation of love to each other
- John 6:8 "to whom shall we go you have eternal life"

- if possible a kindred spirit may develop
- Rev 21:2,9 "I will show you the bride (the church) the wife of the Lamb of God"

> Story: Rita had a hip implant surgery that required me to be her caregiver for some 12 weeks. I was her *reacher*. She was not to bend past her knees, nor bend her hips past 90 degrees. I did her personal care, made meals, helped her in and out of bed and even tied shoelaces for her. One business-minded visitor said, "Boy, Rita is going to owe you big-time for all you've done for her!" My response was: "No, Rita owes me nothing. She's invested in our marriage-friendship for 49 years. She's now receiving dividends on her investment!"

Intimate friends "*pray for one another*" and pray *with* one another! One guy told me (after he broke up with the girl he had planned to marry) that in two years of dating they had never prayed together. Hello? Never! In two years. What were they doing that caused them to think of getting married?

Intimacy, in marriage or friendship, requires a mutually agreeable *movement towards one another with* mutual truth and mutual trust. Scripture says: "*...confess your sins to one another, and pray for one another so that you may be healed...*"—(James 5:16). Most faults are usually obvious to everyone else more than they are to us. But, when you do confess them to others, it confirms your credibility if you admit a fault, and your integrity if you do something about it to become a different person!

The context of our verse from James 5 is related to details for healing. It can also apply to the healing of friendships, a misunderstanding, an unkind word or a jealous response. Rita and I are *perpetual mutual forgivers*. Virtually all bonds require forgiveness to maintain the relationship. Even more so in marriage!

Options for Men's Ministries in a Local Church

Men's Ministries is too large a need and men have too many needs for any one model to work. To say our church only does Men's Ministries one way is at best naïve, arrogant at worst and destined for failure. No one model meets the needs of all men today! On top of Home Bible Studies shared with other couples and women, men need times together as men! Let me suggest they need three overlapping simultaneous models.

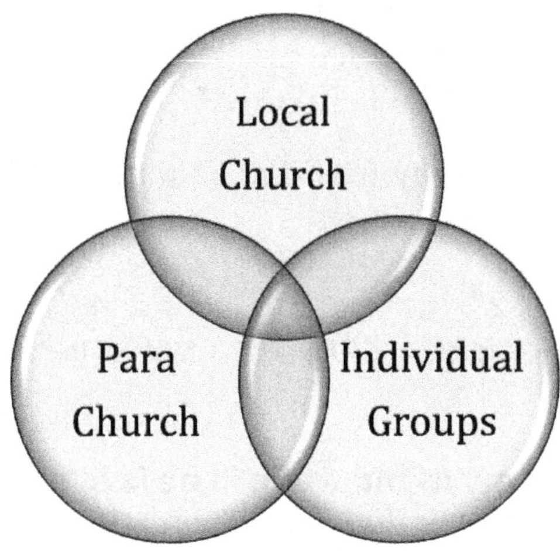

- **Local Church** (Your Local Church's Men's Ministry).
- This includes: Retreats, Breakfasts, Speakers, Challenges, Evangelism, Prayer Groups, Bible Studies, Service Projects, Fishing weekends, times of bonding and Fun!

- **Para-church** (Your Denomination or Inter-Denominational Men's Ministry).
- This includes: Insightful Speakers, Cross-Denominational, Challenging Topic, plus Outdoor Challenges and Community Service Projects

- **Individual** (Your Smaller Men's Ministry Accountability Team).
- Similar to the model developed in *The Company You Keep* by David Bentall, Bob Kuhn and Carson Pue. Smaller Accountability Groups (three to five guys) meeting regularly with honesty and intimacy with a variety of study texts to focus discussion for times together.

Overall Goal

To be conformed to the Image of Jesus Christ

Help make it happen my brothers!

Competencies Required for Role of FRIEND

Personal Checklist
Circle the best answer for each to determine your score

Do I have…

1. The ability to love my friend at all times?—*"A friend loves at all times"*— (Proverbs 17:17).

1	2	3	4	5
Not at all	A little bit	Usually	Most of the time	Always

2. Availability to my friend when in he is in need?—" *there is a friend who sticks closer than a brother"*—(Proverbs 18:24).

1	2	3	4	5
Not at all	A little bit	Usually	Most of the time	Always

3. A willingness to confront my friend in a spirit of gentleness?—*"Faithful are the wounds of a friend…"*—(Proverbs 27:6).

1	2	3	4	5
Not at all	A little bit	Usually	Most of the time	Always

4. A desire to see my friend grow and mature in his Christian walk?—*"Iron sharpens iron, so one man sharpens another"*—(Proverbs 27:17).

1	2	3	4	5
Not at all	A little bit	Usually	Most of the time	Always

5. A sensitivity and awareness of the right time to say and do certain things with my friend?—*"He who blesses his friend* *with a loud voice early in the morning, it will be reckoned a curse to him"*—(Proverbs 27:14).

1	2	3	4	5
Not at all	A little bit	Usually	Most of the time	Always

6. The ability to offer wise counsel to my friend?—*"Oil and perfume make the heart glad, So a man's counsel is sweet to his friend…"* – (Proverbs 27:9).

1	2	3	4	5
Not at all	A little bit	Usually	Most of the time	Always

7. Loyalty to their character development?

1	2	3	4	5
Not at all	A little bit	Usually	Most of the time	Always

8. Trustworthiness in keeping confidential information?

1	2	3	4	5
Not at all	A little bit	Usually	Most of the time	Always

Total divided by 8 =

Evidences, the Role of FRIEND, Fulfilled

Personal Checklist
Circle the best answer for each to determine score.

Have I demonstrated…

1. A number of individuals at all 7 Levels of Friendship whom I regard as my friends with the assurance they have a similar connection with me?

1	2	3	4	5
Not at all	A little bit	Usually	Most of the time	Always

2. People whom I can call at 3:00 AM in the morning in an emergency and they will come—or visit unannounced and uninvited in any time of need or concern and know they will give me a warm welcome and an open door?

1	2	3	4	5
Not at all	A little bit	Usually	Most of the time	Always

3. A depth in my relationship with people that is personally significant enough to use the word 'Friend"?

1	2	3	4	5
Not at all	A little bit	Usually	Most of the time	Always

4. Unsolicited and unexpected personal evidences to me of others friendship? (e.g., calls, visits, gifts, expressions of remembrance that serve as a partial barometer of our mutual movement toward one another, beyond Christmas cards and Facebook!

1	2	3	4	5
Not at all	A little bit	Usually	Most of the time	Always

5. The development of a *"kindred spirit."* (See 1 Samuel 18:1; 20:41-42 and 2 Samuel 1:26).

1	2	3	4	5
Not at all	A little bit	Usually	Most of the time	Always

6. An openness to confess or correct, discuss or disagree without fear of betrayal, rejection, withdrawal or hostility?

1	2	3	4	5
Not at all	A little bit	Usually	Most of the time	Always

7. An evidence of respective input and movement toward one another in character development? (He may have encouraged you to exercise; you may have helped him refrain from vulgar language).

1	2	3	4	5
Not at all	A little bit	Usually	Most of the time	Always

Total divided by 7 =

The Role of a Friend

Projects for Investigation and Discussion

[__] Five Friendship Challenges:

- List three friends who aided your journey through school
- List three friends who helped you through a difficult time as an adult.
- List three friends who have been a mentor to your character development.
- List three friends who make you feel appreciated and extraordinary.
- List three friends who you enjoy *"just hanging out with"* – without an agenda.

Send each one a personal, handwritten note of thanks

[__] *A husband should be his wife's best friend.* – Do you agree or disagree? Share reasons.

[__] Many men admit to not having one intimate male friend! Why do you believe this is true? What factors affected your answers?

[__] What are some of the differences between a Friend – and a Mentor? What are the values and limitations of being a Mentor?

[__] Homosexuality appears to be increasing in our society. As a man, what do you believe are reasons for this shift in morality among people? What might you consider to be a positive response to those engaged in the LGBTQ lifestyle?

[__] A friend says to you: "I have tried to be friendly with George, but I just can't get anywhere in building a friendship with him. I just don't know what to do." What is your counsel to your friend?

[__] Write the name of your most intimate male friend. Look at APPENDIX A. All 22 items should be natural for you IF an intimate friend.

Chapter 5

Single • Relationship to Living Alone

Make sure that your character is free from the love of money, being content with what you have; for He Himself has said, "I will never desert you, nor will I ever forsake you," • Hebrews 13:5

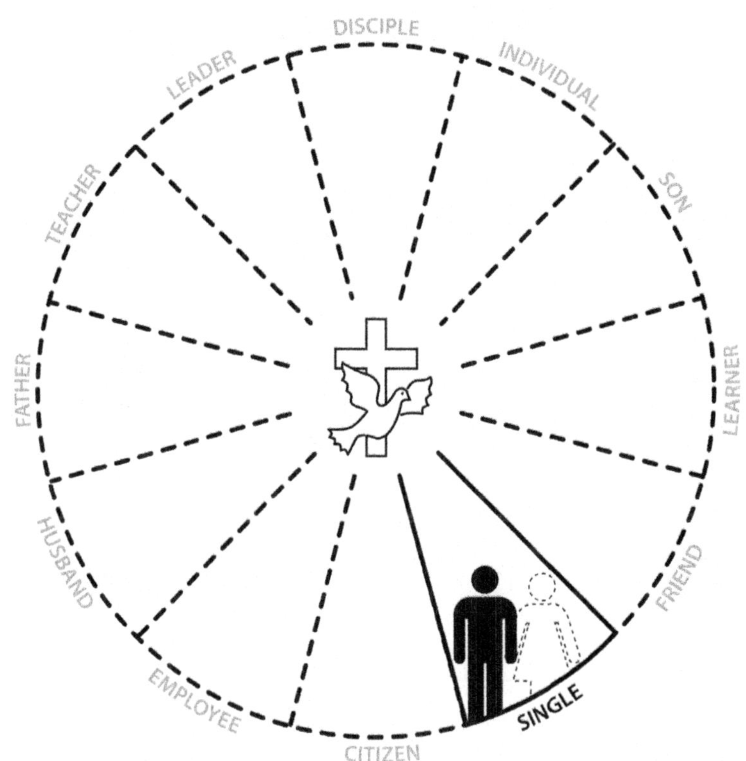

Who Are The New Singles?

The definition of Single has morphed from unmarried to include any man living alone. It now includes Bachelors who never married; Widowers who went through the death of a spouse; Separated who are not currently living with their spouse and Divorced who had a wife but for multiple reasons ended the marriage. All now live on their own as Singles.

Every man begins life fulfilling his role as a Single Man. Some marry quickly in their teens. Some, like my brother-in-law lived as a never-married single until he was 60! Being Single can be examined from two perspectives: singles in a transitional role and those who have elected to remain single (about 5% of the male population).

Our role as a single man: From observing single men enjoying life here are a few observations:

First, maximize your full potential! Single is a state of being, not a state of mind! Single is not to be equated with lonely, even if there are times of feeling somewhat alone. Transitionally single is the time to investigate, travel, explore new opportunities and put your creativity to work. Many purposeful life activities and projects get accomplished while single. As a single 23-year-old college student, I managed (and lived with) eighteen recovering dry alcoholics in the Quinten Warner Halfway House in London, ON. This assignment would never have been possible had I been married.

Second, direct your talents, strength, and energy into projects of service to others. Serving others brings dividends that are disproportional beyond any investment of time you may make.

Third, preserve a clean, transparent lifestyle. The volitionally single men we know enjoy their life to the full. They direct their time and energy into projects that use their talents and gifting. They remain open to the possibility of marriage should the Lord bring the right woman of His choice into their life at His appointed time. They do not view being single as an incurable disease. However, with the rise of the homosexuality, single straight men are increasingly held up for suspicion in today's hedonistic society.

Fifth, maintain Philippians 4:8 as your life verse. The Apostle Paul writes: "*Finally, brethren, whatever is true, whatever is honorable, whatever is right, whatever is pure, whatever is lovely, whatever is of good repute if there is any excellence and if anything worthy of praise, dwell on these things.*" Loose living, sexual promiscuity, fornication, pornography (even masturbation) require a mind that is diametrically opposed to the verse above.

Sixth, avoid the appearance of evil to minimize gossip and slander of your reputation. Some single men will not drive with a married woman alone in the same vehicle unless a third party is present. Legalism? No. Reality! People watch. People talk. Saying you *do not care what people think* does not stop people from thinking.

Seventh, keep an open door for hospitality mixed with freedom for privacy as needed. Build open friendships with men and women. If you want a single woman in your home, invite a married couple as well.

Eighth, maximize the development of your spiritual gifts. *There is only one spiritual gift* (The Holy Spirit) given to us when we are born again (John 3). But, the Holy Spirit has a multiplicity of spiritual gifts. He can give us whatever gift we need to suit the task. The key is: allow the Holy Spirit to fill you and control you!

A single man who invests his time wisely is a treat to meet. The opposite holds true for a foolish and undisciplined, single man – at any stage in life.

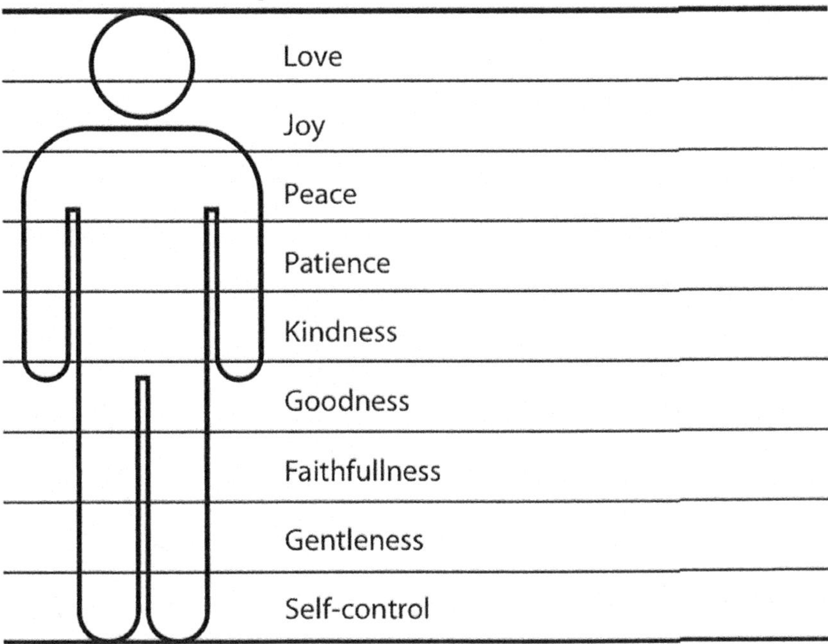

Ninth, exercise (practice) the character qualities required to be a servant-leader-elder. Look at the chart on the next page (below). It is my rendition of what I call The 10 Commandments for Elders. Each Commandment has attached below related character qualities of an Elder. At one conference I had these 10 Commandments printed, so each one was on a business-card-size piece of paper. I gave each man the ten pieces. Then I told them, "Put these in order so the one you have the MOST issues with is on the ***bottom***. Then place the one you find the easiest to do or the LEAST issue in your life on the ***top*** of the pile with the others in ascending/descending order in between. They did. Then I told them the story of Mathias Rust flying his little Cessna from Helsinki through the heaviest Soviet air defense system in Russia and landing in Red Square[66] I added: "The card on TOP, the one area you feel is most protected could also be the area from which the Enemy of our soul attacks us without warning!"

---

[66] https://en.wikipedia.org/wiki/Mathias_Rust#Later_life

1
No other gods before me

There is one God Jehovah.

Holding firm to scriptural truths
1 Timothy 3:9;
Titus 1:9

Tested
1 Timothy 3:10

2
No idols In any form

Sports – Money
Materialism – Hobbies

Upright and holy
Titus 1:8

Not given to drunkenness
1 Timothy 3:3, 8;
Titus 1:7

3
No taking the Lord's name in vain

End swearing and/or minced oaths

Self-controlled
1 Timothy 3:2;
Titus 1:8

Sincere
1 Timothy 3:8

4
Remember the Sabbath day

Keep it holy vs. 'working'

Able to teach
1 Timothy 3:2; 5:17;
Titus 1:9

Hospitable
1 Timothy 3:2;
Titus 1:8

5
Honour your father and mother

Live long with obedience & respect

Managing family well
1 Timothy 3:4, 12;
Titus 1:6

Having obedient children
1 Timothy 3:4-5, 12
Titus 1:6

6
You shall not kill

Avoid hating and being "mean-spirited"

Not quarrelsome
1 Timothy 3:3

Not violent but gentle
1 Timothy 3:3; Titus 1:7

Not quick-tempered
Not overbearing
Titus 1:7

7
No adultery

End lusting and "image"ing

Having one wife
1 Timothy 3:2, 12

Disciplined
Titus 1:8

8
No stealing

Time theft/deceit tax manipulation

Not a pursuer of dishonest gain
1 Timothy 3:8;
Titus 1:7

Not a lover of money
1 Timothy 3:3

9
No false testimony

Gossip or Slander

Good reputation with outsiders
1 Timothy 3:7

Respectable
1 Timothy 3:2, 8

10
No coveting

Jealousy or Envy

Above reproach
1 Timothy 3:2, 9;
Titus 1:6
Loving what is good
Titus 1:8

And for Elders/Deacons
Not a new convert
1 Timothy 3:6

I Just Don't Have Time

Let's consider the medium of exchange we call time. We offer temporal services, skills or activities to an eternal time market. In exchange, we receive opportunities to have our needs met.

Figure 5-A

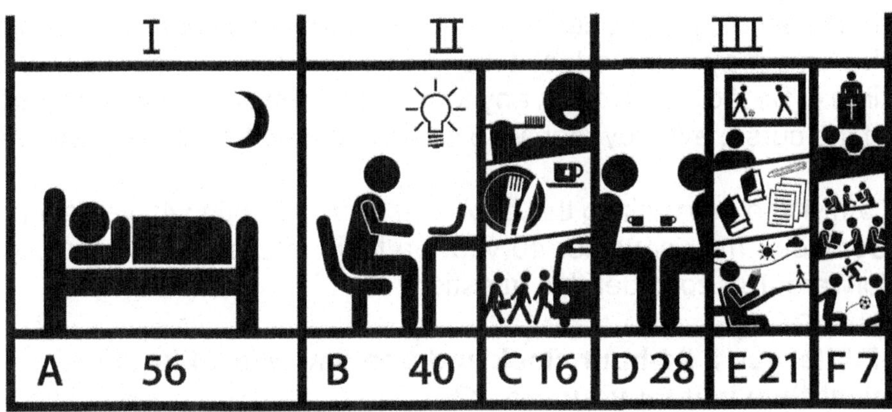

Look at the Chart above:

Section I – A = Sleep based on 8 hours a night	7 X 8 =	56
Section II – B = Work	5 X 8 =	40
Section II – C = Preparation and Travel	5 X 3.2 =	16
		56
Section III = Personal Time such as:		
Section III – D = Meals / Home / Family	7 X 4 =	28
Section III – E = Free Time / Hobbies / Screen Time	7 X 3 =	21
Section III – F = Church / Service Activities	7 X 1 =	7
		56
TOTAL (3 x 56) equals one week		168 hours

Life for many men is: *Rest during A so they can Do B & C to earn money to Enjoy D, E, and F.*

Each man is given the same amount of time to exchange to fulfill his chosen goals. Perhaps the word redeem is better than exchange. We have a pre-determined, God ordained amount of time on this Earth. [67] God designed time. He created the 24-hour day. He created darkness at night – for a portion of the 24 hours. He designed our bodies to require rest and exercise and nourishment. Therefore everything that requires time is part of God's plan for man to have purpose and significance. Men often find their greatest joy in Section III but begrudge time spent in Section II. Some may even reduce time in Section I and II to spend more time in Section III. Work in any form is still viewed by many as part of the curse, even by men who do not claim to be Bible believers!

I am sitting here writing this book that I started writing 40 years ago. Someone may consider 40 years a long time at age 30 looking forward! But consider this question:

IF Life was a 24-hour clock and one day was 24 hours – what time is it on your clock?

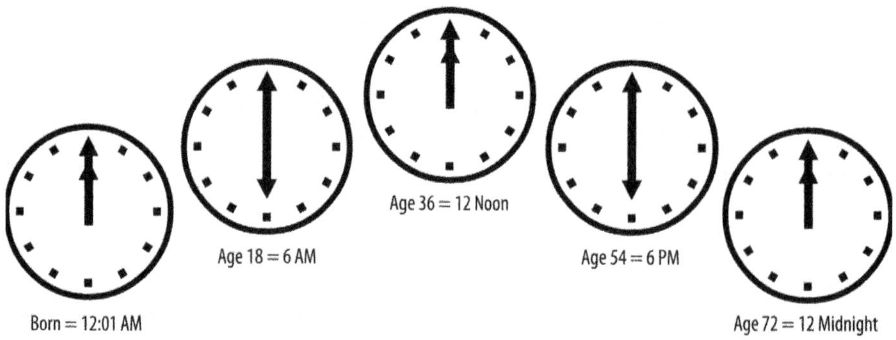

Time – The Gift of God to All Men

Have you ever read a book where the author writes something like: "This is being written from 35,000 feet (12,000 meters) as I am flying from City A (usually their hometown) to City B (usually far away). Perhaps they are trying to impress upon us the readers how disciplined they are in their use of time. Paul announced

---

[67] Psalm 31:15a

he was writing from prison, chained between two Roman guards. [68]Writing from prison holds less appeal as a place of inspiration. Regardless of our surroundings we need to be wise stewards of our time.

The adage *"You cannot teach an old dog new tricks,"* may be suitable for dogs but not humans. Adults can learn. Some men can rule a nation in a 12-hour period, while other men can barely cope with their day's limited activities. Why is there such a contrast in their accomplishments?

The answer lies in two concepts: Responsibility and Priorities. Each of us must assume responsibility for the next 24 hours. Consider how much time we are going to invest in front of a screen today. Screens include television, computer, mobile phones, tablets and whatever others may be invented before finishing this book!

Concept number two is that we program our time to do whatever we consider a priority. Look what happens when there is a tragedy. A family member needs emergency surgery or there is death. A Single man can often re-arrange his time to meet these responsibilities and new priorities. For married men with children it becomes more challenging,

> Story: I once landed at an airport and was approaching a car rental booth. In front of me was a pastor friend from a far-away city. After renting our vehicles, we sat and had a coffee together. He told me why he was in town. His youngest son had run away from home. Some time later the son's old car had broken down near the city we were in, and the son had phoned his dad to see if he could come back home. We prayed together, and he left to meet the son. I mentally added up the cost of this event. Airfare, car rental, hotel, towing charges, meals, pulpit supply to cover his absence all because his son was in need of help. His responsibilities were radically altered. His priorities of time and finances took on a new perspective.

[68] Acts26:29; Ephesians 6:20 2 Timothy 1:16

What are priorities for a Single Man?

- A right relationship with God as a Disciple of Jesus Christ
- A right relationship with Parents/Family
- A right relationship with Employer
- A right relationship with Friends
- A right relationship with Neighbors/Government

And, Keep a Journal. Write what God is doing in your life. It becomes your Personal History Book of answers to prayer, events that happened and how God used them for your good. [69]

***

[69] See Chapter 12 for more information on keeping a Journal

Competencies to Fulfill Role of SINGLE

Personal Checklist
Circle the best answer for each to determine score

Have I…

1. Never been married? Traditional meaning of being single or bachelor (A secondary meaning has evolved that includes men who are divorced, separated, widowers, or living on their own without a wife or children.)

1	2	3	4	5
Not at all	A little bit	Usually	Most of the time	Always

2. Recognized that God is my strength? (Habakkuk 3:16-19)

1	2	3	4	5
Not at all	A little bit	Usually	Most of the time	Always

3. An awareness of the special calling God has for me as a single man? *“Not all men can accept this statement, but only those to whom it has been given. For there are eunuchs who were born that way…also eunuchs who made themselves eunuchs for the kingdom of heaven. He who is able to accept this let him accept it.”* (Matthew 19:12) Happy is the single man who knows ‘why’ he is single!

1	2	3	4	5
Not at all	A little bit	Usually	Most of the time	Always

4. The ability to respond in praise to the Lord for being single? (Nehemiah 8:10 – *“the joy of the Lord is your strength.”*)

1	2	3	4	5
Not at all	A little bit	Usually	Most of the time	Always

Total divided by 4 =

Evidences, the Role of SINGLE, Fulfilled

Personal Checklist
Circle the best answer for each to determine score.

Have I demonstrated…

1. Personal satisfaction with being single? (The man who has remained single in disobedience to the will of God or through a personal fear of women or marriage or accepting responsibility will be unable to check this one.)

1	2	3	4	5
Not at all	A little bit	Usually	Most of the time	Always

2. Evidence that I am a maturing person, leading a balanced life? (Every bachelor has his own 'idiosyncrasies' – so do many married men – but when the role is properly fulfilled, there will be an evidence of stability in your lifestyle.)

1	2	3	4	5
Not at all	A little bit	Usually	Most of the time	Always

3. Recognition of the unique calling or task God has given to me to do? Often this will be an assignment that would be unsuited to a married man.

1	2	3	4	5
Not at all	A little bit	Usually	Most of the time	Always

4. Utilization of the time, resources and energy God has given to me to be involved in the ministry of the kingdom of heaven.

1	2	3	4	5
Not at all	A little bit	Usually	Most of the time	Always

Total divided by 4 =

Role of SINGLE

Projects for Investigation and Discussion

[__] From the section on Time, compare how a married man and a single man invest the hours in a week. What would be the difference in terms of how hours can be invested by both to the maximum glory of Jesus Christ? Note also where both might 'waste time'.

[__] For most adult ages, the number of single men is less than the number of single women. Discuss the apparent reasons for this and the implications it has in our society and in our churches.

[__] Have a panel discussion with three single men and three married men. Ask them to discuss the topic "Reasons why I enjoy being single or married."

[__] Jesus Christ remained single throughout His earthly ministry. Discuss why this was necessary.

[__] From a public library or church library, find a book written for single men, by a single man. Review the book by comparing the principles the author suggests with those of Scripture. Share the report with a men's class to give them a further insight into the Role of a Single Man.

[__] Invite a single man to your home for a meal (if married.) Invite a married couple(s) to your home (if single.) Use this visit as an occasion to gain new understanding of how you might be able to mutually build up one another in the body of Christ, the Church.

Chapter 6

Citizen• Relationship to Our World

I urge that prayers…be made on behalf of…all who are in authority… • 1 Timothy 2:1

Let every soul be subject to the governing authorities… • Romans 13:1

New Earth Island - 2017

© 2017 by James D. (Jim) Cunningham, Ed.D. jdcunningham@telus.net

Population 1,000 - Area 20 Sq. Km.

Based on Ratio of 7,500,000:1 (*)

MOTHER-TONGUE LANGUAGE TOTAL: 300+ LANGUAGES

1. 160 - Chinese	5. 33 - Arabic	9. 17 - Japanese
2. 57 - Hindi	6. 29 - Portuguese	10. 13 - Punjabi/Farsi
3. 53 - Spanish	7. 23 - Bengali	+ 308 speak 88 Languages
4. 48 - English[a]	8. 23 - Russian	+ 236 speak 200+ Languages

[a] 114 live in areas where English is the official language

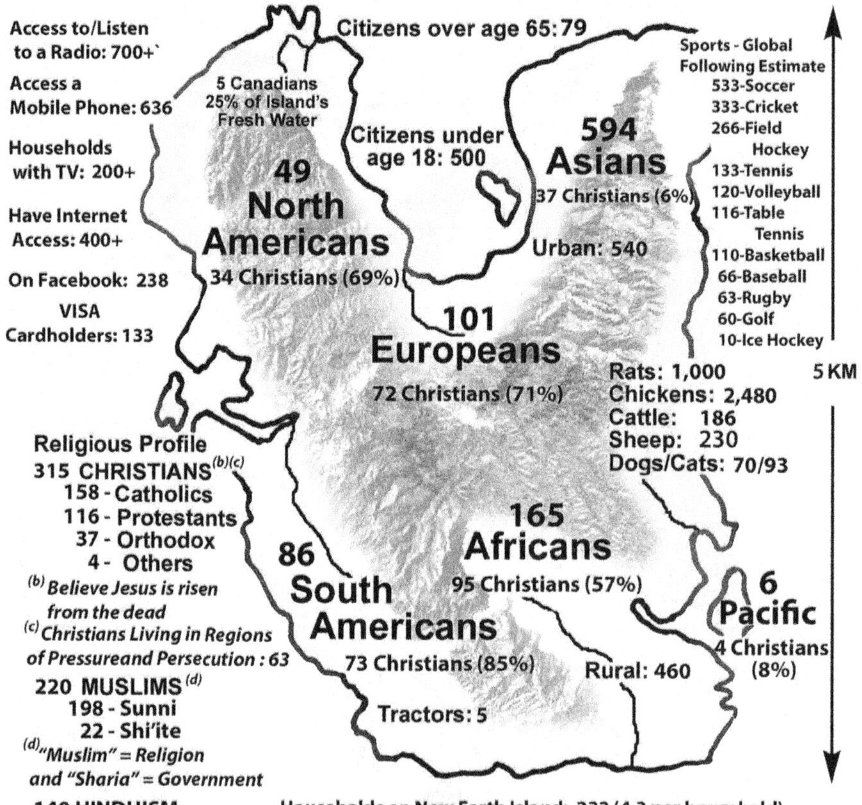
Access to/Listen to a Radio: 700+`
Access a Mobile Phone: 636
Households with TV: 200+
Have Internet Access: 400+
On Facebook: 238
VISA Cardholders: 133
Citizens over age 65: 79
5 Canadians 25% of Island's Fresh Water
Citizens under age 18: 500
49 North Americans
34 Christians (69%)
594 Asians
37 Christians (6%)
Urban: 540
101 Europeans
72 Christians (71%)
Sports - Global Following Estimate
533-Soccer
333-Cricket
266-Field Hockey
133-Tennis
120-Volleyball
116-Table Tennis
110-Basketball
66-Baseball
63-Rugby
60-Golf
10-Ice Hockey
5 KM
Rats: 1,000
Chickens: 2,480
Cattle: 186
Sheep: 230
Dogs/Cats: 70/93
Religious Profile
315 CHRISTIANS[b)(c)
158 - Catholics
116 - Protestants
37 - Orthodox
4 - Others
(b) Believe Jesus is risen from the dead
(c) Christians Living in Regions of Pressureand Persecution : 63
220 MUSLIMS(d)
198 - Sunni
22 - Shi'ite
(d) "Muslim" = Religion and "Sharia" = Government
86 South Americans
73 Christians (85%)
165 Africans
95 Christians (57%)
6 Pacific
4 Christians (8%)
Rural: 460
Tractors: 5

140 HINDUISM
150 NON RELIGIOUS
60 BUDDHISTS
50 CHINESE RELIGIONS
50 ETHNORELIGIONISTS
8 OTHERS
4 SIKHISM
2 JUDAISM
1 BAHA'I

Households on New Earth Island: 232 (4.3 per household)
New Earth Island Birthrate: 3.3 per family
Adult Literacy Rate: 86% - 70 adults are illiterate

Students enrolled in New Earth Island Colleges: 10 (4 are women)
Citizens deaf or blind: 22
Citizens with leprosy: 3

(*) Computed figures are based on currently available data

← 4 KM →

New Earth Island

As a child, I used to live in a small Canadian village of some 300 people called Carlisle, Ontario. The year was 1943. Canada was at war with the Allies against Nazi Germany. Wives were left at home while their husbands went off to war. My maternal grandparents, Norman and Mina Mills, helped raise me till my father returned from Europe.

Our little village had four quadrants formed by the main intersection of Centre Road and the 9th Concession. Grandpa Mills owned, operated and lived above the General Store/Post Office on the southeast corner of the village. To the southwest was a Bank and on the northwest corner was another General Store. A private home stood on the remaining northeast corner. This village was my immediate world.

Each year I gained access to more of the community. Up the hill to the east lived my mother's sister (my Aunt Margaret Rasberry), her husband and my four rather special first cousins. Everyone knew my mother, Marie Cunningham. Mom worked in the local gathering place for news of the war: the Post Office.

Folks tended their gardens, cheered for the hometown baseball team and showed up for the annual July 1 Community Garden Party in the park behind the Methodist Church. A few commuted to the big city of Hamilton, to work in the steel mills. Such was life in my little home village.

Tombstones in the church graveyard had British sounding names like Campbell, Grey, and Eaton. A few Ukrainian Fulchucks and Italian Trigonas made it on the mailboxes – but Asians, Africans, and South Americans must have lived on another planet. To be Chinese was synonymous with owning a city restaurant or laundry!

How little we knew in our village of the outside world. We knew each other but precious little about anyone else. A few pre-kilometer miles from our home was a ridge of shale like rock formation that rose above the surrounding countryside. This escarpment, named *The Mountain* rose some 200 meters high.

Years later I moved to Vancouver, British Columbia, and lived within eyesight of Mount Baker, a 10,000 foot (3,300 meter) Giant. That was a real mountain. I climbed and hiked alpine meadows, to experience the reality of life above the tree line.

Then in 1994 I made my first trip to Lhasa, Tibet. I stepped off the plane at 12,000 feet (4,000 meters) in the land of Mount Everest and the towering 29,000-foot (10,000-meter) Himalayas. I discovered that how one views reality and life is often a matter of perspective.

I cannot comprehend 7.5 billion people on our planet Earth.
I cannot comprehend 1 billion people.
I can better understand 1,000.

So I decided to visualize Earth as an Island of 1,000 people and consider numbers for the year 2017 AD based primarily on Patrick Johnstone's text Operation World with an approximate world population of some 7.5 billion. I was able to reduce these humongous numbers for easier comprehension.

Let's look at the map of New Earth Island and consider ways this impacts our lives.

First, we note that half of the 1,000 inhabitants of New Earth Island (500) are under the age of 18! This number compares to a much smaller percentage (7.9%) over the age of 65. Notice also that Canada has only 5 Citizens on the Island (5 x 7.5 million = 37+ million people). Ironically the city of Tokyo, Japan, ranked the largest city on Earth also has 5 Citizens. Tokyo equals Canada's entire population! Small wonder Japanese think Canada is uninhabited!

Now let's examine the Religious Profile of New Earth Island.

Of the 1,000 citizens on New Earth Island, 535 believe in:

- Some god - other than Jesus of Nazareth; and read
- Some holy book - other than the Bible; and follow the teachings of
- Some prophet, or guru - other than the Jewish prophets of the Old/New Testaments who spoke on behalf of God; and accept
- Some form of angelic/demonic activity - other than the defeat of Satan by the resurrected Christ; and believe
- Some criterion for eternal life - other than the Bible's command to confess with your mouth the Lord Jesus and believe in your heart that God has raised Him from the dead and you will be saved; and put their hope in
- Some system of future rewards for decisions/actions in this life - other than heaven or hell.

Some may ask what is meant by the term "Christian". I am using the term as defined by Operation World: A Christian is *"Anyone who professes to be Christian. The term embraces all traditions and confessions of Christianity. It is no indicator of the degree of commitment or theological orthodoxy. The primary emphasis utilized is that of recognizing self-identification as well as accepting the Scriptural principles illustrated in Matt 10:32 and Romans 10:9."* http://www.operationworld.org/glossary

Pray for Those in Authority

In my opinion, it is highly plausible that by the time Jesus Christ returns to Jerusalem to rule as King of Kings and Lord of Lords, [70] virtually every nation will have had an opportunity to be a world leader and failed. Look at the historical record: China-Mongolia-Japan-Greece-Turkey-Italy-Spain-Portugal-France-Hungary-Austria-Norway-Holland-England-Germany-Russia-America-Aztecs-Incas-Mayans-Ethiopians-Egyptians-Babylonians-Persians etc. etc. etc. They each had an Empire of varying size, strength, and influence. And they each crumbled and failed to survive.

---

[70] See Zechariah 14:4 and entire Chapter 12-13 and 14

God works through these human efforts to exercise His Sovereign will and prove that Man is incapable of ruling with justice, mercy and humility (see Micah 6:8). Man's failure in all methods of government, from Monarchy to Marxism, proves that only the wisdom of the Holy Spirit can enable any system of human government to meet the needs of his fellow man.

Lessons From Previous Civilizations

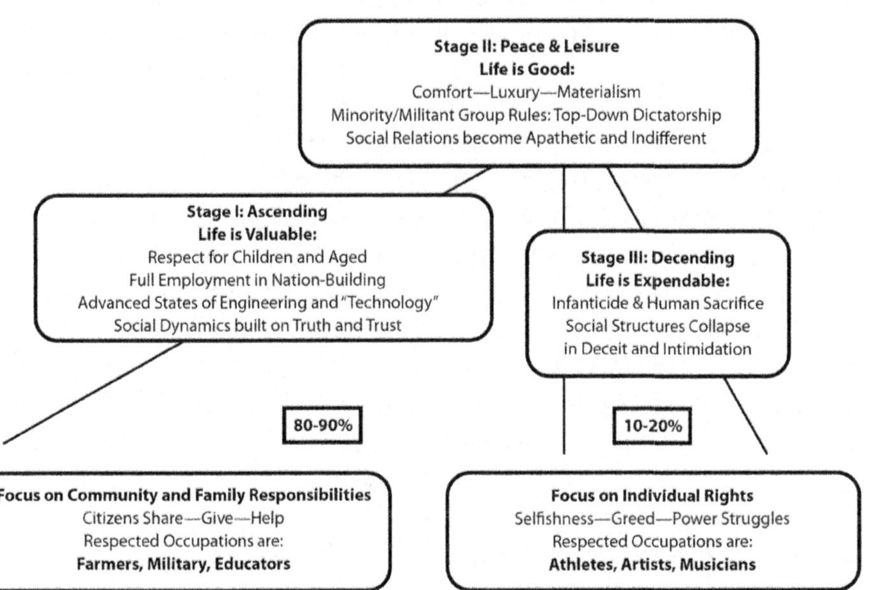
Stage II: Peace & Leisure
Life is Good:
Comfort—Luxury—Materialism
Minority/Militant Group Rules: Top-Down Dictatorship
Social Relations become Apathetic and Indifferent
Stage I: Ascending
Life is Valuable:
Respect for Children and Aged
Full Employment in Nation-Building
Advanced States of Engineering and "Technology"
Social Dynamics built on Truth and Trust
Stage III: Decending
Life is Expendable:
Infanticide & Human Sacrifice
Social Structures Collapse
in Deceit and Intimidation
80-90%
10-20%
Focus on Community and Family Responsibilities
Citizens Share—Give—Help
Respected Occupations are:
Farmers, Military, Educators
Focus on Individual Rights
Selfishness—Greed—Power Struggles
Respected Occupations are:
Athletes, Artists, Musicians

Three Stage Rise and Decline of a Civilization

Stage I – Ascending Civilization – Life is Valuable

We need people at every age and stage to 'build the empire' so to speak. Nobody is expendable! Children, adults, and wise elders – everyone counts. There is full employment as the resources of the country are focused on Nation-Building. Ever increasing advanced states of engineering and technological ingenuity move the society forward. This appears in virtually every civilization from the Aztecs and the Mayans to the Romans right through to European Commonwealths. The social dynamics of an Ascending Civilization rest on two foundational principles: Truth and Trust. People tell the truth. And we trust one another. Handshakes seal deals. The front door is unlocked. Ascending Civilizations seek to enrich community and family responsibilities. Citizens choose to share, give, or help their neighbors – sometimes risking loss or hardship to help others. The occupations admired by young and old are: Farmers – to feed the citizens; Military – to protect our gains and Educators – to teach life skills. In an Ascending Civilization Educators pass on to the next generation skills, knowledge and wise values from previous generations to permit survival by ensuring each citizen knows the truth – and trusts the authorities to implement justice with mercy.

Stage II – Peace and Leisure – The Good Life

There is now freedom, peace and a new commodity called Leisure Time. Freedom redirects time and energy towards developing the arts, music, and drama plus sports and recreational activities. Life is all about me: my comfort, my luxury, and my materialism. Individualism says: *just leave me alone.* We have implicit social contracts. You don't bother me, and I will leave you alone. Apathy and indifference appear tattooed into our social conscience. Self-absorbed materialism leads to a disenchanted fog of disconnection by the masses in the affairs of government. An increasingly top-down dictatorial form of government provides a veneer of security by capitulating to moral blackmail from militant, minority special-interest groups. The attitude of the masses appears to be: *who cares, pass the grapes.*

Stage III – Descending Civilization – Life is Expendable

What took 80 – 90% of the time in the Cycle of a Civilization is now about to disappear in a matter of years. The time of descent appears to be approximately 10-20% of the life cycle. Speaking of life, the three words to sum a descending civilization are *Life is Expendable.* Infanticide/Abortion and Human Sacrifice/Euthanasia replace respect for life and the preservation of truth and trust. Social structures begin to collapse through deceit and intimidation. *Rent-a-crowd* mobs quickly assemble to promote whatever agenda the wealthy powerbrokers desire to retain power. The focus shifts from the Family and Community to the rights of the Individual, ignoring the responsibilities that go with them. Teaching a person only their rights, eventually leads to rebellion. The human heart (to quote the prophet Jeremiah) "*is deceitfully wicked*" leading to selfishness and greedy struggles for control and power. It is ironic that respected occupations in a declining civilization become overpaid Athletes, bizarre Artists, and out-of-tune Musicians.

Educators need to fulfill a prophet-like role in a descending civilization to show, not tell, the next generation how to learn from History, before repeating History with a devastating loss.

Daniel clearly taught and believed that it is God Himself who raises up one king and puts down another (see Daniel 2:20-23). God permits one king to become strong and uses that King as a judge against a disobedient nation. God said He would rise up *"my servant Nebuchadnezzar"* to judge Israel for the 490 years they had disobeyed Him. One year for each of the 7th years they had not let the ground lie fallow! King Neb took them captive for 70 years! Then the Lord said, *"This is what I say to (my) anointed, to Cyrus, whose right hand I take hold of…"* [71] -*"I am the Lord…"* (10 times he says this phrase) *"I am the Lord…"* and adds: *"and there is no other…"* he (Cyrus) is going to punish Babylon for being too harsh on my people! God is in control. Accept it!

God can direct a King so that he has a bad night's sleep, asks for someone to read to him and "poof" and Haman gets hung, and Esther protects the Jews from a Holocaust! (See Esther Chapter 6.) Or perhaps dear sweet Mary was resting in Nazareth in the 9th month of her pregnancy unaware that Micah had prophesied that Messiah had to be born in Bethlehem of Judah (Micah 5:2). So in the sovereignty of God *"Caesar Augustus issued a decree that a census should be taken of the entire Roman world…and everyone went to his own town to register…"* [72] "and Jesus was born in Bethlehem. Wait. Hosea the prophet said: *"…out of Egypt I called my son…"* [73] so an angel awakens Joseph in a dream and tells him to *"take the child and flee to Egypt…for Herod is going to search for the child…"* [74] Once again, the decrees of authority (even an ungodly authority) are used to move people about to be where God wants them to be to accomplish His plan.

Whenever the government of any country makes a law, God is able to work through that law to bring ultimate glory to Jesus Christ even if it appears to be (in our eyes) a bad law! Jesus was born during the reign of a despot (Herod). Why would God choose this time in history as *"the fullness of time"* [75] for His Son to be born? Herod was a terror. He massacred all heirs to his throne. He killed two of his sons and his wife. Did God want Joseph and Mary to obey this neurotic, suspicious, bloodthirsty, power hungry, murderer? The answer appears to be yes. And He did. Joseph did not lead a revolt against Herod. He just obeyed God and moved away to Egypt for some three-and-a-half years. Respect for authority is a principle for men to note.

---

[71] Isaiah 45:1

[72] Luke 2:1-3

[73] Hosea 11:1

[74] Matthew 2:13

[75] Galatians 4:4

Even when David was pursued by a mad, jealous, paranoid King Saul, David refused on at least two occasions to kill Saul and claim the throne. David's response was: *"Do not destroy him (Saul) for who can stretch out his hand against the Lord's anointed and be without guilt?"* [76]

Here's a short word of caution for my zealous political activist friends. I commend you for your prayers *for those in authority.* I praise God for those in government offices who are followers of Jesus Christ. So let me say this carefully. Guard your criticism of *those in authority* both in government and in the church. Scripture says (Ecclesiastes 10:20): *"Furthermore, in your bedchamber do not curse a king, and in your sleeping rooms do not curse a rich man, for a bird of the heavens will carry the sound and the winged creature will make the matter known."* How, you might ask would a person in leadership ever know what you have said to a person in your bedroom? The answer is simple. Your countenance (eyes, face, spirit, demeanor) changes every time you meet someone against whom you have gossiped or slandered. They appear to sense (don't ask me how) that I have spoken against them!

God is at work though all leaders. Leaders are permitted to be there by God's grace. So be careful. *"Do not judge...in the way you judge, you will be judged..."* [77] Another example of God controlling politicians is seen in Luke 2:19. Herod died. Joseph was instructed by an angel in a dream to bring the Christ-child back to Israel. But now Archelaus, Herod's son, was ruling in Jerusalem and he was worse than Herod! So Joseph was instructed (for his safety) to return to Nazareth and so all three somewhat conflicting Messianic prophecies about the birth of Messiah were fulfilled in a short period (perhaps seven years)! Messiah was: born in Bethlehem. Called out of Egypt. Known as a Nazarene.

Our responsibility as individual men is to do three things under whatever government or authority system we live.

---

[76] 1 Samuel 26:19

[77] Matthew 7:2

First, obey those in authority. They are placed there as part of God's omniscient plan. As Corrie Ten Boom says: 'God governs all things, even those that appear to us as senseless or cruel. Lord, because I do not have the answers to these things I do not, therefore, conclude that there are no answers. You know Lord, and when I am strong enough, wise enough, and loving enough, you will show me too." [78]

Second, submit to those in authority. Learn to know when to assert your authority and when to submit to the authority of others. I would guess that more men have found themselves in 'hot water' for resisting authority than for submitting to authority. The whole of scripture teaches responsibility to be submissive. That's hard for us as men, because we like to think of our wives being submissive to us (after all that is scriptural); but many verses tell us that we as men must learn how to submit.

- I Peter 5:5 – *"You younger men, likewise be subject to your elders."*
- I Peter 2:13 – *"Submit yourselves for the Lord's sake to every human institution, whether to a king as the one in authority or to governors as sent by him for the punishment of evildoers and the praise of those who do right."*
- I Peter 2:18 – *"Servants be submissive to your masters with all respect, not only to those who are good and gentle but also to those who are unreasonable."*
- Romans 13:1-3 – *"Let every person be in subjection to the governing authorities…he who resists authority has opposed the ordinances of God; and they who have opposed will receive condemnation upon themselves."*
- Romans 13:5 – *"It is necessary to be in subjection, not only because of wrath but also for conscience sake."*
- I Corinthians 16:16 (to the church members) "…be in subjection to such men {church leaders) and to everyone who helps in the work and labors."

[78] Corrie Ten Boom, The Hiding Place: The Triumphant True Story of Corrie Ten Boom, Washington Depot: Chosen Books, 1971.

Submission realizes and accepts that God is using any occasion of you having to submit as a test. How you pass this test will determine how much *exalting* God will allow you to receive. James 4:7-10 notes: *"...submit therefore to God...humble yourselves in the presence of the Lord, and He will exalt you."*

If God will not share His glory with anyone else and is a very jealous God, it is reasonable to believe He will not allow anyone to be exalted who might take glory to himself. But when a man has proven his ability to submit to God, and then to those God has placed in authority over him, God regards this man as one He can trust with a little exaltation. When a man humbles himself before God and before his earthly authorities, he will be able to handle it when he receives honor or blessing, by giving the praise for the honor back to God. This gives God, even more, glory, and evidence that His servant can handle more recognition, authority, praise, exaltation, and power. Learning to submit to authority is the first rung on the spiritual ladder to power. [79]

Third, Pray for those in authority. God's reasoning for this is laid out in I Timothy 2:1-2. *"First of all then, I urge that entreaties and prayers, petitions and thanksgiving be made on behalf of all men, for kings and all who are in authority, in order that we may lead a tranquil and quiet life in all godliness and dignity."* Consider what God requests:

- **God wants us to *thank Him* for all authorities!** This proves to Him that we recognize them as being placed there by Him. (See Daniel 2:20-23).
- **God wants us to *intercede* for those in authority.** He is then willing to work through our prayers to have those in authority accomplish His perfect will.
- **God wants us to *pray earnestly* for those in authority.** This is not a "Now I lay me down to sleep, God bless the President" type of child's prayer. It is to be intense, carefully

---

[79] Harold Butt, The Velvet Covered Brick, New York: Harper and Row, 1973. (Chapter 4. Submission: Key to Power develops the relationship that exists between "authority" and "submission").

thought out pleading with God to work in specific ways through those in authority to His glory.

Praying for those in authority is perhaps the highest responsibility a man can have as a Citizen. God wants us to pray, so there might be peace – so that the gospel of Jesus Christ might come for all men to be saved and come to the knowledge of the truth.[80] Sharing the Gospel is challenging when there is war, fighting or noise and confusion. Evangelistic campaigns appear easier to conduct when there is peace (like the Day of Pentecost when 3,000 accepted Christ as their Messiah). Riots usually lead to death or imprisonment, which slows the spread of the gospel to a one-to-one process (such as Paul and Silas in the jail at Philippi). The gospel will not cease, but we know that it may spread more rapidly if there is peace to give it full attention and support.

At this time in church history, it appears that Christian women in many countries are the ones with the burden to pray. One thousand women once met near my hometown to have an eight-hour workshop on the topic of Prayer. Rarely do we hear of that many men meeting to Pray! Women author many of the books on prayer. Campus Crusade's Great Commission Prayer Crusade began as a vision God gave to a dedicated group of women. Where are the men on their knees? Is *"praying for those in authority"* a woman's job? My desire is that we are given a burden, unprecedented in history, to pray.

E. M. Bounds says: "*What the church needs today is not more machinery or better, not new organizations, or more novel methods, but men whom the Holy Ghost can use – men of prayer."*

"Therefore be careful (or look carefully) *how you walk, not as unwise men, but as wise, making the most of your time, because the days are evil"* – (Ephesians 5:15,16). One of our greatest investments of time as men is to *"pray for those in authority."*

---

80 Timothy 2:4

As men, our mandate is to equip and empower others to achieve peace and reconciliation for community transformation. This idea came from a conversation with Brother Andrew, founder of Open Doors International (see Light Force, Revell, 2004, pp. 57-60).

First, we need a ***Heart at Peace.*** As individual Christians, we earnestly desire to have *A Heart at Peace*, free from guilt, free from anger and free to forgive. We can then practice biblical disciplines that evidence our love for one another based on personal reconciliation to our Lord Jesus Christ.

Next, we seek a ***Home at Peace.*** As practicing Christians when we have our hearts at peace we desire to have *A Home at Peace*, free from abuse and violence. We base our adherence to biblical principles and reconciliation with one another within our family.

Then we pursue a ***Habitation at Peace.*** After establishing our hearts at peace and our homes at peace – disciples of Jesus Christ desire to have our *Habitation* [81] *(Community) at Peace,* free from fighting and conflict. We base our relations on principles of prayer and reconciliation with one another within our church, community, and country.

Who is My Neighbor?

One verse from the Old Testament quoted eight times in the New Testament, says: ***"...you shall love your neighbor as yourself."*** [82]

Let's consider how this is possible.

1. Matthew 5:43 – *"You have heard that it was said, you shall **love your neighbor** and hate your enemy. But I say unto you, love your enemies and pray for those who persecute you in order that you may be sons of your Father who is in heaven; for He causes His sun to rise on the evil and the good and sends rain on the righteous and the unrighteous."*

---

81 The place where a group lives

82 See Leviticus 19:18

Our God loves everyone so much He sends rain and the sunshine regardless of whether we deserve it. Being a follower of Jesus Christ and a Citizen on Earth means I must also love my neighbor and my enemies as much as God does! Some reading this book are regrettably full of hate. They hate someone. This person plagues them. They think of this person when they walk, sleep, eat and even when they are trying to enjoy intimacy with their wife! He possesses them. You hate him for whatever he said or did to hurt you. You have to forgive!

When you forgive, God helps you love the person who caused the harm or the betrayal. I have had to do it. It works.

2. Matthew 19:19 (16-22) – To the question "What must be done to receive eternal life?" Jesus answered: ***"You shall love your neighbor as yourself."*** When the young man replies that he has done all these things from his youth, Jesus adds: *"Go, sell all you have, give to the poor and come follow me."* The Bible says he went away grieved for he had much property. A new insight emerges from this teaching. The rich man claimed that he loved his neighbor – and undoubtedly thought he was right in his mind. Jesus cut through his fuzzy thinking and gave him a clear marker to measure the index of his love – his money!

What does money have to do with loving my neighbor? Consider that Jesus taught: *"No one can serve two masters, for either he will hate the one and love the other, or he will hold to the one and despise the other. You cannot serve God and Mammon* (money)." [83]

Jesus knew that a man's behavior towards money was one of the greatest aids in establishing a proper perspective of his values, attitudes, and priorities. A man's monthly bank statements reveal more of his eternal priorities than what he writes in his Daily Journals. *"If we have food and covering, with these we shall be content"* – (I Timothy 6:8). *"But seek first His kingdom and His righteousness and all these things* (food, clothing, and shelter) *shall be added to you"* – (Matthew 6:33). *"But godliness actually*

[83] Matthew 6:24

is a means of great gain, when accompanied by contentment" – (I Timothy 6:6).

The disciple of Jesus Christ must have a right relationship to the receiving, spending and giving of money. His principles of "*owing nothing to anyone except to love one another"* must be fought out in a world of consumer materialistic madness with lines-of-credit insanity! [84] His setting aside on the first day of the week as the Lord has prospered him is a life action in a pressurized *spend-it-now* marketplace. The man who solves the money riddle is on his way to becoming a man alive unto God with fresh insight and enthusiasm. The rich young man had good intentions, but a wrong attitude towards the one thing he could have used to the glory of God – his money!

Being the disciple of Jesus Christ that God wants demands that nothing (no thing) and no-one have any higher place in our life than God Himself! Easy to say, and easy to write, but it's a daily lifelong challenge to do it! While fulfilling our role as a citizen of Earth we're on our way to becoming an eventual citizen of Heaven.

3. Matthew 22:39 (36-40) – Someone challenged Jesus: "Teacher, which is the great commandment in the Law?" And He said to him, "You shall love the Lord your God with all your heart and with all your soul and with all your mind. This is the great and foremost commandment. And the second is like it, **'You shall love your neighbor as yourself.'** On these two commandments depend the whole Law and the Prophets.'"

4. **Mark 12:31** – (parallel passage). If any man thinks he can be a disciple of Christ's or a man worthy of God's acceptance and not obey these two commandments, this is deception. It is impossible to call oneself a Disciple of God, a follower of Jesus Christ, or a Christian and be full of disobedience to God's word, or hate towards another human being.

---

[84] Romans 13:6

I once heard Jay Adams, in a counseling seminar in Vancouver, tell the story of a man who came for marriage counseling. He said: "I hate my wife, and that's that." Jay looked at him for a moment and said, "You do hate your wife, don't you?" To which the man replied, "You bet." "Well," Jay continued, "The Bible says that you have to love your wife. Right here in Ephesians 5:24 it says *'Husbands love your wives.'"*

"I don't care," said the man, "I still hate her."

"Well, think of her as your neighbor. After all, she is the closest person .to you. You sleep with her. Why not think of her as your neighbor. It says nine times in the Bible that you are to *love your neighbor as yourself,* so I guess you have to love her."

"Nope," said the man. "If she were my neighbor I'd move!"

"Boy, she is really an enemy to you isn't she?"

"Yes, that's it," said the man. "She's my enemy. I hate her."

"Well," said Jay, "I guess you are just going to have to love her regardless, for it says in the Bible, *'Love your enemies and pray for those who persecute you.'"*

No matter how we cut it, the Bible says we are to love. If a man cannot love another person whom he can see – made in the image of God – how can he claim to love God whom he has never seen?

5. Luke 10:27-37 – In this passage a young lawyer (an expert in the law) approaches Jesus and asks what he must do to receive eternal life. The answer includes this verse (27):

"You shall love the Lord your God, with all your heart and with all your soul and with all your mind and ***your neighbor as yourself****...but willing to justify himself he said to Jesus, 'And who is my neighbor?'"*

Jesus tells the famous story of the Good Samaritan. Now, you have probably heard this story many times. Here's a quick review. This is not the time to skip reading scripture. Read carefully. There's a plot twist coming!

30 Jesus replied and said, "A man was going down from Jerusalem to Jericho and fell among robbers, and they stripped him and beat him, and went away leaving him half dead. 31 And by chance a priest was going down on that road, and when he saw him, he passed by on the other side. 32 Likewise, a Levite also, when he came to the place and saw him, passed by on the other side. 33 But a Samaritan, who was on a journey, came upon him; and when he saw him, he felt compassion, 34 and came to him and bandaged up his wounds, pouring oil and wine on them; and he put him on his own beast, and brought him to an inn and took care of him. 35 On the next day, he took out two denarii and gave them to the innkeeper and said, 'Take care of him; and whatever more you spend, when I return I will repay you.' 36 Which of these three do you think proved to be a neighbor to the man who fell into the robbers' hands?" 37 And he said, "The one who showed mercy toward him." Then Jesus said to him, "Go and do the same."

Did you notice that the questioner was an expert in the law? He knew his Hebrew Bible better than anyone around. And way back in 2 Chronicles, there was a story told that would have been familiar to this lawyer. Read the following story, pretending you are that lawyer. Think of the Chronicles story you know and then re-read the story Jesus told. Don't focus on pronouncing names correctly. Get the historical lesson in your mind.

***12** "Then some of the heads of the sons of Ephraim—Azariah the son of Johanan, Berechiah the son of Meshillemoth, Jehizkiah the son of Shallum, and Amasa the son of Hadlai—arose against those who were coming from the battle, **13** and said to them, "You must not bring the captives in here, for you are proposing to bring upon us guilt against the Lord adding to our sins and our guilt; for our guilt is great so that His burning anger is against Israel." **14** So the armed men left the captives and the spoil before the officers and all the assembly. **15** Then the men who were designated by* *name arose, took the captives, and they clothed all their naked ones from the spoil; and they gave them clothes and sandals, fed them and gave them drink, anointed them with oil, led all their feeble ones on donkeys, and brought them to Jericho, the city of palm trees, to their brothers; then they returned to Samaria" – (*2 Chronicles 28:12-15).

Now re-read the story Jesus told and ask: "What does it mean to be a citizen-neighbor?"

- We must be aware of the needs of people experiencing trauma wherever they are.

- We must express compassion for people – not anger – not bitterness – just pure, genuine love spelled

C-O-M-P-A-S-S-I-O-N.

- We must act carefully and wisely with whatever resources we have available.

Notice the sequence of Compassion in Jesus' story: *...he came to him* (involvement) *and bandaged his wounds* (assistance), *pouring oil and wine on them* (utilizing his own resources), *and put him on his beast* (inconveniencing himself to help others), *and brought him to an inn* (helping him by finding additional resources beyond his own*) and took care of him* (kindness) *and paid the innkeeper* (putting his finances into action to help those in need). The neighbor (citizen) was the one who showed mercy in a time of need. A neighbor is anyone we meet in need. And Jesus said (my paraphrase): "Citizen – Neighbor – Follower of Jesus – *Go and do the same!* – (Luke 10:37).

6. Romans 13:9 (8-11) – *"Owe nothing to anyone except to love one another; for he who loves his neighbor has fulfilled the law and if there is any another commandment, it is summed up in this saying,* ***'You shall love your neighbor as yourself.*** *Love does no wrong to a neighbor; love, therefore, is the fulfillment of the law."*

Story: As a Canadian, I have watched the black-white racial situation in the USA with varying degrees of smugness, interest, detachment or judgment. "Sure glad we Canadians don't have any problems like you Americans," seems to be the internalized feeling of many of my fellow Canadians. But a test was presented in the late 1960's to the 70% of English Canadians to prove they know how to love the less than 25% who are our French neighbors. Suddenly a government policy demanded ***Bilingualism and Biculturalism.*** Virtually every region of the country, every box of cereal, every government document would now be written in two Official Languages: English and French. 50-50. No debate. Just accept it. Canadians eventually passed that test. Now as we approach our 150th Anniversary as a nation, a new test is upon us: accepting Sharia Law, plus Hindu, Sikh and Buddhist immigrants as neighbours. Canada has morphed to become a New Canada.[85] Who is my neighbor? In our shrinking global village, the neighbors are getting closer. How we respond to the starving neighbors *two-countries-down-the-street* will soon affect how they respond to us! Where is our Compassion?

7. Galatians 5:14 (13-15) – *"For you were called to freedom brethren, only do not turn your freedom into an opportunity for the flesh, but through love serve one another. For the whole law is fulfilled in one word in the statement,* ***'You shall love your neighbor as yourself.'*** *But if you bite and devour one another take care lest you be consumed by one another."*

It appears the Bible focuses on our relationships, either with God, or with Man made in the image of God! The greatest freedom

[85] Preston Manning's book entitled "The New Canada" says: Reformers seek a New Canada—a Canada which may be defined as "a balanced, democratic federation of provinces, distinguished by the sustainability of its environment, the viability of its economy, the acceptance of its social responsibilities, and the recognition of the equality and uniqueness of all of its citizens and provinces." New Canada must include a new deal for aboriginal peoples and a new Senate to address the problem of regional alienation. New Canada must be workable without Quebec, but it must be open and attractive enough to include a New Quebec.[3]

we can have is freedom to love one another and be at peace. Proverbs says: *"When a man's ways are pleasing to the Lord, He makes even his enemies be at peace with him."* [86] Paul says: *"If possible, so far as it depends on you be at peace with all men."* [87]

A relationship of peace is our goal: peace within, peace with others, and peace between countries. A relationship is like weather, hard to describe but we know when it is bad. We know what it is like to have a strained relationship. You walk in the room and the other person avoids eye contact or deliberately turns away.

Galatians 5:13 commands us *"to serve one another."* Many wives exhibit a servant-spirit ahead of their husbands. He may have spent time that day being *served* by employees, secretaries, waitresses, stewards, and bellhops. When he comes home he thinks, "When you're on top, others do it for you!" Wrong!

When I love my neighbor, I will find ways to serve him, not speak against him or gossip about him. 1 John 1:7 tells us: *"If we walk in the light as He Himself is in the light, we have fellowship with one another and the blood of Jesus Christ His Son cleanses us from all sin."*

> Story: Reality Check! When I cannot have fellowship with another man who claims to be a follower of Jesus Christ then one of us or perhaps both of us are not walking in the light of God's Word. As a young Christian, I became the Manager of a Rehab Center for recovering alcoholics. I recall two Board members contacted me soon after I accepted the job. Both knew I was a student at a conservative, Evangelical Seminary. They each had a word of advice. The first said: "Many of the men here are new Christians. They are walking in the light of God's Word to the best of their knowledge. If you also walk in the light of God's Word, you will be able to have fellowship with them, no matter how good you think you are or how bad

[86] Proverbs 16:7

[87] Romans 12:18

they may have been. Remember, the blood of Jesus Christ makes us equally forgiven brothers in His love." The second Board member was more blunt and brusque in a phone call: 'Read Matthew, Chapter Seven, Verse One Sir. Good Day,' and hung up." [88]

Let me suggest what I believe may be the biggest hindrance to fellowship between two brothers: Jealousy! Jealousy breeds rapidly in the swamp of personal pride! It enters a relationship like an infectious virus, weakening the very heart of love that gives life to the body. It will keep two brothers from talking to each other for years! It saps spiritual strength. Result? We have a biting, snapping, gossiping, bitter, grumpy old man. Scripture says: Stop! Clean it out. Ask the Holy Spirit to fill your heart with love that motivates you to go, meet, humble yourself, ask forgiveness and rebuild a new relationship. [89]

8. James 2:8 – *"If however you are fulfilling the Royal Law according to Scripture,* ***'You shall love your neighbor as yourself,'*** *you are doing well. But if you show partiality you are committing sin and are convicted by law as transgressors."*

This is the Royal Law according to James. Rarely in the Bible does God say something is a sin. Texts like Romans 14:23 say: *"whatever is not from faith* ***is sin****..."* and James 4:17 says: *"to one who knows the right thing to do and does not do it, to him it* ***is sin****..."* But, here we see a new kind of sin named and branded for identification: showing partiality. It's hard for us as men to stand in public and be greeted by a light, polite handshake by someone you regard as a friend, and then watch the gorilla give the man next to you the biggest hug you've ever seen. Obviously, the hugged friend received a little more partiality than the limp handshake we received. Right? Oops. I have done the same thing.

---

[88] Matthew 7:1 says: *"Do not judge so that you will not be judged."*

[89] See Matthew 5 and Matthew 18

Remember the Pharisees (See Appendix B) who were called
Teacher. [90]
They loved to
...walk around
[*visibility*];
...in flowing robes
[*ego-status*];
...to be greeted in the marketplace
[*prestige*];
...and have the most important seats at meetings
[*power*];
...and the places of honor at banquets
[*honor*].

Be aware of those around you, your neighbors, and love them as you would love yourself. It could change your actions. It could alter your beliefs. And it will affect your character. It could make you and me more like Christ. Hallelujah.

Obedience Outside My Comfort Zone: My Judea/ Samaria

We first meet our early church witnesses in Jerusalem; waiting for power; so they could be witnesses in Jerusalem, Judea, and Samaria and to the ends of the earth. They had fulfilled the first part but neglected the second part of the assignment. Do not stay in Jerusalem. Go directly to Judea and Samaria and tell them about Jesus Christ, the Messiah. Peter and John are at the Temple in Jerusalem, healing beggars and teaching the people and setting up all the administrative duties of the deacons when suddenly the Jewish leaders get upset and arrest Stephen. This part is so typically human. The disciples stayed in Jerusalem, as told. They experienced the power of the Holy Spirit, as told, and everything appears to be going OK. The disciples are like many of us today, enjoying our modern, cozy Christian family and friends in the local church fellowship. They were personally blessed.

---

[90] See Luke 20:45-47

We believe in the sovereignty of God—of course. But, do we believe that God is in full control and works all things after the counsel of His will? Do we accept that all things work together for good, to them that love Him and are called according to His purpose – as long as there's not much personal sacrifice? When God gives us a command, and we only partially obey, God then orchestrates events to gain our attention and teach us complete obedience. Consider what happens next. *"On that day a great persecution broke out against the church at Jerusalem, and all except the apostles were scattered throughout Judea and Samaria."* [91] Judea and Samaria, exactly where the disciples were under command to go! The Samaritans were the people outside the disciples' comfort zone even though they spoke the same language and lived in the same community. Close, known, same language, similar culture, but different than us. Do we know anyone like that? Notice how the Holy Spirit did it. He gave them a little persecution to get them on the move. To their credit, it says they preached the word everywhere they went. They were excited. They were powerful. They were witnesses.

Obedience to the Word of God requires submission to the Will of God.

As a Christian citizen today what represents our Judea and Samaria? Consider the following:

Relationship with Employers and Employees

"All who are under the yoke of slavery (or employed by an employer) *should consider their masters worthy of full respect, so that God's name and our teaching may not be slandered…Those who have believing masters are not to show less respect for them because they are brothers. Instead, they are to serve them even better,*

[91] Acts 8:1

because those who benefit from their service are believers, and dear to them." [92]

Every job becomes a place of ministry. The marketplace is a primary place to establish our Christian integrity.

Relationships with Neighbors

What verse from the Old Testament is repeated seven times in the New Testament? Leviticus 19:18b - "Love your neighbor as yourself..." The phrase is repeated in Matthew 5:43; Matthew 22:39; Mark 12:31; Luke 10:27; Romans 13:9; Galatians 5:14; and James 2:8. When God says something *eight times* we begin to get the message! One of the greatest areas of ministry in the world is to our neighbors. A Christian may be praying for the salvation of their cousin who lives next door to you! Neighbors are part of our Judea and Samaria, the ones outside our comfort zone.

Relationships with Government: Praying For Those In Authority

"I urge, then, first of all, that requests, prayers, intercession and thanksgiving be made for everyone, for kings and all those in authority, that we may live peaceful and quiet lives in all godliness and holiness ..." Notice the next sentence in this section—"*This is good and pleases God our Savior, who wants all men to be saved and to come to the knowledge of the truth, for there is one God and one mediator between God and men, the man Christ Jesus, who gave Himself as a ransom for all men..."* [93] God is pleased when we accept His mandate to pray for kings and all those in authority. We begin to know them as individuals made in the image of God—with worth and value. We become interested in their world and their needs.

It is time for a call to obedience outside our comfort zone

---

[92] 1 Timothy 6:1-2

[93] 1 Timothy 6:1-4

How Do We Teach Citizens To Pray For Those In Authority?

Insert name of leader. "Lord, we intercede for [ ] and ask that he/she will:

- *"Act justly, love mercy and walk humbly with our God"* (Micah 6:8).
- Have a wise and understanding heart to judge the people and discern between good and evil.
- *"Develop common sense and good judgment"* (Proverbs 4:7).
- Have a strong healthy family life with safety, and support from their spouse and children.
- Not become *"weary in well doing" (*2 Thessalonians 3:13).
- Meet Christians who radiate the love of Jesus Christ (see 2 Corinthians 2:14-17).
- Recognize the valuable contribution made by Christians in the economic development of their area of responsibility.
- See Christians as people who keep their word (see Matthew 5:37).
- Search for understanding and find knowledge and wisdom in God's Word.
- Accept that *"...where there is sensible leadership, there is stability..."* (Proverbs 28:2). Pray leaders who live in darkness will receive a personal message of God's love. Pray God reveals Himself to them and *"...that which had not been told them shall they see..."* (Isaiah 52:15).
- Will grow weary of the continual bloodshed in their country *"...The Lord, my God, has given me rest on every side..."* (1 Kings 5:3-4).
- Realize their power comes from God. Daniel told King Nebuchadnezzar, *"...He (God) removes kings and sets up kings..."* (Daniel 2:19-21). Proverbs 21:1 says: *"...the King's heart is in the hand of the Lord...He turns it wherever He wills..."* and Paul *says, "authorities (are) established by God..."* (Romans 13:1-7).
- Ask God for Wisdom. *"If anyone lacks wisdom, let him ask of God, who gives generously to all without finding fault and it will be given to him"* (James 1:7) and *"wisdom from*

above is pure, peace-loving, considerate, submissive, full of mercy and good fruit, impartial and sincere" (James 3:18).

- Maintain compassion. Politics is a hard life at times. It is too easy to become cynical and critical and disgusted with the power, the manipulation, the games, and the abuses to the system.
- Be wise!—Pray an unjust leader will make many mistakes in decisions that involve evangelistic efforts in their area. *"...Let them cover themselves with their confusion..."* (Psalm 109:29).
- Be diligent!—Pray leaders, who despise God and His Son, Jesus of Nazareth, will fall from power through improper advice. The Psalmist prayed, *"...O God, let them fall by their counsels..."* (Psalm 5:10).
- Be holy! Pray leaders who head corrupt governments will recognize their evil ways and turn to God—as Manasseh did—*"...Then Manasseh knew The Lord; He was God..."* (2 Chronicles 33:12-13).
- And pray that Christians will be an active encouragement to leaders who do right *"You are the salt of the earth. But if the salt loses it saltiness, it is no longer good for anything"* (Matthew 5:13-14).

The older I get, the more I appreciate a phrase that hung in our hallway as a child, growing up in Toronto, Canada. It simply said:

Just One Life
'Twill Soon Be Past
Only What's Done
For Christ Will Last

Competencies to Fulfill Role of CITIZEN

Personal Checklist
Circle the best answer for each to determine score

Do I have...

1. A readiness to risk the consequences of becoming involved in the needs and lives of other people? (Matthew 10:28)

1	2	3	4	5
Not at all	A little bit	Usually	Most of the time	Always

2. A willingness to pray for those in authority? (1 Timothy 2:1-4)

1	2	3	4	5
Not at all	A little bit	Usually	Most of the time	Always

3. Awareness of the issues concerning the people in my neighborhood, community, city, province/state, country, and the world.

1	2	3	4	5
Not at all	A little bit	Usually	Most of the time	Always

4. Knowledge of the Biblical principles as they relate to the 'social issues' of the world in which I live? *"Be shrewd as serpents and innocent as doves"* (Matthew 19:16).

1	2	3	4	5
Not at all	A little bit	Usually	Most of the time	Always

5. Love and friendliness, with a measure of grace and tact in being able to present my ideas verbally and in writing? (Colossians 4: 5-6)

1	2	3	4	5
Not at all	A little bit	Usually	Most of the time	Always

6. Concern and empathy for the needs of people, matched with a willingness to 'become involved in helping to meet those needs'? *"For I was hungry, and you gave Me something to eat, I was thirsty and you gave Me drink, I was a stranger, and you invited Me in; naked and you clothed Me; I was sick, and you visited Me; I was in prison, and you came to Me."* (Matthew 25:35-36) (see also James 1:27).

1	2	3	4	5
Not at all	A little bit	Usually	Most of the time	Always

Total divided by 6 =

Evidences, Role of CITIZEN Fulfilled

Personal Checklist
Circle the best answer for each to determine score

Have I demonstrated…

1. Expression of my personal views related to Biblical principles within the context of the political system?

1	2	3	4	5
Not at all	A little bit	Usually	Most of the time	Always

2. Awareness of the names and needs of those people who are my 'authorities' at a local level (mayor, school board, etc.) and a provincial/state or federal level?

1	2	3	4	5
Not at all	A little bit	Usually	Most of the time	Always

3. Personal separate times of prayer for those 'in authority' with an indication of concern for them publicly?

1	2	3	4	5
Not at all	A little bit	Usually	Most of the time	Always

4. Participation at meetings, presentation of papers or writing letters to those in authority over issues evidencing a need for a Biblical position?

1	2	3	4	5
Not at all	A little bit	Usually	Most of the time	Always

5. Hospitality shown to those outside of the membership of my church? (i.e. neighbors, acquaintances, members of the community, teachers, politicians, etc.)

1	2	3	4	5
Not at all	A little bit	Usually	Most of the time	Always

6. The initiative taken to meet neighbors (especially in apartments)?

1	2	3	4	5
Not at all	A little bit	Usually	Most of the time	Always

7. Compassion shown to those in need within my immediate area? (Hospitals, jails, missions, homes for the aged)

1	2	3	4	5
Not at all	A little bit	Usually	Most of the time	Always

8. Support of agencies, service clubs, etc. that are evidencing a worthwhile contribution to my community?

1	2	3	4	5
Not at all	A little bit	Usually	Most of the time	Always

9. Involvement in some manner with a project that ministers to people outside my country through prayer, gifts, letters or giving of my skills and time for a project?

1	2	3	4	5
Not at all	A little bit	Usually	Most of the time	Always

Total   divided by 9 =

Role of CITIZEN

Projects for Investigation and Discussion

[__] Make a bulletin board for your church, and for your home, showing on a map pictures (from newspapers, etc.) of the people in authority at the municipal, provincial/state and federal level.

[__] Discuss: "Politics is dirty, and a Christian should have no part of it."

[__] Invite a Christian leader in your community/government to speak at your church, on the topic of Praying for Those in Authority. Allow time for questions.

[__] Write a letter to a Christian giving leadership in some position of 'authority' (i.e., policeman, teacher, politician) and encourage him or her by making them aware of the specific items for which you are praying.

[__] Set a hospitality goal of inviting one non-church family from your community into your home for a meal, barbecue, etc., during the next two months.

[__] Visit a school production/open house/ PTA meeting.

[__] Invite your child's teacher to your home to share a meal with you.

[__] Plan a visit to a nearby jail, hospital or nursing home with a team of adults from your church to conduct a special meeting.

[__] What should be the Christian response to life and death moral issues like abortion, euthanasia? (Plus other social issues?) Discuss.

Chapter 7

Employee • Relationship With His Employers

Whatever you do, do your work heartily, as for the Lord rather than for men; knowing that from the Lord you will receive the reward of the inheritance. It is the Lord Christ whom you serve" • Colossians 3:23-24

The Challenge of Living Under the Curse

Few actions in history have altered the destiny of man more than a mere act by Adam, the first man and his wife Eve, the first woman. Adam was in charge of the Garden and Eve was his helper. They were in fellowship with God. And they lived in a perfect environment. No weeds. Lots of food and a perfect relationship between husband and wife! But, with their disobedience came an alteration of the roles that have affected every man and woman since that day. There were four penalties for disobedience that forever altered the working conditions here on earth.

- First, the ground was cursed.
- Second, we would work by the sweat of our brow all the days of our lives.
- Third, there would be thorns and thistles (and not mentioned but also mosquitoes, snow, and cold winds – that never appeared in the Garden of Eden!)
- Fourthly everyone was going to die!

Instead of accepting the curse, Man has initiated endless effort to avoid the implications of the Fall. These actions bring a new set of complications.

Man has to work the land – but it is now subject to bugs, weeds, and natural disasters. However, if man either neglects to control the Earth or abuses the land, he upsets the balance of Nature. The end result is pollution, climate disasters, wasted resources and productivity loss.

Story: One of Marxist-Man's greatest Natural disasters is the Aral Sea Project. Soviet engineers decided in the 1970's to drain water from the lake to irrigate cotton fields in Uzbekistan. "Steadily, over the past 40 years, around 60,000 square kilometers of water, in places 40 meters deep, has evaporated into thin air. The Aral Sea, in Central Asia, used to be the fourth largest lake in the world, after the Caspian Sea, and Lakes

Superior and Victoria. Now barely 10% of it is left." [94] Man without God's wisdom ends up destroying the very land God gave him to manage.

Man has to work to earn his daily bread. Many men equate their work with power and have turned their work into their life. Since Men tend to pour so much time and energy into their work, the wives begin to think, "If work is so important, then I am going to get a job as well." Few women understand how many men feel unfulfilled in their job. Career dissatisfaction is rampant throughout many businesses. A man possessed by his work has little time for prayer, meditation, fellowship, hospitality, Bible study or family relationships. Work must have a higher fulfillment than earning wages to exchange for goods and services. Scripture is clear: *"If a man will not work, neither should he eat..."*

My friend Craig Murdoch says, "Some might suggest our 'Vocation' is where we work and our 'Calling' is to make Christ known through every aspect of our life, but the word distinction is false. Calling and vocation are interchangeable. Vocation comes from Latin *vocare* 'to call.' Where many of us get into trouble is seeing the task(s) which we do on a day-to-day basis as being an end in themselves, something by which we measure our worth (financially, socially, etc.) rather than a role to which God has called wherein we may *'proclaim the excellencies of him who called you out of darkness into his marvellous light'* (1 Peter 2:9). I need to see every aspect of my life as an opportunity to reflect the image of Christ — the goal toward which God has predestined me (cf. Rom 8:29)." [95]

Man has to work by the sweat of his brow. Men today are masters at scheming how to avoid work. Lotteries, gambling, fraudulent schemes, sick-days, stealing, wasting time, turning up late for work, sleeping on the job, extended coffee breaks, welfare, unemployment insurance, drugs, alcohol, travel, name it. Someone will

---

[94] http://www.bbc.com/news/resources/idt-a0c4856e-1019-4937-96fd-8714d70a48f7 (accessed 11 March 2017).

[95] Personal email from Craig Murdoch, August 4, 2017 at 3:58:55 PM PDT

have discovered it as a way to avoid work and still justify eating—with an advanced standard of living.

Man The Manipulator sounds like a title for a book. Subtitle: *The Story of How Man Beats Working!* It is never ending, in virtually all cultures. Let's agree at the beginning: Work is part of the Curse on Adam. And having to sweat was part of the curse as well. [96] Some men have spent their lifetime avoiding both work and sweat. They have made the pursuit of *work-sweat-avoidance* their lifelong challenge. And they are not always lazy. Some work harder at avoiding work than others do working.

Society is inundated with fraudulent schemes to deceive and steal our money. Some manipulators are *healthy, capable people* begging for spare coins. Others are illicit technicians making phone calls wanting remote access to come on our computers to "*fix a problem*" while they empty the victim's bank account.

Men in a right relationship with Jesus Christ can see a purpose to their job that goes beyond the expenditure of time and sweat. God commanded us to manage the Earth (its people and resources) to produce goods and services that benefit citizens of Earth. That exchange of productive physical and mental energy for food, clothing, and shelter is God's plan for us to experience life more abundantly.

Larson suggests questions a man should periodically ask about his job:

- Why am I doing this job? By accident? By choice?
- For whom am I working? God? Man? Self?

---

[96] Genesis 3:17-19 – "Then to Adam He (God) said, 'Because you have listened to the voice of your wife, and have eaten from the tree about which I commanded you, saying, 'You shall not eat from it'; Cursed is the ground because of you. In toil, you will eat of it all the days of your life. Both thorns and thistles it shall grow for you, and you will eat the plants of the field. By the sweat of your face you will eat bread, till you return to the ground because from it you were taken; for you are dust, and to dust, you shall return."

- For what am I working? Wages? Prestige? Benefits?
- With whom am I working? Fellow Employees?
- What kind of place am I in? Is it Important?

Scripture commands, *"Whatever you do in word or deed, do all in the name of the Lord Jesus, giving thanks through Him to God the Father."* [97] Two questions help determine our job satisfaction, personal morale and productivity. First, am I doing my job in the name of Jesus Christ? Does He receive glory for what I do and the way I do it? And second, am I giving thanks to God the Father for this job and the tasks I am asked to do?

Story: In China, I met a Christian medical doctor we called Aunty Esther. Here's her story as told by Paul Estabrooks in his book Lion's Den. [98] Aunty Esther was a little elderly Chinese medical doctor with a soft, kind voice that masks the many years of suffering through which she has passed. During the Cultural Revolution, she says, I was called in by my superior one day. At that time I was in charge of eight large pediatric wards in my hospital. The communists were cracking down on people who did not toe the current party line. My superior warned me that I should deny my faith and join the communist party or I may have to face the serious consequences of job demotion and salary reduction.

"A few days later, I was rudely awakened by four nurses who roughly pulled me from my bed and marched me to the hospital. En route they stopped at a barbershop and shaved off half of my hair. In front of the rest of the staff, I was confronted to renounce my faith in Christ and join the communist party.

"I responded, 'I can't deny Jesus. I love Jesus!' At the mention of His name they threw me down on the ground and cursed. Later, the communist cadre at my hospital tore the stethoscope

---

[97] Colossians 3:17

[98] "Daily Devotional by Open Doors" <usa@opendoors.org> Subject: January 14 - Standing Strong Through the Storm Devotional, Date: January 14, 2017.

from my neck and said, 'You are no longer Esther; you are now The Fool.'"

Esther continues. For the next eleven years, she lived in the basement of the hospital and obediently submitted to her new task—cleaning the floors and toilets of the hospital wards that she previously headed. Her already meager salary of 50 dollars per month was reduced to 15 dollars. And she had to buy the cleaning materials from it. The rest was used up on food. But Esther practiced the presence of Jesus in her job. She sang as she toiled. With a twinkle in her eyes, she adds, "My hospital had the cleanest floors and cleanest toilets in all of China!"

Hospital staff would come to her and with great envy question her source of joy in spite of her troubles. Esther responded, "When you have Jesus in your heart, it doesn't matter what job you do or what position you have. It only matters that you love Him and are faithful and loyal to Him!"

When the Cultural Revolution period ended, Aunty Esther was reinstated in her original job and given back pay for all that she had been deprived during those eleven years. This amount enabled her to send one of her children for higher education. She faithfully carried on her public witness for Jesus until the day she died in her late nineties.

"When you have Jesus in your heart,
It doesn't matter what job you do or what position you have.
It only matters that you love Him and are faithful and loyal to Him!"

My longtime friend Dr. Fred Romanuk prepared the following chart to show the attitudes of different age groups towards being an Employee. (See Footnote)[99]

---

[99] Used with permission (23 January 2017). Chart created by Fred Romanuk, Ph.D.

World View	Traditionalists-1900-1945	Baby Boomers-1946-1964	Generation X-1965-1990	Millenials- 1991-2010
Influencers	War, Great Depression, Hard Times, Conformist Society	Civil rights, Divorce, American Dream, Radicalism,	Dual Job Parents, Single Parents, Rebellion	Terrorism, Child Focused World, Protected, Schedules
Core Values	Trust Authority, Hard Work, Loyalty, Duty, Patriotism	Anti Everything, Equal Rights, Make A Difference	Work-Life Balance, Pragmatic, Self-Reliance	Achievement, Tolerance, Fun, Optimism, "Me Generation"
Attributes	Conservative, Dedicated, Ethical, Sacrifice, Respectful	Ambitious, Competitive, Challenge Authority	Independent, Pampered, Entitlement, Work-To-Live	TeamWork, Multi-Cultural, Globalism, Meaning-In-Work
Entitlement	Through Seniority	Through Experience	Through Merit	Through Contribution
Work	Fair Days Pay for Fair Days Work	Workaholics	Get Paid For Results	Fill the time Between Weekends
Work-Life Balance	Hard Work For Job Security	Work Comes First	Focus Upon Work-Family Balance	Achieve Balance with Life, Community, Self-Development
Work Focus	Quality	Long Hours	Productivity	Contribution
Work Values	Duty Before Fun	Live-To-Work	Work-to-Live	Extreme Work-To-Live
Work Is ...	An Obligation	An Adventure	A Difficult Challenge	A Means to An End-Fulfillment
View of Authority	Respectful	Impressed	Unimpressed	Relaxed
Career Development	'Nose-to-The-Grindstone'	Loyal To The Company	Loyal To Themselves	Extreme Loyalty To Themselves
Motivated By ...	Respect & Security	Money	Time Off	Freedom

I was born during that period called: Traditionalists 1900-1945.

> Story: Part 1: My father, Harold Cunningham, went to work in Wholesale Hardware at the age of 18. After serving his WW2-time in the Canadian 2nd Army, he returned to the same company and worked his way up in the accounting office. One day, at age 49 he sat down at his desk and everything went blurry. Wet macular degeneration was the diagnosis in both eyes. Within 24-hours he went from a full-sighted, fully employed Cost Accountant to a legally blind Employee. After re-training, the company transferred him to their pre-computerized catalogue-binding Print Department. He also worked part-time in the Maintenance Department. Humbling? Yes. But he stayed with the company until he officially retired at age 68 after fifty years of service with the same company. My father was a true Traditionalist.

Is it too simplistic to say that a man can find fulfillment in his role as an Employee by being in a right relationship with God through Jesus Christ? Why not? Some people enjoy snow! Wait, you ask, what relationship does snow have to job satisfaction? Do you believe that Adam's curse led to the eventual judgment of the Earth by the Flood? If so, that Flood altered the Earth's axis causing four previously unknown seasons, with snow as a by-product of the curse. (My personal theology adds a few other items not found in the pre-cursed Garden of Eden!) Adam and Eve were naked in the Garden. Snow was not part of the original plan. I meet people who tell me they enjoy skiing, skating, hockey, snowshoeing, and a host of winter activities in that cursed snow!

Clothing is another adjustment to the curse. Clothing has become "a means of defining the self socially" according to McLuhan, [100] as well as a "heat control mechanism." A person in rebellion against the curse of having to wear clothes may advocate removal or minimal modesty for maximum stimulation of the inner sin nature of a man. Seductive clothing may arouse the Male in us but not the Man. However, most people admit they enjoy clothes.

If one can adjust to snow and wearing clothes then a man can adapt to a right perspective of work. When he does, fulfillment follows with a minimum of rebellion against the plan of God. He can thoroughly enjoy his job. More than an artificial theory, it is a way of life.

A Good Name is Better Than Riches

What does it tell us when one of the world's wealthiest men answers: "Just a little more..." to the question: "How much money does a man need to be happy?" Forbes magazine makes an annual list of the wealthiest people on earth. One recent edition showed that eight individuals had a combined personal net worth equal to that of the bottom 50% of the world's population!

Why does Scripture say, *"A good name is more to be desired than riches"?* Abraham, Job, Solomon and Boaz gave evidence of combining both. Many men in Scripture, like John the Baptist and various prophets, had a good name without any apparent riches. And

[100] "The medium is the message" is a phrase coined by Marshall McLuhan meaning that the form of a medium embeds itself in any message it would transmit or convey, creating a symbiotic relationship by which the medium influences how the message is perceived. From Understanding Media by Marshall McLuhan

we have a record of Ananias and Sapphira, and the Rich Young Ruler, who, while they had riches, failed spiritually. So wealth (or lack thereof) is not a barometer of spirituality.

A person's attitude towards money will determine his attitude towards God. "*No man can serve God and Mammon" (riches).* [101] Scripture warns us that the pursuit of riches has led many men to ruin and destruction. [102] Just as the emotion of anger can lead quickly to sinful responses, so the love of money leads to all sorts of evil. [103]

How does a Man build a Good Name as an Employee?

1. All work is done for the Lord. *"Whatever you do, do your work heartily, as for the Lord rather than for men."* [104] *"And whatever you do, in word or deed, do all in the name of the Lord Jesus, giving thanks through Him to God the Father."* [105]

Freedom to choose one's occupation is a true luxury. Many men in many societies are forced by family or the state to be a slave to the economic system without choice. Paul wrote biblical principles (above) for Christians living during the Roman Empire when people were treated as property. Slavery was in full bloom. Paul even referred to himself as a slave or bondservant of Jesus Christ, to attach cultural significance to the servant-relationship he had to Jesus Christ as His Lord.

2. All submission to Employers is with respect. Peter tells Employees to *"be submissive to your masters, with all respect, not only to those who are good and gentle but also to those who are unreasonable."* [106] Employers in Roman times were (by our

---

[101] Matthew 6:24-34

[102] See 1 Timothy 6:6-10

[103] 1 Timothy 6:10

[104] Colossians 3:23

[105] Colossians 3:17

[106] 1 Peter 2:18

standards) beyond reason in their expectations for their servants, not to mention the working conditions and stress they would place on their Employees.

In our North American society labor unions have moved past Child Labor Laws and Work Safe laws. They now seek to control the Employee's actions almost as much as Management, demanding loyalty and obedience to the Union. Ask a Union member who has defied an illegal strike (disobeyed the Union), gone to work (obeyed his Employer), and come home to find the trees in his front yard cut down with a chainsaw and given the silent treatment for disobeying the Union. Peter says: *"But if when you do what is right and suffer for it (and), you patiently endure it, this finds favor with God."* [107]

3. All tasks require a full effort of heartiness and praise. What a dreamer, I can hear some reader saying to himself: "That guy never had to work in the conditions I face each day. Come and do my job for one day. Meet my boss, and you will soon revise your views for Employees!"

Believe me brothers; this chapter was the toughest to write. I do not want it to sound like an authoritative, philosophical, theory without connection to reality. I am writing this after 50+ years in the marketplace. I have worked for a salary and I have been self-employed. I have served in a Union and in Management. I have had some supervisors who were a *dream to work with* and others who were a *recurring nightmare.* I have applied for jobs, been short-listed and rejected because I was the wrong gender or too religious (a.k.a. a Christian) or over-qualified or whatever reason one can legally give. I have hired staff, and I have fired staff. I have run for public office—and been rejected by the public. I have experienced being promoted in one job and *terminated without cause* in another. I am not speaking in a vacuum. These are not my theories. This is clear Scripture. And I believe Scripture is true!

---

[107] 1 Peter 2:20

Either the Word of God is God-breathed and trustworthy with sound principles that work, or it is not. The choice is yours.

"Do all things without grumbling or disputing" [108], is not negotiable. It is a command. Every time you do a task with Praise on your lips, you evidence that Jesus Christ is Lord. In essence, we say: "No matter how difficult the task may be, or the supervisor, we do it *'to the praise of His Glory.'*" [109]

What will people remember about us after we die? How hard we worked? How much we earned? How brilliant we were? Let me suggest they will remember: *"as much as possible, and as far as it depended on him, he was at peace with everyone."* [110]

What gives us a Good Name?

- A competency to do and learn assigned tasks.
- A "pure (sincere) heart." [111]
- A "merry heart" giving a happy countenance.
- A positive attitude towards changes, adjustments, new staff, and new relationships.
- An approachable spirit.
- An evidence of ethics and integrity regarding the exchange of time for compensation.

Enjoy whatever liberties God has given you in your job. Give God daily praise for the freedom you have to work and enjoy life. At my age and stage in life, I can look back and tell younger men there are three things you must have to minister effectively as a servant of Jesus Christ. They each start with "M."

---

[108] Philippians 2:14

[109] Ephesians 1:6 and 12

[110] See Romans 12:18

[111] See Psalm 24:4 *"He who has clean hands and a pure heart, who has not lifted up his soul to falsehood. And has not sworn deceitfully."* And 1 Timothy 1:5 *"But the goal of our instruction is love from a pure heart and a good conscience and a sincere faith."* And Hebrews 10:22 *"…let us draw near with a sincere heart in full assurance of faith, having our hearts sprinkled clean from an evil conscience, and our bodies washed with pure water."*

1. **Mobility:** You must have Mobility. Some part of your body has to move to communicate with others.
2. **Money:** You must have Money. Some income/resource is needed to survive...and...
3. And you must have...ahh. You must have...let's see. Oh yeah, third thing, you must have **Memory!**

Dealing with Change.

Every Man's life is guaranteed to have Changes. From your first breath to your last breath, life is a series of changes. For some, these changes are called *reasonable adjustments*, like your hair changing color. But some changes are considered a crisis. And how we deal with change can affect our health and our spiritual life. Our bodies have a limited capacity to deal with the stress of change. But what amazes me is how two people can face similar situations and have different results.

> Story: During the 2nd WW, German U-boats sunk many merchant ships in the North Atlantic. The sailors on these ships were often ordinary workingmen with no military training, no preparation. After a ship sank, the survivors would bob around in the ocean for hours or days until some other ship came and rescued them. Rescue ships discovered that many of the survivors were older sailors and many of the dead were young sailors (still in their life jackets without any physical injuries). Why did the young guys die? Answer: they had never faced stress and fear before their ship sank. Therefore many just gave up and died. Thus began a program called Outward Bound [112] to put a merchant sailor through controlled stress activities to learn how to persevere and not lose hope.

[112] I took and thoroughly enjoyed the Outward Bound short-10-day course for Professionals back in 1973 in Keremeos, British Columbia Canada. I can attest that skills learned gave me great appreciation for the capacity of the human body to endure pain and stress and survive! Christians I meet in regions of persecution reflect to me that same peace from knowing that all things work together for good to those who love God. (See Romans 8).

Changes in Physical Development—All men age. The mid-40's is the time men begin to fight the physical Battle of the B's (Baldness, Bifocals, Bladder, Bulge and Bunions). Crows feet beside the eyes and bags underneath accentuate the physical change from adolescent to aging. Some men begin a lifelong losing battle against getting older: new clothes, new glasses, new hair pieces, new car, and even a new wife, all the while vainly denying the changes apparent to all who watch.

Changes in Virility and Vitality—Most men experience a natural decline in sexual activity as they age, but in our super-sexed, pornography-addicted society many men can neither accept nor understand their decreasing virility. Embarrassment flows through the aging male's tired bloodstream. Some men find it difficult to accept the physical changes in their wife: obesity, enlarged breasts and more body hair than normal. They stop rejoicing in the wife of their youth!

Changes in Family Relationships—One could define middle age for men as the time between teenage kids on one end and aging parents on the other. One major adjustment for parents of school age children is having the first child leave home. Another happens when the last child leaves home. One comedian liked to say, "Life begins when the last kid leaves home and the dog dies! We can now sleep with the bedroom door open!" However, if men have spent their time at a job and women have invested time in rearing children, the spouses may suddenly find themselves living with a stranger.

Change in Employment Relationships—Changes in technology, shifts in the economy, globalization, and the list goes on. Notice on our New Earth Island page that only 8% of the people on Earth are over age 65. By age 45 a man in North America is considered an older worker. In some countries, the average life expectancy for men is under 50!

Death is More Comprehendible—A contemporary dying of a heart attack seems to snap a middle age man back to alert. He may even start practicing healthier habits regarding diet and exercise.

Middle Age is a time for re-evaluation. One's values are re-examined and re-assessed for the next season of life. One author said, "Young men seek security, middle-aged man seek power and old men desire honor." Each Change permits men to make the necessary adjustments for the time ahead.

I was fascinated with a study, years ago, by Dr. Thomas Holmes.[113] He scaled out what he called *Life Changing Units* and attached a value to each: death of a spouse, rated highest, then divorce and marital separation, right down to points given for minor stress-related events like vacations, Christmas, and a traffic ticket. One could add up a personal total of the changes they had experienced within a period of time (one year I believe). His theory is that once a person hits a certain level of change units, he is vulnerable to diseases, many of them emotionally charged, that begin to happen in a person's life. Interesting theory. What struck my attention was that a percentage of citizens (exact number unknown) could experience two or three times the upper level of the stress limit and not suffer either physical consequences or emotionally based diseases.

Can a man develop an internal safety zone that can absorb stress through life changes, travel, job changes, daily tensions, family adjustments, and ground them out before they overload the circuit and cause a disease to start? The answer has to be "Yes." The question has to be "How"?

How can one find fulfillment in employment and life without allowing avoidable stress to cause health issues? Philippians 4:4 says, *"Rejoice in the Lord always; again I will say, rejoice! Let your gentle spirit be known to all men. The Lord is near. Be anxious for nothing, but in everything by prayer and supplication with thanksgiving let your requests be made known to God. And the peace of*

113 http://www.stress.org/holmes-rahe-stress-inventory/ (Accessed 18 Feb, 2017)

God, which surpasses all comprehension, will guard your hearts and your minds in Christ Jesus.

"Finally, brethren, whatever is true, whatever is honorable, whatever is right, whatever is pure, whatever is lovely, whatever is of good repute, if there is any excellence and if anything is worthy of praise, dwell on these things. The things you have learned and received and heard and seen in me, practice these things, and the God of peace will be with you."

It's worth considering. To fulfill the role of an Employee requires all the help we can get.

Competencies to Fulfill Role of EMPLOYEE

Personal Checklist
Circle the best answer for each to determine score

Do I have…

1. Adequate skills, training, and knowledge to assume the tasks or responsibilities related to my job?

1	2	3	4	5
Not at all	A little bit	Usually	Most of the time	Always

2. A willingness to learn those new skills that will enable me to fulfill my vocational assignment?

1	2	3	4	5
Not at all	A little bit	Usually	Most of the time	Always

3. The realization that all work is to be done "heartily, as for the Lord rather than for men?" (Colossians 3:23)

1	2	3	4	5
Not at all	A little bit	Usually	Most of the time	Always

4. Dependability and loyalty to my employer and my assigned responsibilities? (Colossians 3:22 –"in all things obey those who are your masters on earth, not with external service, as those who merely please men, but with sincerity of heart, fearing the Lord.")

1	2	3	4	5
Not at all	A little bit	Usually	Most of the time	Always

5. An attitude of praise with an absence of grumbling or disputing? (Ephesians 6:7; Philippians 2:14)

1	2	3	4	5
Not at all	A little bit	Usually	Most of the time	Always

6. A clear record and a 'good name'? "Prove yourself to be blameless and innocent, children of God, above reproach, in the midst of a crooked and perverse generation, among whom you appear as lights in the world." (Philippians 2:15) (See also Proverbs 22:1; Ecclesiastes 7:1)

1	2	3	4	5
Not at all	A little bit	Usually	Most of the time	Always

7. A willingness to work effectively and efficiently? "And whatever you do in word or deed, do all in the name of the Lord Jesus, giving thanks through Him to God the Father" (Colossians 3:17).

1	2	3	4	5
Not at all	A little bit	Usually	Most of the time	Always

Total divided by 7 =

Evidences Role of EMPLOYEE Fulfilled

Personal Checklist – (Circle the best answer for each to determine score)

Have I demonstrated…

1. A degree of recognized appreciation for my service from my employers? "When a man's ways are pleasing to the Lord He makes even his enemies to be at peace with him" (Proverbs 16:7).

1	2	3	4	5
Not at all	A little bit	Usually	Most of the time	Always

2. Personal satisfaction that I have done my job to the glory of Jesus Christ? (Colossians 3:17)

1	2	3	4	5
Not at all	A little bit	Usually	Most of the time	Always

3. Responses of respect and submission to my employers, "not only to those who are good and gentle but also to those who are 'unreasonable'" (1 Peter 2:18).

1	2	3	4	5
Not at all	A little bit	Usually	Most of the time	Always

4. Full productivity for the task assigned, "with all your might"? (Ecclesiastes 9:10).

1	2	3	4	5
Not at all	A little bit	Usually	Most of the time	Always

5. Fulfillment in seeing the job done as a means of gaining personal satisfaction, plus a medium of exchange to provide for my family? (See 1 Timothy 5:8; 2 Thessalonians 3:10 – "if anyone will not work, neither let him eat.")

1	2	3	4	5
Not at all	A little bit	Usually	Most of the time	Always

6. Openness to the Lord's leading into new areas of responsibility and service based on the skills acquired, training received or proved faithfulness in my given assignments? (Luke 16:10)

1	2	3	4	5
Not at all	A little bit	Usually	Most of the time	Always

7. Adequate performance level when evaluated by my employer? (Matthew 10:10; 1 Timothy 5:18)

1	2	3	4	5
Not at all	A little bit	Usually	Most of the time	Always

Total divided by 7=

Role of EMPLOYEE

Projects for Investigation and Discussion

[__] Discuss: When a Christian joins a labor union, which is his authority: Christ or the Union? Should he ever disobey the union (or the company)?

[__] Job and career dissatisfaction are rampant throughout the executive and managerial suites of American business. (From A.M.A.) Discuss the implications of job dissatisfaction on the various roles a man must fulfill.

[__] 1Timothy 6:8 says: “If we have food and covering, with these we shall be content.” What are the factors that are causing a national epidemic of materialistic greed? What is the ‘striving for more goods’ doing to our lifestyle?

[__] Discuss: What can a man do if he is in a job that he hates?

[__] Develop a journal of the lifestyles of several wealthy men. Note what they have done with their wealth – and what their wealth has done to them. Share your observations.

[__] “Work is part of the curse and can never be enjoyed.” How would you answer a man who makes this statement? (See Genesis 3:17-19)

[__] Interview two Employees who you regard as enjoying their job. Ask them to identify the reasons for their job satisfaction. What causes a man to enjoy his job? List the factors.

[__] What does 2 Corinthians 6:14 mean to you as an employee?

Chapter 8

Husband • Relationship to His Wife

Husbands love your wives • Ephesians 5:25, 28-33

What do we do with "the weaker vessel"?

Few verses incur the wrath of aggressive women faster than Peter's admonition to husbands found in 1 Peter 3:7. It says:

"You husbands in the same way [likewise] ***live with your wives in an understanding way, as with someone weaker*** [lit. a weaker vessel] ***since she is a woman; and show her honor as a fellow heir of the grace of life, so that your prayers will not be hindered."***

"**You husbands**..." Those who are married to the wives mentioned in verses 1-6.

"...**likewise**..." You have some responsibilities to obey lest you take the idea of wives submitting to you as a selfish excuse to Lord it over your wives.

"...**live with your wives**..." Make your wife number one in your life. Not your job, your career or your profession. One man built a *Man Cave* in his garage filled with man-toys: large screen TV, latest tech games, posters of sports teams, refrigerator, cold drinks, food, etc. The neighborhood men thought that was an excellent idea, so some of them built one in their garage. Soon the boys were going from cave to cave watching sporting events, drinking beer, and enjoying each other's company more than being *at home with the little lady.* Need I add that the owner of the first *Man Cave* is now divorced?

"...**in an understanding way**..." That knowledge includes accepting the fact your wife and my wife are different.

Story: During my research in Israel, I was a guest for a week on a Marxist Kibbutz in Northern Israel, where a couple hundred Marxist, atheistic Jews established their kibbutz, based on full equality and adherence to Marxist ideology. The results, while intellectually honest were in reality quite humorous. Members had a job rotation every six weeks at different tasks on the kibbutz. For example, one man might get six weeks in the orchards, then six weeks in the kitchen, six weeks in the sewing room and another six weeks in the chicken barns. At the weekly Thursday assessment meetings the women started to say, "Keep the men out of the sewing room. Those klutzes have five thumbs and schmuck up the bobbins on the sewing machines, and we then waste days fixing them." Then the women complained the blue denim standard outfits each person received were harsh. It rubbed on their breasts and was affecting their nipples! Could they have money to buy brassieres? The immediate objection came from some of the men. "If they have money spent for bras, what do we get of equal value?" Gradually over the years a strange thing happened among the so-called Marxists on this kibbutz. The men gravitated towards the physical jobs that earned money for the kibbutz (orchards, manufacturing) and the women gravitated with full *Thursday Meeting Agreements* towards the jobs we would call the service jobs. Not even strict Marxist idealists could maintain equality between men and women.

Think of how *the wife of your youth* is different from her husband:

- ***Wives are physically different.*** Hallelujah! They can menstruate, bear children, and nurse a baby. Try that some year, guys! These three features alone remain exclusively feminine roles! And, there are differences attached to these roles. They have moods, feelings, and emotions that have no male equivalent! Any husband married more than 28 days soon understands this. As young boys, my sons thought the letter P on my office calendar meant Pay Day. Little did they know that for dad P-Day was in reality *Prepare, have Patience, and Pray.*

- ***Wives are emotionally different.*** Women activists would have us believe this is purely the result of the environment or culture. Few men would admit there is no difference emotionally between them and their wife. Wives tend to be responders. Husbands are more the initiators. To fulfill the sex act husbands must initiate to penetrate. Wives must respond to receive. If the husband cannot initiate it is called *Erectile Dysfunction*. If the wife does not respond to her husband, it could be called *Rape*. Men tend to move about, travel, and initiate plans and decisions more often than their wives. My observation is that when the wife is the initiator the husband may give up his role and become passive. Some men even quit their job and let *Mamma* earn money. Some merely accompany a more aggressive wife wherever she leads him. If we as men are going to fulfill our God-ordained role as initiators we need to think carefully about how our decisions affect our wife and children. It usually causes high levels of stress for a wife to give up her nest and move. Likewise, a job change (*"we're moving to Jeddah next month…")* can generate stress for your wife. So can some of the riskier male ambitions such as: *"think I'll try para-gliding this year."*

- ***Wives often have more discernment.*** My wife Rita has a legendary level of insight into people's character. As a nurse entering a room of psychiatric patients she had been trained to read body language, eyes, and tone of voice for her physical safety. But as a godly spirit-filled woman she elevated this training to a higher level of spiritual discernment. She once met a Christian educator in a public meeting. After spending less than five minutes in his presence, she said to me, "Make sure you never leave me in a room alone with that man." "Why?" I asked, like a dumbfounded husband. "What did he do?" "He did not *do* anything." Then she added, "I cannot respect him. He came across very aggressive like a dictator and asked inappropriate questions. And, I do not trust his eyes." Later we discovered this man lost his leadership of a Christian agency for having sexual relations with both his secretary and her mother! His eloquent speech and credentials distracted the directors of the ministry who hired him. Rita discerned something was wrong by his demeanor in a *blink!* [114] She discerned he was unable to walk humbly with respect. [115]

- ***Wives are often more compassionate than husbands.*** When she says, "It's time to spend more time with (insert name)," she means it. Likewise whenever she begins a sentence with "I've been thinking..." take her next sentence seriously. When she has been thinking, this is not a spur-of-the-moment, *throw away* thought. She has good reasons for what she's saying. We need to listen carefully rather than overruling our wives with our perceived greater insight or more spiritual-sounding response.

Story: I agreed one time to take on an assignment of raising money for a Christian ministry. Big mistake. But worse yet, I did not listen my wife. Bigger mistake! When I told her I had taken the job, she asked me "Why did you ask me for my opinion and then not accept it?" She had said, "The person you are reporting to cannot raise money. That is why they want you in the job. So face it, IF you're successful, they will take the credit, and you will be raising money the rest of your life. Is that why we sacrificed those years in university learning how to teach adults – so you could be a fund-raiser? And IF you are unsuccessful, they will fire you. Either way, you lose." She was right. 18 months later I was released from the job!

In scripture, I can find examples of where the wife had a greater discernment than the husband. The story of Abigail needs to be

---

[114] Gladwell, Malcolm, Blink: *The Power of Thinking Without Thinking,* 2005. Gladwell argues that one's intuitive judgment based on experience, training [add for the Christian, the indwelling discernment power of the Holy Spirit] can often overrule what he calls "analysis paralysis" based on having too much information. Gladwell believes that simplicity of information is often better than too much information. Rita discerned this man's character in a "Blink!"

[115] See Hebrews 5:14

studied. [116]And note the wise advice given to Pilate by his wife. [117] However there are examples of where a godly wife agreed with her husband and they were both wrong as in the case of Ananias and Sapphira. [118] But in the majority, godly wives are a "help-meet" more than a hindrance. Men, Husbands, it pays to listen carefully to your wife's concerns, views, and suggestions!

"...**as with a weaker vessel**..." In scripture, the word "weaker" does not mean "inferior." On the contrary, it means finer or more valuable as in a valuable piece of china. Aggressive women dislike this term and concept. Rather than celebrating their differences, they seem determined to prove they are physically capable of doing whatever a man may do. Peter is saying, husbands, protect your wife from the hazards of evil men around her.

"...**since she is a woman**..." In no manner does Peter imply or leave himself open to be interpreted that women are therefore inferior. Yes, they are uniquely different. And they gain their full *mystique* and attraction when they are accepted as being different. Not the same, but equal in the eyes of God. *"Male and female made He them...in His own image..."* When a loving husband meets the needs of a wife, she in turn will help him achieve godly character qualities. It's a symbiotic[119] relationship.

"...**grant [show] her honor**..." Respect her and elevate her to a position of honor in the eyes of your children and friends. Do not call her *The Wife.* She is not an object. She is a person. Your wife is a person with a name that you love. Help your children see that she is the most important person on earth to you even above any of them. My lifelong friend Paul Estabrooks still calls his wife "My Bride" - after 52 years! And my Rita is still "My Angel" - after 50 years!

---

[116] See 1 Samuel chapter 25

[117] See Matthew 27:19

[118] See Acts 5:1-11

[119] Symbiotic as in a "mutually beneficial relationship."

Story: When I was a young father, a single friend asked me one time, "Who do you greet and hug first when you get home after a long time away?" I answered, "Usually my boys as they run ahead of Rita to greet me…" He replied, "Help them see and understand that Mom is Number One in your books, not them. Disobey Mom and you deal with Dad!" Good advice from a single guy! I like to remind him of what he said, now that he is married with three daughters.

"…**as a fellow heir of the grace of God…**" By God's grace, through faith in the atoning work of Jesus Christ we have become one in spirit with all Christians. We are neither bond nor free, man nor woman in our personal relationship with Jesus Christ. We are equal. Scripture teaches that the husband is to be *the head of the wife* as Jesus Christ is *the head of the Church.* Husbands are partners with their wives in a ministry ordained by God Himself, rather than a *master-slave* relationship.

"…that your prayers be not hindered…" A man's relationship with his wife determines the quality of his relationship with the Lord. [120] Some Christian men try their best to do everything right except the way they treat their wife. Some may be very insightful. Some may even be pastors and leaders. But the Bible says that a man's prayers are affected by his relationship with his wife. Happy is the man who is one with the wife of his youth. They can pray together with sincerity, honesty, and openness. Husbands in a right relationship with their wives have met one of the qualifications for giving spiritual leadership in their church. If a church is failing [121] spiritually, it may be time to clean up the husband-wife relationships at home.

---

[120] See also Mark 11:25; Ephesians 4:26-27; 1 Timothy 3:2-7 and Titus 1:6-9.

[121] Backfire: verb 1. a mistimed explosion in the cylinder or exhaust of a car or vehicle. 2. (of a plan or action) have the opposite effect of what was intended.

Husbands, love your wives

Story: Rita had an intense discussion with a pastor who believed Jesus was not the *Head* of the Church, as an authority, thereby giving men a parallel-permission to be the *head* (a.k.a. authority) over the wife. He believed Christ was just the *"source"* of the Church much like a mountain stream is the headwater *source* of a river. And he suggested Man (Adam) was the *source* of Eve (as she came from his rib). Rita was shocked at his theology compared to the many verses that say Christ is the Head of the church and started the Church. She felt it was dishonoring to Christ to say He was *just a source*. Jesus gave His life for the Church. No one has done more to earn that title than Jesus did. When it comes to obeying Scripture, we cannot play word games. Either we believe it or we don't. Moses went out of his way to tell the Children of Israel they should remember *"the whole way the Lord commanded you."* (See Deuteronomy 8:1-2). Early in our marriage Rita observed that in Ephesians 5:22-23, husbands are told FOUR times (her emphasis) to *love their wives*, but wives are never commanded to love their husbands. Her view, as my wife, is that wives know how to love their husbands intuitively, whereas husbands have to learn how to do it. I am not certain how that excites you as an idea but the following chart is an attempt to show us as husbands how we are to love our wives.

HUSBANDS LOVE YOUR WIVES (from Ephesians 5)		
HOW?	**EVIDENCE**	**RESULT**
1. ***"...as Christ also is the head of the church,*** *He Himself being the Savior of the body…"* (Ephesians 5:23).	Christ accepted His God-ordained assignment by giving His life as a servant and as a ransom for the body (the church). (See Matthew 20:28 and 26:39.)	Christ made decisions as the head of the church that brought glory to the Father and personal fulfillment to His earthly life ministry.
"(So) *the husband is the head of the wife…"*	A husband is to accept his positional assignment as head of his wife, by exercising the authority and fulfilling the responsibilities God assigned to him in this role as Husband.	The husband is to initiate in love the plan God has for him and his wife. He gives himself (body, soul, and spirit) to his wife so they might become one in Jesus Christ bringing glory to God the Father.
2. ***"...as Christ loved the Church..."*** (Ephesians 5:25).	Christ gave Himself up for the Church. (See 1 Peter 2:24.)	Christ gave His life to sanctify the Church and cleanse her so she might be holy and blameless to present to Himself, so that He might be one with her (Revelation 21:2-3 and Ephesians 5:26-27).
"(So) husbands are to love their wives."	A husband is to give his time, his energy and his life if need be for his wife. (See John 15:13.)	A husband is to give himself up for his wife. He is to help her become clean, holy and blameless by sanctifying himself as Jesus did for the Church (John 17:19).
3. ***"As your own body...just as Christ also does the church"*** (Ephesians 5:28).	*"for no one ever hated his own flesh, but nourishes and cherishes it, just as Christ also does the church, because we are members of His body…"* (Ephesians 5:29) (See also Leviticus 19:18 and Proverbs 5:18-19.)	Christ surrendered His will, time, plans, energies, and opportunities for power, prestige, and honor to obey the will of His Heavenly Father to: • Teach (John 16:13) • Comfort (John 16:7) • Heal (1 Peter 2:24) • Protect (Hebrews 13:5) • Feed (1 Peter 5:2 & John 21:16) • Quicken (Ephesians 2:1-5) and • Disciple (Hebrews 12:6) His body, The Church.

HOW?	EVIDENCE	RESULT
"(So) ...husbands are to see their wives as part of their body – and meet their needs." (See Ephesians 5:29.)	*"The two shall become one flesh..."* (Ephesians 5:31). Husbands are to provide for the needs of their wives (1 Timothy 5:8) such as food, clothing, shelter, plus physical, social, mental and spiritual development in Jesus Christ.	When a husband invests, time, money and energy to meet the needs of his wife (like he does his own needs), his wife will know she is loved and grow as an individual. Her strength makes the husband stronger in his other roles and relationships thereby strengthening his qualifications to offer spiritual leadership in the church (1 Timothy 3:2-7 and Titus 1:6-9).
4. **"As Himself..."** (Ephesians 5:33).	Christ provided for fulfillment of His needs: • Physical (Mark 6:31) • Social (John 2:1-2) • Mental (Matthew 22:33 and 46) • Spiritual (John 17:4-5)	Christ was a balanced person who knew how to live love in all situations. He loved us first (Romans 5:8) and gave Himself for us as the Perfect Passover Lamb, a model of sacrificial love. That is why we love Him (1 John 4:19).
"(So) ... husbands are to love their wives the same way" (Ephesians 5:33).	A husband's goals should be to minister to the needs of his wife ahead of anyone or anything else here on Earth.	The husband that truly loves his wife and dwells with her *according to knowledge* will discover emanating from her (as he meets her needs), a balanced, growing, loving individual who increasingly, and willingly, submits to him in the joy and the fear of the Lord.

When my sons were younger, they read through the David C. Cook *Picture Bible for all Ages.* When they finished reading the whole Old Testament, I asked them: "What impressions do you get about God's character, after seeing the Old Testament pictorially?" Their response was: "God sure gets angry when people disobey Him!" True, but He also displays His "steadfast love." It is only by His grace that His judgment is held back from handling people today the way He did in the Old Testament. God expects obedience. When, in the New Testament, He tells husbands to love their wives and wives to submit to their husbands, He means it. This obedience is not a negotiable option or cultural anomaly. Voluntary obedience brings the benefits and blessings of God in numerous ways when we follow His plans for fulfilling our role as husbands.

THE FOUR FACES OF ADULTERY: A Fresh Look at the Seventh Commandment

Have you heard? This question usually precedes an announcement of someone's cancer or adultery. Both are on the increase in our society.

Infidelity: It May Be In Our Genes blazes TIME magazine's cover headlines . [122] **Wife Should Have Heard Secret Before Marriage,** advises America's renowned Ann Landers. Do the tabloids and the media address topics that Christians are reluctant to discuss?

I had one of those *Why-am-I-saying-this* moments the first time I tackled the subject of adultery in a public forum. It had an impressive result. The men were tired. The drive to the conference was long and the time was late. I was finishing a talk on the character of King David and felt a prompting to add these words: "Men, let me take a few more minutes and examine why David is not the only one to be considered in his adulterous relationship with Bathsheba. There were three other people involved."

Within moments of the session ending, three different men noted this was true in their life. One man had separated from his wife. Another had just gone through the process of getting a divorce, and a third related an incident from within his family that backed up the pattern of the Biblical account.

The topic of adultery and pornography affects a man's fulfillment of his role as a faithful husband. In this age of adultery and pornography addiction when marriages dissolve in a moment's notice, it's time to look at the principles in this well-known story of Michal and David, Uriah and Bathsheba.

The names sound like the title of a modern adult movie. They are the characters in the Bible's best-documented account of an adulterous relationship.

---

[122] See note at end

Face Number One: Michal – A wife despises her husband

Principle 1
A wife who despises her husband will lose respect for him and his behavior

"Now Saul's daughter Michal was in love with David…" [123] This innocent expression of romance began a series of chained events in the life of David. Saul wanted desperately to eliminate his despised successor to the throne and received this news about Michal with great delight. Saul's distorted dowry of one hundred Philistine foreskins had only one motive, to have David killed. But David's love for Michal compelled him to deliver twice the required quota.

As his new wife, Michal loved and protected David. She risked her father's wrath by warning David to flee for his life during the night. Their separation and King Saul's forced re-marriage of Michal to another man did not reduce David and Michal's love for each other. By the time they met again, Saul and Jonathan were dead. The house of Saul was at war with the house of David. Things were changing. During his absence from Michal, David fathered six sons: Amnon by his wife Ahinoam, Chileab by Abigail, Absalom by Maacah, Adonijah by Haggith, Shephataih by Abital and Ithream by Eglah. Now, why would I mention six sons from six different wives to men reading this book who likely have only one wife? Here's the reason. Before David would consider becoming King of Israel, his one unconditional request was: *"Give me my wife Michal, to whom I was betrothed for a hundred foreskins of the Philistines."* [124]Michal was still his first love. Men, there is something spiritual almost mystical about your *first love.*

You would think David would have been content. At thirty he was King of Israel and Judah; united again with the wife of his youth and living in the King's Palace. He took more concubines and

---

[123] 1 Samuel 18:20

[124] 2 Samuel 3:14

wives from Jerusalem and added eleven more children to his family tree.

Did he have an invincibility complex that led him to believe that the Lord was on his side, and he could do nothing wrong?" Scripture does say: *"Let him who thinks he stands* (arrogant pride) *take heed lest he falls."* Is it possible to believe we are immune to a sinful action because we have avoided it for so long? We do not know. We do know that David had an attraction to women. But we also know that David's heart had a God-orientation. When an opportunity came to recover the ark of the Lord, David was ecstatic. He wanted the Lord's presence within the walls of Jerusalem.

It was a joyous moment in David's life. As he approached the Holy City, his excitement rose higher than the smoke from the sacrificial offerings. He rejoiced, sang and danced before the ark of the Lord *with all his might.* He put everything into it. Up in the window, *"Michal saw Kind David leaping and dancing before the Lord and she despised him in her heart."* [125] This heart attitude was a significant turn in their relationship.

David returned home from a super spiritual experience to bless his wife and family. Instead of rejoicing, he heard these bitter words from his first love: *"How the King of Israel distinguished himself today, disrobing in the sight of the slave girls of his servants as any vulgar fellow would."* [126] She was angry. In modern English it could read like this: "You really think you are Mr. Spiritual Big don't you? (Hear the dripping sarcasm?) I can't stand the way you try to impress the women. (A slight touch of jealousy perhaps?) If they only knew what you are like around this palace, Hah!" (Go ahead Michal; give David a good verbal beating! A tad bitter perhaps?)

Michal's relationship with David just hit the ditch. A wife with a jealous attitude and a bitter tongue is like a wrecking-ball to a marriage. Solomon, who later understood this story from inside

---

[125] 2 Samuel 6:16

[126] 2 Samuel 6:20

the home, wrote: *"It is better to live in a desert land than with a contentious and vexing woman."* [127]

Face Number Two: David – A bitter, angry husband

Principle 2
Unresolved bitterness by the husband produces alienation and loss of affection towards his wife.

Listen to David's response. Does this sound like a soft-spoken family psychologist turning away his wife's wrath? Not really. David poured out his feelings like gasoline on a fire: *"It was before the Lord who chose me rather than your father or anyone from his house when he appointed me ruler over the Lord's people Israel. I will celebrate before the Lord. I will become even more undignified than this and I will be humiliated in my own eyes. But by these slave girls you spoke of, I will be held in honor."* [128]

In modern language, his emotional rationalization would sound like this: "Listen, woman, I'm more tuned into the ways of God than you or your old man Saul! (Pride). So get off my case about what I do (Anger). If you think I'm bad now in front of other women, then fasten your seat belt, (Threatening) because I haven't begun to go into action yet. So back off, I don't need this. You understand me?" (Lack of affection).

The warmth of David's love was fading fast: from two hundred foreskins for her hand in marriage to a verbal slap across the face of the one he loved the most. The Scriptures say that from that day on: *"Michal, the daughter of Saul had no children to the day of her death."* [129] A thoughtful Jewish way of saying they never had sexual relations again.

---

[127] Proverbs 21:19

[128] 2 Samuel 6:21-22

[129] 2 Samuel 6:23

In spite of these marital tensions, the Lord's grace and mercy was upon David: *"The Lord gave David victory wherever he went."* [130] He defeated his enemies, captured gold, gained popularity and *"administered justice and righteousness, for all his people."* [131] He possessed what many 30-year-old men dream of getting: a wife, wealth, power and prestige. But, one thing was missing, the affection, acceptance, and respect of the first woman he loved, Michal.

David's appreciation for the goodness of God needed to find an alternative recipient. Someone had to become a substitute for Michal. *"Is there anyone left in the house of Saul, that I may show him kindness, for Jonathan's sake?"* [132] David asked. Hello, David, your first wife Michal is the daughter of Saul! But no forgiveness and reconciliation was about to happen. Instead, David located Mephibosheth, the disabled son of Jonathan, and told the people: *"All that belonged to Saul and to all his house, I have given to Mephibosheth."* [133]

Misguided emotion is deadlier than a misguided missile. David starts to rationalize his actions. He terminated his relationship with his wife Michal and ended up sharing meals with her nephew, *crippled in both feet.* Not the setting for a romantic candlelight dinner!

Face Number Three: Uriah – Career first - wife's needs second

Principle 3
A man who places his career ahead of his wife may lose both.

Uriah was a man's man. He was the poster image of military strength and intelligence. He gave unswerving loyalty to serve his commander-in-chief in any situation. Uriah would be the one

---

[130] 2 Samuel 8:6

[131] 2 Samuel 8:15

[132] 2 Samuel 9:1

[133] 2 Samuel 9:9

featured in a combat ad: *Don't-go-to-war-without-him.* (See list of David's 30 mighty men.) [134]

Uriah lived in a society where men were required to go away to war and leave their wives home alone for extended periods of time. Today's *Frequent Flyers* are the closest parallel to Uriah. Women might accuse this kind of man of being *married to his job*. It appears some husbands care more about their jobs and their boss' requests than the needs of their wives.

Workaholic men often find their priorities out of order. Job and career enhancement usually become number one. Getting ahead and enjoying life outranks being home on time for dinner. The distracted body that walks through the door, late again, has little time, energy or interest in *meeting her needs*.

We have heard (or perhaps made) these comments: "What do you want, woman? I bring home real money. You have everything you need. What more do you want? I have a major project due, and I'll be home when it's finished." Ouch.

We must be sympathetic to Uriah. He paid with his life for his loyalty to King David. And as far as we know from scripture he remained faithful to his wife and faithful to his marriage vows.

If there was any hint of weakness in Uriah's relationship with his wife it may have been when David called Uriah back from the front for a report on the battle. After the reporting, David said to Uriah, *"Go down to your house and wash your feet."* [135] In other words, "Go home to your wife, man, enjoy the evening and report back to your post in the morning." But there was no way Uriah would enjoy a night with his wife while *"my lord's men camp in the open fields."* He chose to sleep outside the King's palace rather than go home to Bathsheba.

---

[134] 1 Chronicles 11 – Note: Just to be named, as one of these thirty was the highest of honors. These men were not only physically strong, but brave, mentally acute, and strategically brilliant! You'd want them on your side in a battle.

[135] 2 Samuel 11:8

While we respect Uriah's integrity and his loyalty, husbands like Uriah often place personal discipline ahead of the emotional needs of their wives. Does this sound familiar today? An ignored wife married to a man who does not meet her emotional needs?

Face Number Four: Bathsheba – A lonely, vulnerable woman

Principle 4
An emotionally vulnerable wife left alone finds it easier to respond to another man's attention

Scripture says Bathsheba was *"very beautiful in appearance."* [136]Unfortunately, there is more written in Scripture about her beauty than her character. We know she was alone, again and may have felt neglected and lonely. We do not read of her having a family so she may have been a younger woman, perhaps recently married. We do know that her home was within eyesight of the palace. Scripture tells us that it was *"in the spring, at the time when kings go off to war..."* If David had led his army, as was his official duty, he would have been away from the palace. The timing was significant.

Bathsheba may have assumed the King was away with her husband, and that no one would be walking on the roof of the King's palace, or she may have known the King was home and was seeking his attention. We do not know her motive for bathing within eyesight of the King's palace.

"But David remained in Jerusalem..." [137] What an innocuous statement. David was in the wrong place at the wrong time, seeing the wrong person with the wrong emotional response and the wrong things began to happen!

---

[136] 2 Samuel 11:2

[137] 2 Samuel 11:1

David saw Bathsheba bathing. We do not know how much he saw or how much she was washing, but it was enough on both counts to arouse his royal hormones.

The scriptures say she *"purified herself from her uncleanness,"* (2 Samuel 11:4), meaning she had just finished her menstrual cycle and was not pregnant when the adultery began.

Bathsheba was beautiful. That is a given. And beauty is a gift from the Lord. The Bible teaches that modesty by women helps prevent the attraction of promiscuous men.

The Muslim faith goes to a bizarre extreme. They require a woman to cover her legs to the ankles, her arms to the wrists, her body to the neck, her head with a shawl and then put a veil over her face. Muslim men leave the most attractive part of a woman uncovered: her eyes. Some Muslim countries still require a light veil over the eyes! But, purity begins in one's mind.

Men having trouble with relationships at home or problems with inappropriate emotional responses to women need minuscule *body language* or eye appeal to get an idea. Later, Solomon, a future son of Bathsheba, wrote about the women of beauty in his Proverbs:

"Do not let her catch you with her eyelids."
(Seductive looks)
Proverbs 6:25
"Do not desire her beauty in your heart."
(Lust)
Proverbs 6:25
"Do not listen to her persuasions."
(Flattery)
Proverbs 7:21

Many lonely, beautiful women are open to the attention of a man, especially a man of perceived prestige or one who shows them kind attention. I asked a psychologist friend, "Why do women commit adultery?" She said: "Often some man pays more attention to her than her husband does." Then I asked: "Why do men commit adultery (or view pornography)?" Her response: "Usually for the pure personal pleasure of sex."

Some women want revenge. Some are dissatisfied with their marriage partner. Some are frustrated with their lifestyle, and some are just plain lonely. Women who sense fulfillment in their marriage and their relationship with Jesus Christ; women who guard their words, dress modestly and behave appropriately, rarely find themselves arousing men sexually.

Bathsheba's story does not indicate rape. Adultery is the fulfillment of mutual desire. Adultery implies a predetermined initiation and a voluntary response. *"...David sent someone to find out about her... then David sent messengers to get her."* [138]David knew what he was doing. David is accountable for consciously initiating disobedience to four of the Ten Commandments.

You shall not commit adultery
You shall not steal
You shall not covet your neighbor's wife - and
You shall not murder

He enticed her by taking an interest in her. Then he abused his position of power and trust by initiating a sexual relationship. *"She came to him, and he slept with her...Then she went back home. The woman conceived and sent word to David, saying, 'I am pregnant'."* [139]

Kings represent influential people. Why should a woman doubt the intentions of a man of power and credibility? Many women have become manipulated victims of powerful spiritual leaders with selfish intentions. Bathsheba in all likelihood knew the story

---

[138] 2 Samuel 11:4

[139] 2 Samuel 11:4-5

of Joseph caught alone in the room with Potiphar's wife. Joseph ran, Bathsheba stayed.

Bathsheba, for whatever personal reasons, responded and complied. Was she Naive? Afraid? Lonely? Bored? Looking for attention? We will not judge. But we can make this observation: the consequences of this adulterous relationship were horrific. *"This is what the Lord, the God of Israel says: 'I anointed you king over Israel, and I delivered you from the hand of Saul. I gave your master's house to you and your master's wives into your arms. I gave you the house of Israel and the house of Judah. And if all this had been too little, I would have given you even more. Why did you despise the word of the Lord by doing what is evil in his eyes? You struck down Uriah the Hittite with the sword and took his wife to be your own. You killed him with the sword of the Ammonites. Now, therefore, the sword will never depart from your house, because you despised me and took the wife of Uriah the Hittite to be your own.*

"This is what the Lord says, 'Out of your own household I am going to bring calamity upon you. Before your very eyes I will take your wives and give them to one who is close to you, and he will lie with your wives in broad daylight. You did it in secret, but I will do this thing in broad daylight before all Israel...but because by doing this you have made the enemies of the Lord show utter contempt, the son born to you will die.'" [140]

Principle 5
Adultery (pornography) in hidden intimate seclusion, eventually results in public open awareness

Freud believed sex is the strongest of human drives. While it may appear so at times, Love is still more powerful. Love protects. Sex outside of marriage destroys relationships.

---

[140] 2 Samuel 12:9-1

Principle 6
God initiated marriage to protect society from self-destruction

Adultery (Pornography) attacks the five primary reasons for marriage

Principle 7
Companion/Friend/ship

Adultery (pornography) betrays the most intimate of all friendships

Marriage gives us an intimate friend to share life's joys and pains. This unique friendship requires adjustments that teach us sensitivity, self-control, patience, and acceptance. This companionship can make us a kinder, gentler, more compassionate human being, if we're willing to learn the lessons.

Adultery (Pornography) says, in a devastating way: "I see you, my chosen marriage partner, to whom I pledged my lifelong love, exposed to me, in intimate vulnerability, yet I decide to reject you for someone else."

Principle 8
Sexual Pleasure

Adultery (pornography) advocates immediate sexual pleasure without responsibility for one another.

Marriage permits us to enjoy sex to the full. Sex is perhaps the highest universal pleasure of all pleasures to be enjoyed by marriage partners regardless of race or economic level. God Himself created sex initially. He made Man. He made Woman. And He said: *...it is good!*

Sexual pleasures do need boundaries and times of self-control. The Jewish Scriptures teach varying lengths of abstinence in marriage: i.e. during the menstrual cycle, after the birth of a child, the evening before worship and during times of fasting. If anything, a brief period of abstinence increases enjoyment of the opportunities for sex.

Maximum pleasure from normal intimacy is how God designed sex. Aberrations and experimentation push marriage partners to new levels of fantasy based more on boredom with a sense of being used, rather than enjoying natural and healthy sexual pleasure.

When a husband engages in pornography/adultery he leaves his wife feeling inadequate. She interprets this as a sign of her failure to meet his needs. Consequently this may lead to depression, or to her looking elsewhere for comfort and/or a solution.

Principle 9
Child Bearing
Adultery (pornography) views sex as pleasure without ownership of children

Marriage permits us to receive one of the dearests of God's creative gifts: Children. They represent perhaps the single strongest reason for the wedding - to multiply Life. Husbands and wives develop a safe, integrated, unit within society to safely give of themselves and procreate.

The joy of having children and grandchildren made in the genetic code image of the father and the mother is worth more laughs, more delights, more pain and more character enrichment for most people than any other human enterprise.

Principle 10
Protection
Adultery (pornography) leaves children and spouses vulnerable to attacks by 'The Evil One'

Marriage can be the greatest possible protection for our emotional, spiritual, physical, social, and psychological wellbeing. Marriage permits freedom for sex with protection from the risk of disease. Marriage gives emotional acceptance and love in spite of our weaknesses. What a tremendous increase to our self-worth. Experiencing unconditional love helps us cope with life's day-to-day pressures.

God wants to protect children from abuse. He wants them to grow up in the fear and admonition of the Lord in a home where the parents love and honor Him and love one another.

Principle 11
A Model of the Church

Adultery (pornography) says, I reject God's plan and Christ's love, and choose to live by my selfish rules

Marriage is a mini-model of God's relationship to the Church. God, our Heavenly Father, chose His Son Jesus of Nazareth to be the Head of the Church. Christ, in turn, loved the Church so much that He died for the Church.

Husbands are to be the head of the wife and love their wife as Christ loved the Church, and husbands are to give themselves for their wives as Christ gave Himself for the Church.

Marriage is a Lifelong Covenant

Principle 12

Marriage is a lifelong covenant not a temporary contract

In 725 BC, prior to the Assyrian invasion of Israel the Lord asked Hosea, to marry a prostitute named Gomer. God's wanted Hosea's marriage to be a living example to the Israelites of their relationship with Him. Hosea married Gomer, and they were blessed with three children. Everything went well for a few years until Gomer decided to return to her former lovers. Gomer rejected Hosea and his children.

Hosea grieved her departure but refused to terminate his love. In Hosea's mind, marriage was a covenant of love and fidelity sworn before God. It was unalterable because of health or circumstances, including adultery. Eventually, Gomer was alone, in debt and ruined. She was imprisoned according to the custom of the day to be sold as a slave at a public auction to pay for her debts.

It so happened that Hosea was walking through the marketplace the same day his wife was on the auction block. Motivated by his love, Hosea paid the price, and took her back as his wife. The result was a restored family and a new relationship between Hosea and Gomer. We as individuals are like Gomer, running away from God to serve other gods. But our loving heavenly Father paid the ultimate price, the death of His Son, Jesus Christ.

A marriage contract identifies agreed areas of responsibility. A marriage contract is in effect as long as both parties fulfill their mutually agreed obligations. In contrast to this, God intended marriage to be a lifelong covenant between a husband and his wife.

A Christian Marriage

Principle 13
A Christian marriage, ordained, and planned by God is ideally the monogamous union between two virgins: one male and one female, in a covenant relationship, as husband and wife, with fidelity, until parted by death.

Principle 14
A Christian marriage models Christ's relationship with His church: the husband (Bridegroom) is to love his wife (Bride) as Christ loved the Church and gave Himself for her, and the wife is to submit to her husband as the Church submits to the Head: Jesus Christ.

Principle 15
Men are not born with genetic factors that make them addicted to adultery (pornography)

Story: The wife of one serial adulterer reported this sequence of events: "We married young, and had four children. As I began to put on more weight, he began taking an interest in his secretary. An affair soon followed. He confessed to me, and I forgave him. We said nothing to anyone else. We moved to another town and kept it a secret. Then I discovered it was happening again. Only this time he was supporting his new girlfriend in her apartment. All that is within me wanted to leave him after 35 years of marriage, but I kept thinking, 'What about the children and the grandchildren?' I loved him and forgave him and hoped he would recover from his addiction."

Story: Church magazines now unabashedly print news articles about adultery addicts that read like sleazy tabloids. One denominational magazine had this article: "Pastor A has resigned from his church. He had been on partial leave, due to marital difficulties. His wife is currently in an illicit relationship with Pastor B who left his church, after having an affair with another woman. Pastor A and his wife have two children. The church has begun a disciplinary process designed to bring about her repentance and restoration. Pastor B's pastoral credentials were removed by the denomination. He has refused to meet with church officials and is in the process of being divorced from his wife. They also have two children. Pray for the restoration of the marriages and all the parties involved." [141]

The Lord told Jeremiah: *"If you can find but one person who deals honestly and seeks the truth, I will forgive this city."* [142] Jeremiah then thought, *"These are only the poor, they are the foolish for they*

---

[141] Source withheld, available from author if needed

[142] Jeremiah 5:1

do not know the way of the Lord, the requirements of their God. So I will go to the leaders...but they too had broken off the yoke." [143]

Then the Lord says: *"Why should I forgive you...I supplied all their needs, yet they committed adultery and thronged to the houses of prostitutes. They are well-fed lusty stallions, each neighing for another man's wife..."* [144]

Did you read those verses? Or, like me, do you speed read the familiar "Bible parts" to get to the author's ideas? Back up a minute. It was the spiritual leaders who were like the *'well-fed lusty stallions.'* King David had more wives than he knew what to do with, yet he lusted after one more women. Why?

Carlin Weinhauer, long-time friend and former Pastor of Willingdon Church in Burnaby, British Columbia, gave me a fresh insight into Proverbs 22:14 (and 1 Corinthians 6:18). *"The mouth of an adulteress is a deep pit; He who is under the Lord's wrath will fall into it." "Flee from sexual immorality. All other sins a man commits are outside his body, but he who sins sexually, sins against his own body. Do you not know that your body is a temple of the Holy Spirit who is in you, whom you have received from God? You are not your own; you were bought at a price. Therefore honor God with your body."*

Carlin would say: "Adultery is a sin a man commits *against his own body*. It destroys his reputation, his credibility and breaks his pride. He may lose his vocation, his family and his health in the process of being humbled before the Lord. It is often the last step the Lord takes to humble a man who is too proud. The Lord lets him fall into a deep pit of his choosing!"

Some men become so proud in their positions of leadership, they move beyond the range of accountability. But God in His grace will accept them back if they confess and repent.

---

[143] Jeremiah 5:4-5

[144] Jeremiah 5:7-8

The role of women in Adultery

Principle 16
Women are significant contributors to the epidemic of adultery

Story: I once heard Scottish Pastor John Moore speak to a group of pastors: "Brothers, you are anointed by God to be a pastor. You and I are marked men as the *'Lord's anointed.'* It is as if we are walking around with a wee circle on top of our heads. And the Adversary is hovering above looking for these targets. When he finds one, he says, 'I know how we can get him – through a woman who finds him attractive.' Brothers, there are women out there who think it is a blessing to be in the presence of the Lord's anointed. They enjoy being with you. They find you attractive. They want to be close to you." At this point, some of the pastors began to laugh. Pastor John looked squarely at them and said with his delightful Scottish brogue: "Aye, it matters not what ye look like. Ye may think you are not sexually attractive to women, but don't ever forget: she's after '*the Lord's anointed.'* Ye can be short; ye can be fat, and ye can be bald, but you're '*the Lord's anointed'!*"

The prophet Malachi wrote: "*Another thing you do: You flood the Lord's altar with tears. You weep and wail because he no longer pays attention to your offerings or accepts them with pleasure from your hands. You ask 'Why?' It is because the Lord is acting as the witness between you and the wife of your youth, because you have broken faith with her, though she is your partner, the wife of your marriage covenant. Has not the Lord made them one? In flesh and spirit, they are his. And why one? Because He was seeking godly offspring. So guard yourself in your spirit, and do not break faith with the wife of your youth…'I hate divorce,' says the Lord God of Israel, 'and I hate a man's covering himself with violence as well as with his garment,' says the Lord Almighty. So guard yourself in your spirit and do not break faith."* [145]

A former Member of Canadian Parliament, Jake Epp used to say, "Divorce is the end of a small civilization." [146] Divorce brings an end to the family lineage, heritage, good name, bloodline and cumulative history. It shatters trust. It removes hope. And it seems to perpetuate the sins of the fathers to the third and fourth generation.

Story: While visiting in a distant city, I stopped at a friend's house. His wife and four kids met me at the door. "Dave is not here," she said with a weak smile. "He moved out and today is our 19th wedding anniversary." I sensed the deep hurt, looked at the youngest son, age 10, playing in the background and offered a feeble: "I'm sorry." Then she told me more: "Would you believe that Dave's dad walked out on Dave when he was 10? He had not seen his dad for years, and all of a sudden his father reappeared in town and asked to meet him. They met at a bar, and he had a soda. His dad laughed at him and said, 'Have a real drink son.' He did and the next thing we knew he was going out drinking with his dad on a regular basis. Then he and his dad began picking up women at the bars, and the rest is history. He now wants to be free and on his own."

I was silent in disbelief. This leader was a model of Christian commitment anytime I met him. He had now consciously cashed in his marriage for an adulterous relationship. His wife continued: "There is more. Dave's grandfather walked out on Dave's dad when his dad was ten years old." Will it ever end? What is this powerful destructive evil we have inside that makes us destroy relationships for a moment of pleasure?

---

[145] Malachi 2:13-16

[146] Author's personal dialogue with the Minister.

Controlling our sex drive

Principle 17
Sexual relations with anyone – or anything! – other than our marriage partner destroys intimacy and sanctity in the marriage relationship

"Can a man scoop fire into his lap without his clothes being burned? Can a man walk on hot coals without his feet being scorched? So is he who sleeps with another man's wife; no one who touches her will go unpunished. Men do not despise a thief if he steals to satisfy his hunger when he is starving. Yet, if he is caught, he must pay sevenfold, though it cost him all the wealth of his house.

"But a man who commits adultery lacks judgment; whoever does so destroys himself. Blows and disgrace are his lot, and his shame will never be wiped away; for jealousy arouses a husband's fury, and he will show no mercy when he takes revenge. He will not accept compensation; he will refuse the bribe, however, great it is." [147]

Principle 18
Control of the sex drive is a mutual responsibility for every male and every female at every age and stage in life

Story: We phoned a Realtor to look at a house. He was married for over 31 years. We knew his wife and beautiful family. He said to me: "I have a house for you to look at, but you will have to go see it on your own, I have a noon luncheon." We discovered later the luncheon was a rendezvous with a woman he found to be attractive. Some days later he walked out of his office, left his appointment book on his desk and 'disappeared.'

[147] Proverbs 27:35

He surfaced years later in another town with the same lunch companion.

When I met his wife after the marriage had collapsed, she said something I remember well: "We had 31 wonderful years together. Had you told me as we celebrated our 30th wedding anniversary, that I would be on my own in two years, I would have said 'Never'. Remember this Jim: 'Never say it can never happen!'"

Just recently a friend's father-in-law abandoned his 49-year marriage and all his grandkids to move in with a younger woman. The words ring again: "*Never say it can never happen...*"

No marriage is immune

Principle 19
No marriage is ever immune to the possibility of adultery (or pornography)

Dr. Billy Graham and a host of other Christian leaders are robust models of healthy marriages over the years. They maintain a commitment to hard disciplines. They will not ride in a car with a woman unless a third party is present. They will not stay in a room alone with a woman or remain in a house alone with a woman. Why? Are they *old fashioned*? Perhaps they have learned how to *"...abstain from an appearance of evil."*

Call us dinosaurs. Call us prudish. Call us anything you wish but most of all, just call us *Happily Married!* And I include myself in this group as I reach my 50th year of marriage to Rita.

Adult educators know that information and the best education in the world is without value unless a person, like Daniel, *"purposes in his heart"* [148] not to defile himself. According to Solomon, the

[148] Daniel 1:8

one who goes into the arms of an adulterous relationship is like "*an ox to the slaughter*," willing, easily led and without recourse. Why are we so foolish?

Principle 20
Three factors behind the grinding motivation for extra-marital sex are:
(1) Dissatisfaction with one's emotional and sexual acceptance at home
(2) A desire to control another person, and
(3) Selfish lust

Do men or women who marry as virgins have a higher potential for escaping adultery (Pornography)? I believe it is true. People, who are willing to acknowledge and address their weakness, become more accountable for their actions. People who pretend *everything is OK* often shock you after they divorce.

If I pretend I am without sin, I fool myself and others into thinking I either don't, won't or can't sin. That is foolish reasoning. SIN as S-I-N: **S**elfish, **I**ndividualism, **N**ow and it can occur at any age or any stage in life.

A PERSONAL REFLECTION

Soon after my birth on April 11, 1943, my father went to Europe with the Canadian 2nd Army until after the war. When he returned to Carlisle, Ontario, in 1946, we lived with my mother's parents until my dad reestablished his career as a cost accountant with Cochrane-Dunlop Wholesale Hardware in Toronto, Ontario. He worked with the Hardware Industry for over 50 years – a distinguished service record!

My parents attended the Methodist (now United) Church of Canada and made their faith commitment to Jesus Christ in that church. When we moved to Toronto, they became members of an evangelical Church near our home. I accepted Christ at the age of nine when Rev. Mel Johnson was the pastor. Mel later conducted a radio ministry for the family called: Young World Radio. At the age of 49, my father's retinas hemorrhaged claiming over 90% of his vision in a matter of hours. It was a major readjustment in his career path. We had to live with my dad's anger at God, whom he questioned: "Why did this happen to me?" I, in turn, abandoned my Christian faith. I became a prodigal living a life of anger, rebellion, and sin. In October 1964, when I was 21, I met Mel Johnson again.

He had three questions: First, "How are things at your parent's Church?" Answer: "I don't go to there any more, Mel." Second, "You must have a better church." Answer: "I don't go to any Church, Mel." Third, "Are you ready to get right with the Lord, Jim?" Answer: "Not yet." Mel did not force me, but graciously gave two passages of scripture to read at my leisure: 1 John 1:9-10 and Psalm 51.

I went alone and read 1 John 1:9-10 - *"If we confess our sins, He is faithful and righteous to forgive us our sins and to cleanse us from all unrighteousness."* Then I read Psalm 51 written when the prophet Nathan came to King David after he had committed adultery with Bathsheba: *"Have mercy on me, O God, according to your unfailing love; according to your great compassion blot out my transgressions. Wash away all my iniquity and cleanse me from my sin…For I know my transgressions, and my sin is always before me. Against you, you only, have I sinned and done what is evil in your sight so that you are proved right when you speak and justified when you judge. Surely I was sinful at birth, sinful from the time my mother conceived me. Surely you desire truth in the inner parts; you teach me wisdom in the inmost place.*

"Cleanse me with hyssop, and I will be clean; wash me, and I will be whiter than snow. Let me hear joy and gladness; let the bones you have crushed rejoice. Hide your face from my sins and blot out all my iniquity.

"Create in me a pure heart, O God, and renew a steadfast spirit within me. Do not cast me from your presence or take your Holy Spirit from me. Restore to me the joy of your salvation and grant me a willing spirit to sustain me.

"Then I will teach transgressors your ways, and sinners will turn back to you. Save me from bloodguilt, O God, the God who saves me, and my tongue will sing of your righteousness. O Lord, open my lips, and my mouth will declare your praise. You do not delight in sacrifice, or I would bring it: you do not take pleasure in burnt offerings. The sacrifices of God are a broken spirit; a broken and a contrite heart, O God, you will not despise..."

God be merciful to me a sinner. That was my prayer. And the Lord heard my cry. He lifted me out of a pit of anger and rebellion and broken relationships and made me *a new creation* in Jesus Christ.

I was teaching Elementary School in Etobicoke, Ontario, in the fall of 1965, when I met David Bell at the London College of Bible and Missions (LCBM) in London, Ontario. His challenge to me was: "Come for three years, learn to know Christ and study the Bible in an intimate way and begin to share your faith with others." It was a great three years. I was bold for my faith for I believed I had to make up for my wasted years! Prisons, choirs, missions, anywhere I could share my faith in Christ, and I did. I gladly accepted an opportunity to manage a halfway house for rehabilitating alcoholics.

Soon after my commitment to Christ, the Lord brought Rita into my life. To me, she was my angel: pure, gentle, and compassionate. I was awestruck! She was training to be a Registered Nurse in Toronto. Her home was in the beautiful orchard lands of the Niagara Peninsula. People from my past would say to Rita: "If you knew what Jim was like before you met him, you would not believe the change." (See 2 Corinthians 5:17.) She would graciously respond: "I like him the way he is." I took that as a signal to be quiet and not talk about my past life or moral failures. That was a mistake.

Rita came to LCBM for a year of studies after graduating from Toronto Western Hospital. Then on Canada's Centennial Day and Rita's 23rd birthday, July 1, 1967, we celebrated our wedding day. I still rejoice in the wife of my youth to this day! In my final year of studies in London, we became house parents at a Salvation Army Children's Village. As newlyweds, we supervised nine children: two teen girls and seven pre-adolescent boys! What a way to begin a marriage.

Jim and Rita - House parents to Nine Children (1967-1968)

I thought I was obedient to scripture, but I was living with my pre-conversion secrets. While some Christians make a ministry out of telling people about the sins they committed and the pain they had inflicted before they became Christians, I was content to be silent.

I went through three years of dating, studies at Bible College and into marriage with memories of my first sexual experience locked in my emotional memory bank. I was sleeping with a ghost.

The less anyone knew, the better I thought it would be for me. But one major problem emerged: the more I established my *Mr. Clean* image, the harder it became to admit anything about my past. I discovered that when the outward visible sins decline, inward sins such as pride begin to ascend.

It bothered me for years, yet I told no one. I rationalized that it would hurt people more to know about my past than not to know. I felt guilty for defrauding Rita and my family and friends. So one night, in deep despair, I poured it all out to Rita. Why wasn't I honest with her before we married? Why did I not tell her? She felt deceived and manipulated. We now had two children. The option to say No to marrying me was gone. It took her time to work it through and forgive me but, thank God, she did. Rita extended to me the same grace and forgiveness King David felt.

For some years we tended to avoid talking about the past. I worked at rebuilding a better relationship with my father. I now see where I made many mistakes in my relationships with people. I tended to be *black and white* with my prophet-like boldness. Some enjoyed my passion for "winning and training boys for Christ." But others felt uncomfortable with my intensity. While many people regard me as a capable speaker and teacher, I now see where my greatest strength, relationships with people, can also be my biggest weakness. I need to help people, with gentleness and humility, to *"speak the truth in love"* rather than hit them over the head with it.

Scripture says our Lord was *"full of grace and truth"* [149] And He was *"gentle and humble."* [150] Both are needs in my life and ministry. The adage is true: people do not care how much you know until they know how much you care.

One friend who knew how much we cared for him and his girlfriend confided in us about his past sexual activity and regrets now that he was going to marry a virgin. He wanted to know "Should I tell her?" Rita and I advised him to tell her the truth so the choice to marry a non-virgin would be hers. No deception. No entrapment. Notice how the word non-virgin sounds more politically correct than to call oneself a fornicator, the word Scripture uses! She

[149] John 1:14

[150] Matthew 11:29

forgave him. They married with her full knowledge of his past and continued to work at their new life together.

Then another friend who trusted me asked whether he should marry his girlfriend after she told him she was not a virgin. We reviewed the options, and they also decided to get married.

Next, a young husband came to me and admitted a scenario from his past that was quite similar to what I had faced. Should he tell his wife? I told him my story. I started to realize that confessing my sins and asking people to pray for me is very humbling and potentially threatening. I make myself very vulnerable. I realize how weak and human I am.

Something was happening to me in the process: my secret was out. After all, a secret is something you only tell one person, at a time. Now four more people knew. I then told our two sons so they would hear it firsthand from me. I asked for and received their forgiveness. It has opened new lines of honesty and acceptance in communication with them as well.

I can never set myself up as the Judge of others' immoralities and sins, for I am also a sinner. I am gaining a growing compassion and kindness in my relationships with others for I know that we are all sinners and potential sinners saved by grace. My only regret is the time it has taken me to understand and accept this fact.

In my early days as a Christian, I saw some sins as worse than others. Adultery (Pornography) was fourth after incest, child abuse and sodomy on my hierarchical catalog of moral failures. Now I see that God views all sin as evil. *"There is none righteous, not even one."*. [151]

Scripture says specifically that God hates some sins: divorce, pride, lies, murderers, false witnesses, wicked schemes, evil, and those who stir up dissension (destroying unity). But I tended to rationalize that most of my actions were minor infractions compared

[151] Romans 3:10

to the sins of *those other people.* It struck me that I was like the Pharisee in Luke's Gospel who went up to the temple with the tax collector to pray. The Pharisee said: *"God, I thank you that I am not like other men, robbers, evildoers, adulterers. I fast twice a week and give a tenth and..."* The tax collector would not even look up to heaven but beat his breast and said one sentence: *"God be merciful to me a sinner."*[152] I suddenly found a new identity with the tax collector!

Scripture says: *"Everyone who exalts himself will be humbled and he who humbles himself will be exalted."* [153] That liberates me beyond imagination. God forgave me, but I am not one notch better than you or anyone else on this earth. While I was born in sin, I am free from sin's penalty and bondage by God's grace. I now live my life with the power of God's Holy Spirit in me. Hallelujah.

It is both challenging and a joy to write these words. The success of our marriage these past 50-plus years is due in large measure to God's mercy and grace mixed with Rita's love and forgiveness. Rita is graciously teaching me how to have freedom in my relationships, especially with women. I can now enjoy proper attitudes and behavior towards women as God intended, made in His image, not to be viewed as sex objects.

God has forgiven me. According to Psalm 51, I am to *"teach transgressors your ways and sinners will turn back to you..."* For a long while, I failed to be honest with my friends and associates. I was too proud to humble myself and say, "Yeah, I messed up, but God has forgiven me." I refused to talk about the horrors and the pain that go with sin. Instead, I pretended that I was OK.

Gordon MacDonald wrote a helpful book, *Rebuilding Your Broken World,* after he experienced the implosion of his self-inflicted broken world. He says: "There are far more broken worlds out there than anyone realizes or admits. We do ourselves and others

---

[152] Luke 18:9-14

[153] Luke 18:14

a disservice when we try to pretend that brokenness of experience and spirit is a rare matter or an anomaly."

When we confess the pain in our broken world, individuals in denial of their broken world can relate to us with greater confidence.

It is quite easy to deceive our self and rationalize wrong actions.

Jesus said, "You have heard it said, 'Do not commit adultery. But I tell you that anyone who looks at a woman lustfully (Pornography) has already committed adultery with her in his heart..." For a married man to touch any woman's breasts other than his wife and say: "I did not lust after her, I was only goofing around or curious," is to deny the Holy Spirit's definition of passion and sin. To confess is to agree with God that what He says is a sin is a sin! To not confess that the wrong we did is a sin, is to deny the truth.

In the 1976 Presidential campaign a magazine writer asked Jimmy Carter: "Have you ever lusted after a woman, Mr. Carter?" With Christian honesty, he said: "Yes." The headlines were predictable. In 1994, US President Bill Clinton, already attached to an adulterous relationship with Jennifer Flowers, was accused of an inappropriate sexual assault on a woman. Asked if the accusation was true, Mr. Clinton replied: "I will not dignify the question by responding."

It is easy to develop wrong attitudes that hurt people when we rationalize sin. If I refuse to change my attitude towards my sins, God promises to humble me. I found that out the hard way. For many years I enjoyed a fruitful ministry. I had a respected name and a solid base of support. I enjoyed teaching, writing articles, and speaking at conferences. I was active in ministry in a substantial manner.

Then I received a "termination without cause and instead of notice, a severance package." That is how lawyers phrase it. An older and wiser friend cautioned me: "Do all you can to resolve this situation graciously and peacefully. Do not allow a black mark on your good name."

But I was upset. "I am getting some legal counsel." Off I went. Anger and urgency replaced grace and mercy. My reputation, credibility, and integrity were about to be affected by my response.

I failed to remember what happened to Moses a few thousand years ago. "One day after he (Moses) had grown up" – in the finest of Pharaoh's training and likely with his Ph.D. in Palace Administration – "he went out to where his people were and watched them at their hard labor. He saw an Egyptian beating a Hebrew, one of his own people. Glancing this way and that and seeing no one, he killed the Egyptian and hid him in the sand."

Moses never dreamed that what he did in secret would become public knowledge throughout the countryside and 5000 years of history! Scripture says: "Then Moses was afraid, and went to live in Midian, to tend sheep." My Midian was Cedar Springs Christian Retreat Center in Northwest Washington. Here I wiped tables, picked up swan poo, made fires, served guests, unplugged stuck toilets and functioned as the unknown "Dr. Who?" Who needs a doctorate in anything, to do this job? Slowly I began to calm down and experience the truth of *"Be still and know that I am God."* [154]

Quietness precedes knowledge of God.

A God-centered life finds a balance between the severe isolated sacrifice of the ancient desert fathers and the swamped hectic service of modern Christian leaders. When God became my focus, I lost my sense of fear and rush. Disciplined time with the Lord releases holy boldness for ministry.

---

[154] Psalm 46:10

Story: During the summer of 1989, just after the June 4th massacre on Tiananmen Square, I was with a tour group traveling in China. The Canadian Director of a Christian ministry was also on this tour. The American founder of his ministry was caught visiting prostitutes. As we rode the bus together, I asked him this question: "You met with the founder of the ministry regularly for some years. Did his problem with adultery (pornography?) go without anyone discerning it for all those years?" His response was: "When Brother J went to his knees in prayer for the lost and poured out his heart before the Lord, no one could imagine for one moment the battle going on inside. No one suspected a thing. The Holy Spirit had to reveal it Himself." Interesting answer.

Where was the missing gift of discernment? Where was the accountability? The higher a man goes up the ladder of leadership the harder it is to humble himself, confess his faults, and make himself accountable. The less we confess, the bigger the mess.

I know I am not alone. I know there are men and some women reading this who will say to me: "You are right. No one knows about my secret sin. I asked God to forgive me, but the memories continue. If people find out, they will be hurt. It is better to keep quiet than to confess and risk losing everything."

I empathize with you. What about the brother involved in a morally or emotionally inappropriate relationship with a woman? He may feel he confessed it to the Lord and that is adequate. He may have asked his wife to forgive him, and all is forgotten, or is it? What if *the other woman* goes public someday with her story? He may feel that he has made a fresh, clean start and it will never happen again. Besides, it might ruin his reputation and his career if he was to tell his wife, or her husband or his Board. Better keep it quiet. Right? Wrong!

Principle 21
It is a myth to say: "The sphere of confession need go no further than the realm of affection."

Story: One counselor managed to involve himself sexually with several women during his career. In each case, he confessed his sin to his wife and one friend. Each time his wife (and each time he chose a different friend) forgave him. He promised never to do it again. They agreed to keep it a secret among themselves. Perhaps they felt it better not to hurt anyone else. Imagine the hurt and the pain when it finally became public. He manipulated his wife, his friends and the women involved so that he could remain without public accountability and do it again and again as a serial adulterer. People who sin are individuals who need help.

When I managed the Quinten Warner House, I hosted and attended many meetings for Alcoholics Anonymous. They always gave their name and confessed to being an alcoholic and how long since their last drink. Perhaps we need "J516" Meetings (James 5:16) and confess to a small accountability group our secret sins. It might go like this:

"My name is Jim. I'm a Recovering Sinner. I had my last gossip four days ago!"

Do you see how important it is to confess? Once you know my personal weaknesses, you can hold me accountable: "I thought you wanted to break that habit?"

Remember when Nathan the prophet confronted King David? Did David's confession stay between the two of them? No, the whole kingdom eventually knew the details. In writing about it, the Holy Spirit informed the world of one man's moment of secret sin. There are no secrets in the Kingdom of God, only forgiven sinners saved by grace. Everything will be revealed and judged, when we get to Heaven, so why deny it, bury it or avoid confessing it down here?

I John 1:9 and 10 say: *"If we confess our sin, God is willing to forgive us our sin and cleanse us from all unrighteousness..."* To hide things affects our relationships with people today. We need, to be honest, open and accountable to people in authority. *"Confess your sins to each other and pray for each other so that you may be healed."*[155]

There are many ministry opportunities people would love to fill. However, if taking one of these positions were to destroy the ministry by our weaknesses, it would be a mistake. When people become aware of our faults and pray for us, it helps if they hold us accountable for living according to Biblical principles in our areas of weakness. Some of us may have greater liberty than others depending on our acknowledged areas of need.

Judge not lest you be judged.

Life is too short to play games. Let's agree that we are each susceptible to sin and moral failures. I must neither judge a man nor condemn a woman who commits adultery (or watches pornography). It is a deceptive sin. Unchecked it ruins one's body, mind, and spirit. But God will forgive any sin we confess to Him.

David wrote in Psalm 38: *"...there is no health in my body; my bones have no soundness because of my sin. My guilt has overwhelmed me like a burden too heavy to bear. I am feeble and utterly crushed; I groan in anguish of heart...even the light has gone from my eyes, my friends and companions avoid me....I confess my iniquity; I am troubled by my sin...those who repay my good with evil slander me when I pursue what is good."*

Is this, like David, my Psalm of Confession? What I am writing is an open and sincere attempt to keep a vow I made to the Lord back in 1964. *"...Teach transgressors (the Lord's) ways...(so that) sinners will turn back to (Him)."*

---

[155] James 5:16

What do I do next?

If at this moment, you are in an adulterous relationship these words are offered to give you Hope.

Agree with God, as David did, that adultery (pornography) is sin.

- *"You shall not commit adultery* (pornography)" (Exodus 20:14).
- *"Against you, you alone O Lord did I sin"* (Psalm 51:4).

Humble yourself, as David did, before the Lord.

- *"Clothe yourselves with humility toward one another, because God opposes the proud but gives grace to the humble. Humble yourselves, therefore under God's mighty hand, that He may lift you up in due time..."* (1 Peter 5:5-6).
- *"Speak and act as those who are going to be judged by the law that gives freedom, because judgment without mercy will be shown to anyone who has not been merciful. Mercy triumphs over judgment" (*James 2:12-13),
- *"Humble yourselves before the Lord and He will lift you up... There is only one Lawgiver and Judge, the one who is able to save and destroy. But you -- who are you to judge your neighbor?"* (James 4:11-12).

Confess your sin to the Lord, as David did, and have a clean heart created within.

- *"I have sinned against the Lord"* (2 Samuel 12:13).
- *"If we confess our sins, He is faithful and righteous to forgive our sins and cleanse us from all unrighteousness."* (1 John 1:9)

Pay the price, as David did, for your sinful relationship.
As the King of Israel, David had given the enemies of the Lord cause to rejoice and blaspheme the name of the Lord. There was a price. The child died. The sword never departed from David's house. And God prohibited David from building the Temple because David had Uriah's blood on his hands. (See 2 Samuel 12:10 and 14).

- *"Create in me a clean heart O God...restore to me the joy of Thy salvation"* (Psalm 51:12).

Confess your sin to whomever you offended, and ask their forgiveness.

- *"Confess your sins to each other and pray for each other so that you may be healed"* (James 5:16).

Be filled with the Holy Spirit to bear the fruit of the Spirit - especially self-control.

- *"The fruit of the Spirit is love, joy, peace, patience, kindness, goodness, faithfulness, gentleness, and self-control"* (Galatians 5:22).

Use your experience, as David did, to help others obey God's way.

- *"Then I will teach transgressors Thy ways and sinners will be converted to you" (*Psalm 51:13).
- *"It is God's will that you should be sanctified: that you should avoid sexual immorality; that each of you should learn to control his own body in a way that is holy and honorable, not in passionate lust like the heathen who do not know God; and that in this matter no one should wrong his brother or take advantage of him. The Lord will punish men for all such sins as we have already told you and warn you. For God did not call us to be impure, but to live a holy life. Therefore he who rejects this instruction does not reject man but God, who gives you His Holy Spirit"* (1 Thessalonians 4:3-9).

What can be done to prevent adultery (pornography)?

Pray with your wife.

- Pray together, as often as possible: at meals; by your bed; in the car while driving; by phone; by writing prayers to each other.

Make your wife number one.

- She is more to be loved than either the job or the kids. Show your children that you love their mother more than any other person. Your kids will have added security to know their parents love them.

Protect your wife.

- Do not allow each other to be vulnerable.
- Avoid prolonged times away from home.
- Be accountable to each other.
- Follow your spouse in prayer during times apart.

How do we stop the epidemic?

- Accept Jesus Christ into your life as Lord and Sovereign Controller.
- Determine in your heart with your spouse, that from this moment on you will no longer violate your marriage vows in any manner so as to cause either one to commit Adultery (or view Pornography).
- Never give up. Be willing to forgive. Seek professional help before it is too late.

The less we confess, the bigger the mess!
The moment we repent, God can clean up the event!

Is It Worth It? – 25 Consequences If I Commit Adultery

HEALTH

1. I risk a sexually transmitted disease (STD) or dying from AIDS (Proverbs 6:27).
2. I risk spreading a STD to my spouse (1 Corinthians 7:2-4).
3. I live with the results of guilt and stress (Psalm 38:1-4).

FINANCIAL

4. I risk losing my possessions and future wealth in any settlement plus loss of income from any job loss or health problems (Psalm 6).

REPUTATION

5. I lose my good name and the integrity I have worked hard to establish (Proverbs 22:1).
6. I incur the consequential fury, revenge, and jealousy of the other person's spouse/family (Proverbs 6:33-35).
7. I lose the respect and trust of my wife, children, friends, and fans (Colossians 3:21).
8. I evidence my inability, unwillingness, and failure to control my sexual desires (Proverbs 5).

SPOUSE/FAMILY

9. I betray the most intimate of all friends: my spouse (Proverbs 5:15-20).
10. I teach my wife and my children that I do not care about them or their well-being as my pleasure precedes their needs (Exodus 20:5).

CHURCH/CHRISTIAN COMMUNITY

11. I restrict myself from being a leader in the church (1 Peter 3:7 and 1 Timothy 3:2).
12. I nullify the model of Jesus Christ as the Bridegroom of Heaven loving and dying for His Bride, the Church (Revelation 19:7).
13. I make a mockery of claiming to be a Christian or "*a little Christ*" (Acts 11:26).
14. I destroy and mock my public marriage vows to *forsake all others*, making me a liar and a deceiver (Matthew 19: 4-9).
15. I disregard the commandments of God (Exodus 20:14).
16. I reveal my selfish, individualistic nature (sin) (Jeremiah 17:9).
17. I prove I am under the wrath of God (Proverbs 22:14).

PERSONAL

18. I prove my lack of judgment (Proverbs 6:32 and Proverbs 7:7).
19. I destroy myself by a sin against my own body (Proverbs 6:32 and 1 Corinthians 6:18).
20. I prove I am not satisfied with my sexual performance with my spouse (Song of Songs 2:3-7).
21. I evidence my desire to control other people, especially women, making me a sick person (2 Timothy 3:6).

22. I prove I have no self-control over my lust towards others (I Thessalonians 4:3-5).
23. I demonstrate to future marriage candidates that I cannot be trusted (1 Corinthians 4:2).

COMMUNITY/SOCIETY

24. I contribute to the epidemic of family breakups and social disorder (Luke 12:47-48).
25. I destroy the foundation of Western Civilization based on God's Laws including a monogamous marriage of a man and a woman with lifelong fidelity (Psalm 11:3).

PRAYER

Sovereign Lord God, be merciful to me a sinner.
Help me confess to those I have wronged and watch you heal the relationships.
Make me willing to forgive and become kind and tenderhearted.
Father teach me how to be pure in my mind and my words; to speak the truth with the boldness of a prophet, the obedience of a teacher and the compassion of a healer.
Thank you, Lord, for forgiving my sins, and for making me whole.
May those who are disappointed with my lifestyle, be willing to forgive both.
Help the ones who will benefit the most, to read these words.
Lord bring the silent, tragic, 'Epidemic of Adultery (and Pornography)' to an end.
Restore marriages and heal families I ask.
In the strong name of Jesus of Nazareth,
Amen.

Competencies to Fulfill Role of HUSBAND

Personal Checklist
(Circle the best answer for each to determine score)

Do I have...

1. Conviction that the Word of God has the principles laid out for husband-wife relationships? (As found in Ephesians 5; 1 Peter 3:7; and other related passages)

1	2	3	4	5
Not at all	A little bit	Usually	Most of the time	Always

2. Belief that my wife is the one and only woman with whom I will live and love, until death does us part? (Genesis 2:24).

1	2	3	4	5
Not at all	A little bit	Usually	Most of the time	Always

3. Commitment to the wife of my youth to love her and be satisfied with her for as long as we both shall live. (Proverbs 19:14; 18:22; 12:4).

1	2	3	4	5
Not at all	A little bit	Usually	Most of the time	Always

4. Agreement with God that I hate divorce (Malachi 2:16) **and will not deal treacherously against the wife of my youth.** (Malachi 2:14-16).

1	2	3	4	5
Not at all	A little bit	Usually	Most of the time	Always

5. A commitment to provide for the physical, social, mental and spiritual needs of my wife and family? *"If anyone does not provide for his own, and especially those of his own household, he has denied the faith, and is worse than an unbeliever"*—(1Timothy 5:8).

1	2	3	4	5
Not at all	A little bit	Usually	Most of the time	Always

6. Enjoyment in providing the affection, love, and respect that my wife needs and deserves? (Ephesians 5:28)

1	2	3	4	5
Not at all	A little bit	Usually	Most of the time	Always

7. Ability to express myself in love without anger or retreating to childlike silence? (Ephesians 4:15; Colossians 4:6)

1	2	3	4	5
Not at all	A little bit	Usually	Most of the time	Always

9. A willingness to listen to little things yet assume my responsibility for leadership in the marriage as required in the Scriptures?

1	2	3	4	5
Not at all	A little bit	Usually	Most of the time	Always

Total divided by 9 =

Evidences Role of HUSBAND Fulfilled

Personal Checklist – (Circle the best answer for each to determine score)

Have I demonstrated…

1. An increasing enjoyment in being with my wife while recognizing a reduction in 'periods of hostilities' between us?

1	2	3	4	5
Not at all	A little bit	Usually	Most of the time	Always

2. Mutually beneficial activities (hobbies, leisure activities, common friends, personal goals, growth projects) that we can share and experience together? *"The two shall become one flesh"*—(Matthew 19:6). The more couples enjoy being together, the more they are likely to be ministering to each other's needs.

1	2	3	4	5
Not at all	A little bit	Usually	Most of the time	Always

3. Evidence of my priorities properly established within the framework of vocational responsibilities, family needs, and spiritual ministries?

1	2	3	4	5
Not at all	A little bit	Usually	Most of the time	Always

4. An improved prayer life? 1 Peter 3:7 indicates that the prayers of a husband will be hindered if he is not "living with his wife in an understanding way" and granting her honor as a fellow-heir of the grace of life.

1	2	3	4	5
Not at all	A little bit	Usually	Most of the time	Always

5. A willingness to die for her, or at least give up certain activities to minister to her needs? (Ephesians 5:25).

1	2	3	4	5
Not at all	A little bit	Usually	Most of the time	Always

6. An appreciation, volitional acceptance and submission by my wife to my role as the head of the wife? (Ephesians 5:23)

1	2	3	4	5
Not at all	A little bit	Usually	Most of the time	Always

Total divided by 6 =

Role of HUSBAND

Projects for Investigation and Discussion

[__] Discuss: "Marriage is a covenant made under God and in the presence of our fellow members of the Christian family. Such a pledge endures, not because of the force of the law or the fear of its sanctions, but because an unconditional covenant has been made." (Quote from David Augsburger)

[__] With your wife, make a list of couples (maximum three) you know personally that have split up (either separated or divorced, Christian or non-Christian). List the reasons why you believe this couple split (on separate sheets, by yourself). Then share with one another the items you have listed. What changes could you make in your marriage relationship as means of practicing preventive maintenance and increasing your love and respect for one another?

[__] Dr. James Dobson lists the following ten Sources of Depression expressed by women. Identify how husbands can assist their wives finding solutions to these problems.

( ) Low self-esteem

( ) Fatigue and time pressure

( ) Loneliness, isolation, and boredom

( ) Absence of romantic love in marriage

( ) Financial difficulties

( ) Sexual problems in marriage

( ) Menstrual and physiological problems

( ) Problems with the children

( ) In-law problems

( ) Aging

[ ] Number the item in the order that you think your wife has needs. (i.e. put a #1 beside the area that you believe is your wife's first need for help, then #2, etc.)

[ ] How is a woman like a *weaker vessel*? (Discuss) What are the implications of this statement to husbands and other men?

Chapter 9

Father • Relationship to His Children

And fathers, do not provoke your children to anger; but bring them up in the discipline and instruction of the Lord" • Ephesians 6:4

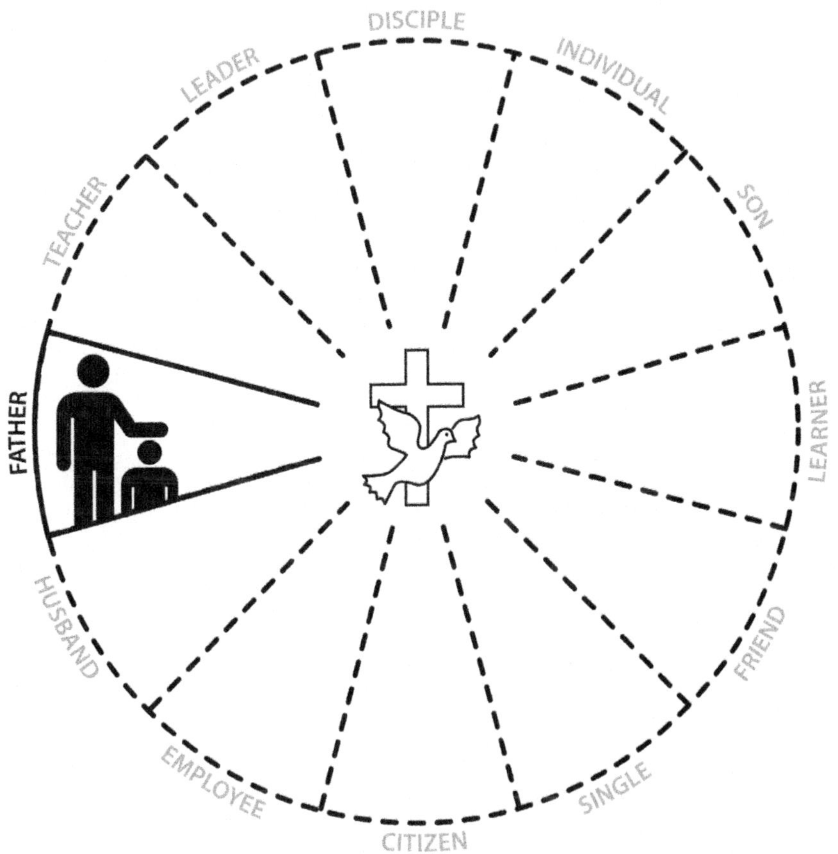

The Humanizing of Father

Story: 12:23 PM 27 December 1968. I joined the ranks of Fatherhood at the General Hospital in Winnipeg, Manitoba. It was an exciting initiation. I agree with those who suggest: *"The greatest aid to Adult Education is having Children!"*

The first *arrow in our quiver* was a boy: David James Cunningham. I had become the guardian counselor of this divinely packaged personality as his earthly Father. Fatherhood was underway. Days later, this little bundle spent his first night in our bedroom. Perhaps I should say, the first part of the night. About 2:30 a.m. a piercing cry set me upright in bed. "He's hungry," came Rita's calm but tired reply.

It didn't take us long to realize he needed a feeding supplement. "Would you like me to get something for him?" I generously offered my exhausted wife. It was nearing 3:00 A.M. as I stumbled into the kitchen mumbling to myself: "How does anyone with kids get any sleep? No wonder old men with five kids have bags under their eyes. They never sleep!" I collected a box of Pablum ® and mixed a *slush* with some mother's milk and poured it into the bottle. He sucked and sucked but got nothing. The nipple was too small. So I grabbed a pair of scissors, snipped off the nipple. "Down the hatch Davy, boy…" and away it went. Wrong!

To enhance my skills as a novice Father, I began to read articles on Fathering. I found fascinating data that was not all that encouraging. E.g. "The number of minutes a father spends each day with his son? Eight"—as I went out the door with my bags (filled with guilt) for another 10-day business trip! I was below the national average!

Slowly, the real role of a Father began to filter into my frontal lobe. God, our Heavenly Father, gives every earthly Father the opportunity to be a finite model of His infinite attributes. Matthew 7:11 sums it up: *"If you then* [Earthly Fathers] *being evil, know*

> *how to give good gifts to your children, how much more shall your Father who is in heaven, give what is good to those who ask Him."*

Our goal is to model His attributes:

The Eternity of God—*The impact of a Father is endless.* The impact of a Father is eternal. My DNA molecules have eternally designed the physical features and inherited qualities of my sons. Likewise, the day-to-day exchanges between a Father and a Child have a lifelong influence on the development of that child as an individual. A Father will shape his daughter's role expectations for her future husband. A Father also role models Fathering skills, or lack thereof, to his children.

The Faithfulness of God—*Fathers are honored for being faithful.* The Father who is *"quick to hear, slow to speak and slow to anger"* [156] says what he means. The Father who *"swears to his own hurt and does not change"* [157] keeps his promises to his wife and children. Broken promises can cause irreparable damage to many family relationships. Faithfulness is like the glue that binds a Family together. When our "yes" means "yes", and our "no" consistently means "no", trust will increase.

The Goodness of God—*Fathers are to be kind.* Children respond more to a single positive word of encouragement than a stream of haranguing and belittling. It was the kindness of God that led us to repentance. The model of our Heavenly Father is a Shepherd not a Drill Sergeant! God is good, kind and gentle with his sheep. His Son, our Lord Jesus Christ was *"gentle and meek."* [158] He learned those traits from His Heavenly Father.

The Grace of God—*Fathers are to give undeserved blessings.* Militant, legalistic, disciplinarian Fathers need to note the quality

---

[156] James 1:19

[157] Psalm 15:4

[158] See Matthew 11:29

of grace shown by our Heavenly Father. The prodigal son had a Father who knew how to forgive and show grace.

Story: A friend's daughter got pregnant by the young man she was dating. My friend arrived home, not knowing the news. His wife met him and said, "Tonight your daughter has something to tell you. Be careful how you respond. How you respond to her will determine your future relationship with her." His daughter said she was pregnant, and then she asked for forgiveness. He had a choice. Get angry, kick her out, or forgive her, accept her and love the child. He chose the latter. He showed grace. He forgave his daughter. She had the child (no abortion!). And now, years later, he and his wife have harmonious relations with his daughter, her husband and their children. This friend taught me more about how God extends grace, by his actions, than I learned through listening to many sermons! What a model for us to follow when our children damage our prized material possessions by accident, or ruin our family image with a divorce or abortion. God extends grace when we ask for forgiveness. We as Fathers must swallow our pride and likewise show grace.

The Holiness of God—*Fathers are to be holy.* God, our Father, is able to expect high standards from us, for He is Holy. Likewise the expectation level for our children cannot exceed our personal performance level, or we become hypocrites in the eyes of our children. Paul was clear when he told the Ephesians: *"Be imitators of God..."* [159] Habits, values, attitudes, and beliefs are many times assimilated by children from their primary male model, their Father, especially if their Father is exhibiting a consistent life of holiness.

159 Ephesians 5:1-5 "Therefore be imitators of God, as beloved children; and walk in love, just as Christ also loved you and gave Himself up for us, an offering and a sacrifice to God as a fragrant aroma. But immorality or any impurity or greed must not even be named among you, as is proper among saints; and there must be no filthiness and silly talk, or coarse jesting, which are not fitting, but rather giving of thanks. For this, you know with certainty, that no immoral or impure person or covetous man, who is an idolater, has an inheritance in the kingdom of Christ and God."

The Immutability of God—*Fathers are unchanging on what is true*. The more we as Fathers think through our options and pray through our decisions the less we have to change our mind or ask forgiveness for a wrong decision. The child who says: "I trust my Dad!" likely has a Father who patterns his life after this divine attribute.

The Infinitude of God—*Fathers' love has no bounds.* There is no end to *"the depth and the riches both of the wisdom and knowledge of God."* [160] Fathers who continue to learn, try new experiences, and adapt to new environments and technology will grow with their children. Happy is the Father who shares life with his children as they build memories together. Take lots of photos of events to aid recall. And consider a significant physical memory item to keep whenever there has been a great spiritual victory won. David kept Goliath's sword in his tent to remind him that God helped him defeat the Giant! [161]

The Justice of God—*Fathers are to be a righteous judge.* "My Dad is just!" is a priceless compliment for a Father to hear. Even better than "My Dad is fair..." Protocol could be defined as the right thing, done at the right time, in the right manner, to the right people. Justice is basically knowing what to see, what to hear, when to speak and when to act. The prophet Micah said we are to *"do justly, to love mercy, and to walk humbly with our God."* [162] On occasions, our Father moved with lightning swiftness to execute judgment (Ananias and Sapphira, immediate punishment [163]) or waited with endurance until individuals had opportunity to repent (days of Noah, at least 120 years of grace while building the ark [164]). Same God. Unchanging. He was just and able to make right decisions to fulfill His will in the lives of His children.

---

[160] Romans 11:33

[161] 1 Samuel 17:54b

[162] Micah 6:8 (NKJV)

[163] See Acts 5

[164] From Genesis 5:32 to Genesis 6:11

The Love of God—*Fathers are to be God's love in the flesh.* Experiencing love from an earthly Father makes it easier to comprehend the love of a spiritual Father. God, our Father, is a loving God. We love Him because He first loved us. A Father's love-model gives credibility to all the words a child will hear about the love of God. *"Husbands, love your wives..."* so that children might see the model of God's love. *"God so loved the world that He gave His only begotten Son."* The Son in turn so loved you and me that He gave His life for the Church. Love is contagious. Love that *gives* is transmittable. The Bible says: *"God is love."* Can our children say: "My Dad is love"?

The Mercy of God—*Fathers have compassion.* Our Eternal Father is *"...mindful that we are but dust."* [165] He became one with us as God Incarnate in Jesus of Nazareth. Wise is the earthly Father who remembers his youth. Who can recall his "growing-up-days?" Who can exercise mercy and compassion according to the age need of his maturing child?

The Omnipotence of God—*Fathers carefully exercise their authority.* The highest authority in a biblical family structure is the Father. *"The husband is the head of the wife, even as Christ is the head of the church."* [166] As Christ was subservient to the Father, so the Husband must be a servant to the Word of God. The power entrusted to the Father is to help develop his child in six areas: independence, security, self-discipline, spiritual maturity, sexual understanding and preparation for adulthood. How the Father fulfills his role as an influential authority figure affects these six areas of growth. Again the wise Father adapts his leadership style to the maturity level of each child.

The Omnipresence of God—*Fathers follow their children in their mind and heart wherever they go.* Earthly Fathers travel with their children in their prayers. God is everywhere, so He knows everything. He knows what we need – before we ask. A Father who seeks to be aware of the world his children live in will be aware

---

[165] Psalm 103:14

[166] Ephesians 5:23

of his child's needs, sometimes before they ask. It may require a visit, a reading or an inquiry to gain awareness of each child's complex environment.

The Omniscience of God—*Fathers know their children's needs.* Jesus prayed with His disciples that the Evil One might not tempt them. And Job offered sacrifices in case his sons had sinned against God. Fathers have a responsibility to use the knowledge they have of their children to pray for them. We learn more about our Father in quiet *one-to-one* times together. Likewise, we find out more about our children when we share life together on a personal basis *one-to-one.*

The Self-Existence of God—*Fathers, filled with the Holy Spirit, have the basics to fulfill their role.* In the beginning was God. Our knowledge of God is rooted in His true revelation to us through the biblical records. Our children need to know us as their Father. Who are we? What has God done in and through us? What have we learned about God and His Goodness and His Sovereignty that we can share with our children and grandchildren *"as you sit down and as you rise"?* [167] Fathers are to *"train up a child in the way he should go."* [168] It was never intended for this role to be abdicated to other people, organizations or government.

The Self-Sufficiency of God—*Fathers are dependent on God.* God, our Father, needs no other. We, His children are not *"adequate in ourselves to consider anything as coming from ourselves, but our adequacy is from God."* [169] God is our Source, not MasterCard® or VISA®. Fathers are commissioned by God to teach their children the worth and value of honest work. The enjoyment and a need for productive leisure activities and fun! A Father who *"does not provide for the needs of his household"* is worse than an unbeliever in God's eyes (see 1 Timothy 5:8). The Father who seeks to serve God rather than Mammon will find his

---

[167] Deuteronomy 6:7

[168] Proverbs 22:6

[169] 2 Corinthians 3:5

energies blessed in partnership with God to develop creative ways of providing for the needs of his family.

The Sovereignty of God—*Fathers are accountable for their freedom.* Few people comprehend the freedom a Father has to teach, influence and mold the life of his children. Fathers need to use that freedom wisely. Maleness is a biological fact. Masculinity is a learned response. The Father's role is to teach the children true masculinity and true femininity understood apart from appearance, occupation, social position or economic value. Fathers will be held accountable for how they use this freedom.

The Transcendence of God—*Fathers show sons a model of God's character.* When our son was old enough to memorize Bible verses, I (as the Father) decided the first verse he should memorize was Ephesians 6:1 *"Children obey your parents in the Lord, for this is right."* [170] My wife Rita (as the Mother) spoke up in his defense and said, "Well I know the second verse he should memorize." I asked, "What would that be…?" To which she quickly responded, *"Fathers, provoke not your children to wrath lest they become discouraged"* [171] How well I remember the little guy looking at me after I had told him to stop doing something and saying, "Daddy, you're making me discouraged."

Our Heavenly Father demands obedience for Himself (which He regards as better than sacrifice). Likewise, He expects His human children to obey their parents. *"Honor your father and mother… is the first commandment with promise, that it may be well with you and you may live long on the earth."* [172] In a society of increasingly isolated, lonely elderly citizens, children need to see Fathers honoring their aging parents.

Story: A politician once took his young son fishing for a day. When a historian cross-referenced the diaries kept by the boy

[170] Ephesians 6:1

[171] Ephesians 6:4 (KJV)

[172] Ephesians 6:23

> (later a famous lawyer) and his father, he found the politician had written: "Went fishing with my son—day wasted." The young boy had written: "Went fishing with my dad—greatest day of my life." Children desire to exalt their fathers. They enjoy being with their parents.

One boy in our group home ran away to go back to his father, who had beaten him regularly. When I asked him, "Why do you want to return to your father?" he looked at me with tears in his eyes, "Uncle Jim, he's still my dad."

The Wisdom of God—*Fathers ask for wisdom.* His attributes are available to man in some limited dimension. *"If any man lacks wisdom* [and what father doesn't] *let him ask of God—and it will be given to him."* [173] *"The wisdom from above is first pure, then peaceable, gentle, reasonable, full of mercy and good fruits, unwavering and without hypocrisy."* [174] Fathers need to be *"as shrewd as serpents and as innocent as doves"* [175]to resolve the conflicts children will face on their journey to adulthood.

Success as a Father is a biblical injunction for a man giving spiritual leadership in the local church. *"He must be one who manages his own household well, keeping his children under control, with all dignity, for if a man does not know how to manage his own household, how will he take care of the church of God?"* [176]

Is it worth it to be a Dad? Let the words of Martin Luther encourage us to fulfill our role with joy and enthusiasm. He says: "Married people should remember that they can perform no better and no more useful work to the glory of God, for the benefit of the church and the state, for themselves and their children, than the proper upbringing of their children." [177]

---

[173] James 1:5

[174] James 3:17

[175] Matthew 10:24

[176] 1 Timothy 3:4-5

[177] Source unknown

Happy Father's Day! A Christian Father is a:

F—Faithful provider of life's necessities for growth.
A—Authority with compassion and justice without partiality.
T—Teacher of survival skills that build security and independence.
H—Helper in handling life's crises from a biblical perspective.
E—Example of a role model committed to the Lordship of Jesus Christ.
R—Refuge for security and protection while growing into adulthood.

***

Grandfathers: A Valuable Aid in Character Development

Larry Fowler, Founder of the Legacy Coalition says: "The incredible potential of Christian grandparents to be influencers of their grandchildren is unrealized in most churches, under-resourced by ministries and publishers, and overlooked by almost everyone."

Dr. Josh Mulvihill, in his book, Biblical Grandparenting, says less than one in four Christian grandparents see their role as a discipler of their grandchildren. The view of a grandparent as friend, cheerleader and helper to the parents dominates their vision of their role. [178]

Many grandparents feel set aside as detached observers of how their children raise *their* grandchildren. Deuteronomy 6:2 in the New Living Translation uses the word *grandchildren* when most translations say your *"children's children."* Moses said: *"These are the commands, decrees, and regulations that the Lord your God commanded me to teach you. You must obey them in the land you are about to enter and occupy, and you and your children and grandchildren must fear the Lord your God as long as you live. If you obey all his decrees and commands, you will enjoy a long life."* In all my years of hearing speakers and sermons, I cannot

---

[178] Notes taken from Executive Summary of the Legacy Coalition, Tuesday 14 March 2017 at a meeting with Larry Fowler in Langley, British Columbia.

recall anyone telling me that I am to be an *Intentional Christian Grandparent* until I met Larry Fowler. [179]

Grandparents can play a huge role in assisting their sons and daughters. Circumstances such as death, divorce, distance, difficulties, and desire affect the influence of grandparents.

My maternal Grandpa Mills was a spirited little Welshman. His no-nonsense worldview was *just let me get the job done.* He probably had a disproportionate influence on my life. My paternal Grandfather Cunningham died before I was born, Grandma Cunningham was in Heaven by the time I was five and Grandma Mills was blind from diabetes and died when I was about 10. My mom and I lived in Carlisle, Ontario, with her parents while my dad was serving overseas with the Canadian 2nd Army in Europe, liberating Holland, Belgium, and France. So Grandpa Mills became a surrogate father to me, and my boyhood hero. He's the one who taught me to hunt and fish. He trained me to help him hunt rabbits in the bush as soon as I was old enough to flush them out by firing my toy Roy Rogers Cap Gun: *"Rabbits will run in a circle and come back to where they started."* He taught me how to walk into the bush, quietly marking the trail, to find my way home: *"Bend the saplings so when you come back they point in the direction you came from…"* And he introduced me to some serious survival skills if I ever got lost in the bush for the night: *"Plastic and elastics: carry a piece of plastic, attach a small stone in each corner by wrapping an elastic around the stone in the plastic, stretch it over a tree bough and you have an instant shelter!"* From my childhood observations of hunting with Grandpa Mills, there appear to be three kinds of hunters.

So when a Hunter makes his kill and approaches his game he has two options: either clean the whole animal (to preserve it), or remove one choice piece of meat for his evening dinner. The Lazy Hunter fails to gut and clean the animal (too messy). And if he refuses to take the time to dry or roast strips of meat for future meals or for sharing with his family and community back home he

[179] Check out www.legacycoalition.com

is not only lazy, he is often selfish. No one else benefits from his skills. That is perhaps what King Solomon meant when he wrote: *"The lazy man does not roast his game, but the diligent man prizes his possessions"* (Proverbs 12:27). Grandpa Mills taught me that it is wise to *"roast the spoils"* pass on whatever skills or things you have learned for the benefit of others. One of his life lessons was: "There is nothing new under the sun, Jimmy, so don't worry who gets the credit. Almost everything you know, somebody else taught you about it first."

Fathers and Grandfathers, let's agree: Integrity blends actions, beliefs, and character to help our sons and daughters become conformed to the image of Jesus Christ. Paul said to Timothy: *"And the things you have heard me say in the presence of many witnesses entrust to reliable men who will also be qualified to teach others"* (2 Timothy 2:2). So let me paraphrase this passage: *"And young Fathers, the things you have heard me, your older Father, say to you in the presence of many witnesses while we lived together, now entrust to your Son, my Grandson so he will teach his friends and family how to teach others"* Grandparents play a major role in affirming biblical principles taught to their grandchildren.

Standards: The Guardrails of Life

Metric is a word that changed a whole generation of Canadians in the 1970's. The Liberal federal government of Pierre Trudeau began implementing metrication in Canada. By the mid-1970s, metric product labeling began.[180] The changeover in Canada created some confusion as drivers quickly converted from the former 60 miles-per-hour to 100 kilometers-per-hour. One cartoon showed a tractor-trailer truck rammed securely under an overpass bridge. The sign indicating the height of the bridge was in meters. The driver's helper in the front seat had a pocket calculator and was trying to make the conversion from feet to meters. With a note of exasperation, the driver drawls to his helper, *"Y'all just have to make them calculations a little faster boy!"*

---

[180] https://en.wikipedia.org/wiki/Metrication in Canada (accessed Jan 17, 2017).

Children, like drivers, need to know the standards for living safely. Life can be exciting and enjoyable and move smoothly and safely when the child knows and adheres to the standards of God's Word. But to have a Father who is constantly changing the rules is a frustration for the best of children.

Scenario: Many of us have driven a vehicle over a bridge. And the majority of us (99+%) have done so without ever hitting the side guardrails. But, if we came speeding up to the same bridge at 100 kilometers an hour and saw it had no guardrails, we would (if you were like me) panic! We would stop the car (if possible), get out, walk to the bridge, look over the edge and say: "No way you'll get me to drive across that bridge without any guardrails." (See Figure 9-A). Reasoning with the driver at that point would be virtually useless. "Have you ever hit the guardrails before?"—"No." "The road is the same width."—"I know." "Why are you afraid to drive across the bridge?"—"Because!" A few brave souls may proceed over this bridge. But the insecurity and frustration for the majority of drivers would soon reduce the flow of traffic over this same bridge.

The Bible reminds us that the road to life is a narrow road and few find it. The path towards death is more like an Expressway, wide and open, full speed ahead. Most Expressways are, in a word, boring. Narrow roads usually have more excitement and beauty but they have a few tricky spots that need clear signage and a few bridges that need sturdy guardrails. Fathers fulfill their role when they provide protective guardrails for their children to get them across a difficult time in their life. Keep in mind these guidelines for guardrails:

Guardrails are...

To improve progress, not slow it. A psychological security as much as a physical security.
Only used in emergencies. Absorb maximum impact yet still hold and at locations of maximum danger.

The same conditions could apply to Standards we create for our children. As Fathers, we:

- **Establish the Standard**
- **Explain the Standard**
- **Exhibit the Standard**
- **Expect the Standard**
- **Enforce the Standard**
- **Evaluate the Standard**

Standards: The Guardrails of Life

1. Establish the Standard—What are the criteria by which we determine when, where and what are the guardrails for our children? The Apostle Paul told the Corinthians, we are not to *"compare ourselves with some who commend themselves, but when they measure themselves by themselves and compare themselves with themselves, they are without understanding."* [181] Do not let the culture deceive you into establishing weak, artificial or unnecessary standards. Put your energies into building guardrails where they are needed, not where others think they should go.

Story: A Christian family had three daughters. The parents made certain they went to a Christian school. The girls wanted to wear blue jeans to school to be like the other girls. The Father approved. The Mother said: "No way. My daughters will wear skirts and dress like young ladies..." The parents argued the issue. During this time, the Mother discovered she was pregnant with their fourth child. The mother became depressed. She went to a Christian doctor. He referred her to a Christian Psychiatrist. They (the Mother, Doctor, and Psychiatrist) agreed that: "Mother is so depressed, she should have an abortion." So she did. Fast forward. Husband disagreed, but it happened anyways. Conflict. Parents divorced. Family unity disintegrated. To say wearing blue jeans is evil but abortion is okay is an example of wrong standards and poorly placed guardrails that failed to protect the family!

Consider the Pressure the Enemy of our Soul is putting on our Children and our Grandchildren to destroy Traditional Biblical Family values:

- Lose virginity—ASAP.
- Experiment with LGBTQ lifestyle – and accept those who think they are.
- Delay marriage – in China one must be 25 years old for a permit to get married.

---

[181] 2 Corinthians 10:12

- Voluntarily choose to have NO children – Become a DINK: Double Income No Kids.
- Or have only 1 or 2 children – compare Islam, where one man could have four wives and 23 children!
- Betray your marriage vows – commit adultery or be abusive.
- Give in – Give up – Get a divorce – or 2 or 3 or more! – Some are up to #7 or #8!
- Get a sexually transmitted disease.
- Work long hours and make MORE money! – Materialism is an epidemic disease.
- Forget God – Skip Church – No Bible Study or Prayer – Just have Fun!

2. Explain the Standard—Our Heavenly Father made certain His Children knew what the standards of His Word meant. Time after time, the Children of Israel tested God's standards and found them to be firm. Our father made certain they understood the rules – and the consequences for disobedience. Once the Father and the Mother have established the standard with an agreement, it needs an explanation at the child's age level of understanding.

> Story: My three-year-old granddaughter once told me, "Grandpa Jim, choices have consequences..." Years later, when she was misbehaving one day, I reminded her of that phrase. She looked at me with a sweet smile and said, "Grandpa, tell me your consequences before I make my choice..." How soon we move from childhood innocence (with obedience) to adult reasoning (with rationalization) for our decisions.

3. Exhibit the Standard—"Children have more need of models than of critics..." (Joubert). It is a wise Father who becomes a model of his agreed family standards. Children are natural born imitators. They love to play and model their lives after what they see around them. If they see anger, they model anger. If they see Father practicing what he teaches, their appreciation level increases for their number one model.

Story: Our five- and four-year-old sons invited neighborhood kids into our unfinished basement to play Neighbors. They drew lines on the floor to show our road, and where each house sat they had a box. I once overheard a dialogue between the new four-and-five-year-old neighbors. Our 5-year-old son said to one of the neighborhood girls: *"Every morning you let your dog out and it comes across the street to my hedge. If that dog pees on my shrubs again, I'm calling the SPCA!"* Wow! Where did he hear that phrase? From one of the Fathers, of course, and I knew which one: Me! Guilty.

4. Expect the Standard—Police say a law unenforced is a meaningless law. The success of a standard is determined by what happens after it begins. Children soon learn when Dad means it and when he was just kidding. Fathers who place guardrails at strategic locations can expect their children to appreciate them and accept them. Fathers who make unnecessary rules find the standards regarded as tedious.

Story: We taught many Proverbs to our sons. One was *"a gentle answer turns away wrath."* [182] After moving to a new school, the local (larger) bully confronted our youngest son in the schoolyard at recess. He lifted Mike up to the wall with his left hand at the top of Mike's shirt and, waving his right hand, said to Mike and the listening crowd, "Hey, Cunningham, know what I'm gonna do to you?" Mike thought fast and gently replied: "Ahh, I don't believe you're gonna kiss me!" The big bruiser began to laugh. So did all who were listening. He lowered Mike and laughing with everyone said, "You're OK Cunningham. That was good. Welcome to our school." Mike passed the test.

5. Enforce the Standard—Usually, when guardrails get hit we call it an accident. Likewise, enforcement of an agreed family standard often comes at an inopportune time. This increases the temptation

[182] Proverbs 15:1

to let it go this time. Adding threatening words to what will happen next time permits the child to bask in a successful detour around the standard. The time to evaluate the rule is after enforcement not before. To alter before is to admit the standard has little value. Faith, in love, enforces standards. Love and control in balance are the criteria for good Fathering. The Father who abdicates enforcement to the Mother misses the opportunity to build a closer relationship with his child. Discipline is part of Discipling.

> Story: For many years we listened to a neighbor raising their children. Their method of enforcement was interesting. "Bobby, dinner will be ready in five minutes. Come in and get ready." No response from Bobby. "Bobby…" (a little louder) "…I said dinner is ready so get in here." Bobby continues whatever he is doing and ignores the second request. Finally, the third time it was, thunderous (that is how we knew the sequence) "Bobby, you get in here right now!" The mother began to count. "10—9—8—I'm counting—7—6—if you are not here by one you are going to your room without dinner—5…" (Bobby begins to move) "…4—NOW!—3," and Bobby would shoot past her in the doorway just before she said, "2—1—0." We heard this scenario so many times it became a joke for us. All I had to say was "3—2—1" and we would laugh. Bobby had his Mother and Father conditioned that the standard meant nothing – until they got louder and screamed. Once we even heard the Father get to 1 without a response, so he began hollering fractions "7/8's—3/4's—1/2" before saying zero.

A word of caution: Never enforce a standard in anger! Let me suggest that anger may be the most destructive force in a father-child relationship. It is amazing to see how many angry parents lose their tempers in public. One can only imagine what happens at home behind closed doors. Can you imagine a Highway official arriving at the bridge and seeing your car has spun out of control and hit the guardrail? Here he comes up to your dented car. Screaming at the top of his lungs. "You stupid driver. Why are you hitting my guardrail?" Unreasonable, isn't it? The same official is likely glad the guardrail saved your life! So likewise we need to rejoice when we have to enforce a biblical standard. It probably prevented a greater tragedy.

Suggestion: Enforce standards with the wisdom of James 3:17.

- Be pure (no selfish interest).
- Be peaceable (not done in anger or malice).
- Be gentle (this character quality is identified three times: once in the *fruit of the Spirit*; second in the qualities of a spiritual leader; and third, as a quality of wisdom. You would think God knew men had a challenge to be *Gentle*.
- Be reasonable (be approachable in spite of the pressure).
- Be full of mercy (discipline is to be redemptive, not in vengeance for hurt pride or loss of status.
- Be full of good fruits (sanctified discipline usually results in improved behavior. Selfish anger often produces alienation).
- Be without partiality (just enforcement of a standard for all concerned without playing favorites or bending the rule for a particular occasion).
- Be without hypocrisy (pure motives are part of Christ-like wisdom)

6. Evaluate the Standard—Now is the time to review the rules—after implementation. Did we obtain the expected results? Fathers can now decide on the value of the standard as an aid to progress. Retain if producing the desired results. Alter or eliminate if it is a hindrance to development. Be ready as a Father to apologize and ask forgiveness of your child if the evaluation reveals a weak standard, an improper communication of expectations, failure to exhibit a proper modeling of the standard or an inappropriate method of enforcement. Each of the five previous sections is up for review during this time of evaluation.

Guardrails alone do not guarantee safe passage across the bridge. Scripture says that Daniel *"purposed in his heart not to defile himself with the King's meat."* [183] Each child must ultimately decide to *drive carefully* in the right direction, the path of righteousness.

As a Father, you may be reading this and believe that you had standards and tried your best and yet your children are living in disobedience to God's Word. They have knocked out the guardrails and hit-the-ditch so to speak. Here's a word of encouragement for you. Few Fathers of spiritually successful children take full credit for what happens. They often regard their children walking with the Lord as the grace of God.

Adam and Eve, living in the post-Garden exile had a near perfect environment to raise their two sons – Cain and Abel. Think of the corruptive influences missing from their society. All they had was their inner sinful nature. No violent screens to watch. No drunken beach parties to attend. No seductive girls to entice. No secular-humanistic high school teacher to blame. Nothing. We can assume that Cain and Abel knew what happened when their parents disobeyed God's commands. Dad and Mom probably instructed them in the things of the Lord. Yet, Cain murdered Abel. Volitionally of his own free will, Cain slammed head-on into the guardrails of his parents and his Creator. His life ended in isolation and rejection. He was cut off from his family without any recorded repentance. We must remember, guardrails are an aid to progress and security for travel. They do not guarantee arrival at the destination. But as part of God's eternal-maintenance-team on the-King's-highway we, as Fathers – and Grandfathers – are required to erect the guardrails and keep them in good repair for each of our children as they travel through life.

Provoke Not To Wrath

Ephesians 6:4 notes: *"Fathers, do not provoke your children to wrath."* Do we as Fathers really "bug" our children that much? If so, how do we do it? Your list may vary depending on the age of the child and whether it's a boy or a girl. But here are a few apparent universals in all cultures.

---

[183] Daniel 1:8

1. Teasing—Many cultures have ways of deceiving children. Western Culture is ripe with occasions such as April Fool's Day, Easter Bunnies, Tooth Fairies and Santa Claus. These all eventually become known for what they are—*artificial realities*. Teasing is different. Often it involves name calling based on a physical characteristic: *Red*, *Curly*, *Shorty*. But often the words are not humorous. Then the Father cuts deeper by saying "What's the matter son, can't you take a joke?" Sometimes the sarcastic remarks come from another adult like an Uncle or family friend who thinks they are funny.

2. Name-Calling—Number Two is branding a child with a registered name that begs ridicule against them: Richard becomes *Dicky* etc. Some nicknames imply character weakness or deficiencies such as *Sissy*, *Slowpoke*, *Lazy*, *Meat-Head* etc. Name-calling is not part of the Christian's vocabulary. Jesus built people up by giving them new names that suggested strength: Peter's name went from Simon (meaning *pebble*) to Peter (meaning *rock*).

3. Inconsistency in Disciplining—God, is Consistent. He is the same: *"yesterday, today, yes and forever..."* [184] Children suffer under a ranting, raving maniacal Father one moment, only to ignore the whole situation for a month! One neighbor would swear and call his son all manner of names from the kitchen window and then appear later at the door and say, "Honey Munchkin, it's time for din-din..." Being consistently inconsistent does not equal consistency!

4. Failure to Keep a Spoken Word (Promise)—One Father who worked for a trucking company shared his philosophy of raising his Children: "Under-Promise—Over-Deliver..." (sounds like his trucking company's philosophy as well).

Building trust is our goal as a Father. We can do it, Men! The whole world is watching. Hollywood and the media have created *Buffoon-Weak-Almost-Idiotic-Fathers*. We have been forced to watch the old Archie Bunker to Homer Simpson and Family Guy.

---

[184] Hebrews 13:8

Now the World is watching. If we can be successful as fathers it doesn't matter as much what else we accomplished. This one role—Father—quickly evidences our level of spiritual maturity as followers of Jesus Christ.

Keep Going my Brothers.

THE NEW SON (A Father Writing to His Son)

Why am I here?
I awake. I breathe.
My eyes are open to the new sun.
I sit. I think.
I know I am here.
But why?

Your Word is before me.
Full of the records of men.
They lived. They fought. They loved. They died.
But why?

My son is standing here.
Asking me to fix his bicycle.
I just told him "Wait a minute."
Do You do that with us?

I am not sure how I am doing as a Father.
He grows. I guide.
But You are different Lord.
You have a plan for me,
And my son.

Your plan involves me –
And my family, and the neighbors
And the country and – and –
It is beautiful to think about.

Here I sit with a pen
And a piece of paper.
There You are "out there" with Your plan.
But You are also "in me" guiding this pen.
It boggles my mind.

You are in me.
You are in the air I breathe.
You are "in" everything.

How do I know You
The words from Your Book and Your Son.
I read them – by faith.
I accept them – by faith.
And then by faith I say,
"I know God."

So here I sit.
Me the finite
Trying to understand the infinite
When all along
Your Holy Spirit is in me.

You want me to live
To have life more abundantly.
Doing what I can
To the limits of Your love.

Right now that means fixing a bike.
He is my son
And that plan
You have for me
Includes discipling a son
Who will affect eternity?

Why am I here?
I awake, I breathe.
My eyes open to the new son.

JDC – October 1973

Competencies to Fulfill Role of FATHER

Personal Checklist
Circle the best answer for each to determine score

Do I have...

1. Acceptance of my child as "a gift of the Lord God," (Psalm 127:3-4) **formed by God** (Jeremiah 1:5; Psalm 139) **and entrusted to my wife and me as human guardians of an eternal soul?** "Whoever causes one of these little ones who believe in Me to stumble, it is better for him...that he is drowned in the depth of the sea." (Matthew 18:6)

1	2	3	4	5
Not at all	A little bit	Usually	Most of the time	Always

2. Acceptance of the responsibility for the birth of my child with the realization that 50% of his inherited qualities come from 'my side of the family'? "Let marriage be held in honor among all, and let the marriage bed be undefiled." (Hebrews 13:4) **God's plan allows childbirth through a sanctioned marriage.**

1	2	3	4	5
Not at all	A little bit	Usually	Most of the time	Always

3. Awareness of the needs and developmental characteristics of my children as individuals? (2 Timothy 3:15).

1	2	3	4	5
Not at all	A little bit	Usually	Most of the time	Always

4. Ability to provide for the fourfold needs of my child? "Jesus kept increasing in wisdom, and stature, and in favor with God and men." (Luke 2:52; 1 Timothy 5:8; Matthew 7:9-11).

1	2	3	4	5
Not at all	A little bit	Usually	Most of the time	Always

5. Readiness to develop a personal spiritual instructional program for my child? (See chapter on the Role of Teacher) (Deuteronomy 6:4-9; Proverbs 22:6).

1	2	3	4	5
Not at all	A little bit	Usually	Most of the time	Always

6...Love and respect for my child?

1	2	3	4	5
Not at all	A little bit	Usually	Most of the time	Always

Total divided by 6 =

Evidence Role of FATHER Fulfilled

Personal Checklist
Circle the best answer for each to determine score

Have I demonstrated…

1. Regular dialogue with my children?

1	2	3	4	5
Not at all	A little bit	Usually	Most of the time	Always

2. Mutual openness, honesty and good will?

1	2	3	4	5
Not at all	A little bit	Usually	Most of the time	Always

3. Evidence that our home is 'a comfortable place to be' to which my children bring their friends to meet me rather than always desiring to 'go out and get away from dad'?

1	2	3	4	5
Not at all	A little bit	Usually	Most of the time	Always

4. Do my children obey me?

1	2	3	4	5
Not at all	A little bit	Usually	Most of the time	Always

5. Proper discipline in love within the basics of scriptural principles? (Proverbs 23:12; 22:15).

1	2	3	4	5
Not at all	A little bit	Usually	Most of the time	Always

6. A commitment to faith in Jesus Christ as personal Savior by my children? "elders...having children who believe, not accused of dissipation or rebellion" (Titus 1:6).

1	2	3	4	5
Not at all	A little bit	Usually	Most of the time	Always

7. Good management of our household, keeping children under control with all dignity. (1 Timothy 3:4).

1	2	3	4	5
Not at all	A little bit	Usually	Most of the time	Always

8. Talk about God, and love for God, as part of a natural flow of our conversation? "...when you sit...and when you walk... when you lie down...when you rise"--(Deuteronomy 6:4-9).

1	2	3	4	5
Not at all	A little bit	Usually	Most of the time	Always

9. Purposeful talk with my child about any topic related to his age level with candidness and interest?

1	2	3	4	5
Not at all	A little bit	Usually	Most of the time	Always

Total divided by 9 =

Role of FATHER

Projects for Investigation and Discussion

[__] Interview three fathers with children the same age (or who have had children the same age) as your kids. Ask them what suggestions or advice they could give to you in the area of:

1) Family recreation	3) Family finances	5) Discipline
2) Family worship	4) Sex education	6) Teaching values

[__] Read a book on Fathering or Grandfathering and make a report to a small group of Fathers or Grandfathers.

[__] Set aside one day with each child / grandchild where the two of you do a particular project, or make a visit, or have dinner together, just the two of you.

[__] Review a copy of CHARACTER SKETCHES (from Basic Youth Conflicts, Box 1, Oak Brook, Illinois 60521) as a tool for family devotions to teach character development.

[__] "The average father in North America spends eight minutes a day with his child." What are the implications of such a statement to you personally?

[__] Four responses fathers often give to their children's requests are: "I'm too tired"; "We don't have enough money"; "I'm too busy"; and "Keep quiet." What are we saying to our children when we use these statements?

[__] If you were Joseph (Father of Jesus) and your firstborn child was the *Son of God*, what changes would you make in your role as a Father?

Chapter 10

Teacher • Relationship to His Learners

You therefore who teach another do you not teach yourself? • Romans 2:20

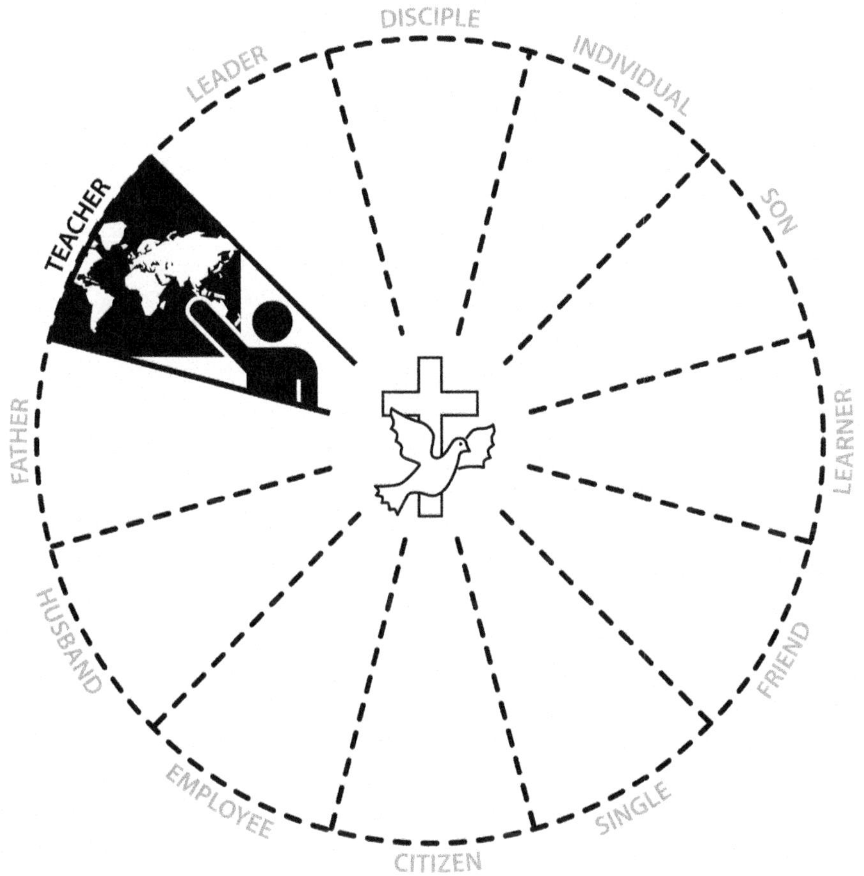

Infusing Life in our Teaching

***"If a teacher is ineffective,
either they do not have the gift of teaching,
are not developing it, or
are not in fellowship with the Lord."*** [185]

What a surprising insight into what may be the greatest cause of ineffective education in our country today.

I love teaching. But I was not born a natural teacher. I was given insights into lesson preparation, how to ask questions, ways to evaluate learning and so forth. This training has been at the Elementary Primary School level and the Adult Graduate level. But does that make me a teacher? Does that mean students left my presence with a sense of having participated in a worthwhile, life enriching experience? Did they *learn*?

Is it possible to be trained academically in *how to teach*, yet not be able to do so? Scripture says every father is to be a Teacher: *"These words which I am commanding you today shall be on your heart, and you shall teach them diligently to your sons...(and grandsons!)"* [186] God intended each home would be a spiritual education center where fathers and sons would share life together. They were commanded to talk about our Heavenly Father, His Word, His commandments and His precepts at all times:

- *"When you sit in your house..."* – at times of relaxation, rest, meals or quiet activity.
- *"When you walk by the way..."* – suggests occasions of traveling, walking or working together.
- *"When you lie down..."* – the time of day before rest and sleep when the rush of routines has come to an end.

---

[185] Roy Zuck, The Holy Spirit in Your Teaching, Scripture Press, David C. Cook, 1984, p.74.

[186] Deuteronomy 6:6-7

- *"When you rise up…"* – means that first thing in the morning, upon waking, the father and son are to be in dialogue about the Word of God.
- *"Bind them as a sign on your hand and the frontals of your forehead, and write them on the doorposts of your house and your gates…"* – Let them always remind us of their life-giving truths.

Story: On one visit to a home, I was amazed to be given a tour and shown commissioned landscaped oil paintings in every room. Each picture had a hand-scripted verse of scripture. Even the mantle of their fireplace had the words of Joshua etched in the wood: *"As for me and my house, we will serve the Lord…"* [187] My erroneous impression was that the Father of this house was the Teacher of the Scriptures. Not true. It was the Mother who had commissioned the paintings. The Father was living a secret double-life: *Mr. Clean* at church and in public, but *Mr. Evil* as a drug dealer and eventual murderer in his private life. The family was devastated by his actions. Some of his children even changed their name to avoid any association with his outrageous behavior. A man in a right relationship with God, his wife, and his fellow man is able to be effective as a Teacher to his children.

As a young teacher and a recent follower of Jesus Christ, I experienced some effective, and ineffective, teachers. To me, any teacher who did not communicate truth with the gifting that goes with being a teacher made the learning time *horrific*. (*Horrific* meaning: *separated from the presence of God).* If teaching was a *gift* given by the Holy Spirit, then anyone teaching without the gift of teaching was teaching without the Holy Spirit's empowerment or enablement to teach. Conversely, if a teacher were teaching without any spiritual enlightenment, it would be *horrific* to sit in their class and try to learn from them.

---

[187] Joshua 24:15 (KJV)

Let's consider for a moment the teachers we have had. Pick the one you call *the best teacher I ever had*. Then think of the one you call *the worst teacher I ever had*. Then make a parallel list of the characteristics of each. Hold on to that list for a moment.

God assigned the role of teaching the children to the Father. But, and this is important, many men find it easier to give the responsibility to *Mamma* and let her do it.

In 1989, the U.N. Convention on the Rights of the Child codified children's entitlements in a document that was adopted by the U.N. General Assembly and subsequently endorsed by more than 100 countries. It spells out rights that children have everywhere. And it acknowledges that parents have the most important role in the rearing of children.

In the *Traditional-Conventional Model of Education* the teacher is the authority. Historically in many other cultures, the model for training and teaching follows this model. (See chart below.)

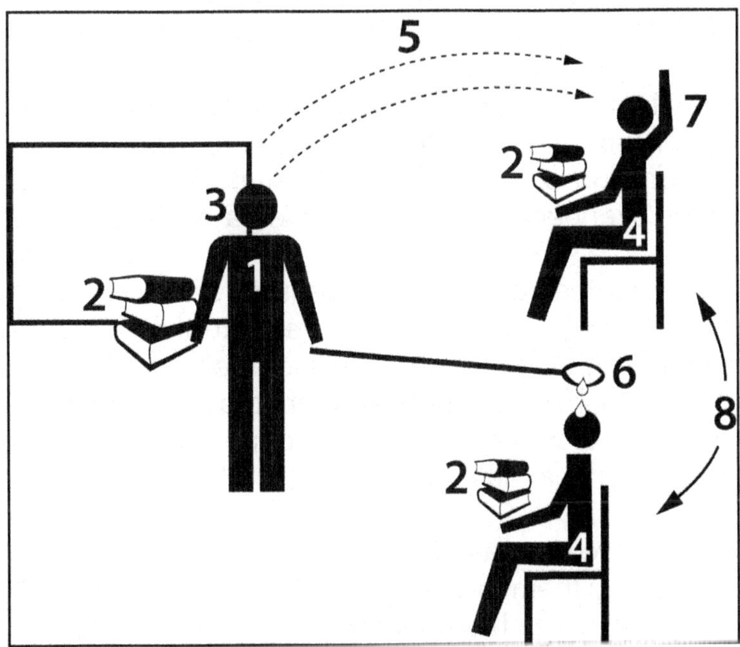

© Cunningham's Chart of Traditional-Conventional Education

(1) Traditional-conventional education begins with the teacher. The teacher is the recognized source of knowledge and authority.

(2) The teacher selects the content. Content may be a skill, knowledge or attitude.

(3) The teacher dominates the class and the learning through authority, power, and grading. The teacher tends to stand when speaking to assure dominance over the seated class members.

(4) Traditional-conventional education students (learners) sit passively in a *be-quiet-and-listen* arrangement.

(5) The students listen to a respected authority. They may take notes. Knowledge and insights come via a monologue lecture. The talk may include a series of rhetorical questions. Sometimes it may include pictures or PowerPoint.

(6) Traditional-conventional education sees the teacher spoon-feeding the learners with the knowledge, and they control the amount of knowledge given to the student.

(7) Information flows from the head of the teacher to the head of the listener (sometimes without a whole lot of processing). So much information is poured in that the student may suffer from an information overload that could be called a *cognitive-stuff.*

(8) The teacher then questions students to verify correct answers or retrieve facts or information poured into the student's head. This questioning leads to a competition between students. The old "ask-me-ask-me" routine helps them prove they know the right answer. Each student becomes an independent competitor with the other students to gain the approval of the teacher.

The challenge we have as men today is to teach our children rather than transferring them to a secular public school system that may run counter-culture to biblical principles.

A. A. Hodge wrote the following—in 1890!

"It is capable of exact demonstration that if every party in the State has the right of excluding from the public schools whatever he does not believe to be true, then he that believes most must give way to him that believes least, and then he that believes least must give way to him that believes absolutely nothing, no matter in how small a minority the atheists and the agnostics may be." [188]

In God's economy, the home is where a father *makes-it-or-breaks-it.* From "Day One" in the child's life, fathers are given the responsibility to give spiritual leadership to their children. Too many turn this role over to *The Mamma*, especially if *The Mamma* is more dominant or aggressive than *The Poppa*. In some homes, *Momma* assumed the spiritual leadership by her nature. In other homes, she has taken charge of the spiritual development of the children because of a lack of interest, or leadership, by her husband. Fathers need to realize this is not a mandate for becoming a religious tyrant or dictator. Parents need a team approach to teaching their children to attain harmony, unity, and balance.

We as fathers can be assisted in our teaching by friends, relatives, club leaders and church members.

The **Aims** of Education focus on three primary areas: Training, Teaching, and Discipling. To train in how *to do* or teach what *to know* without discipling in what *to be* in Biblical morality and character is to create what one author calls "*pin-striped barbarians.*" [189]

---

[188] The Engine of Atheism by A. A. Hodge in Evangelical Theology (first published in 1890). http://hisways.org/about/others-AtheismEngine.htm (Accessed 16 March 2017).

[189] The Patriot: An Exhortation to Liberate America from the Barbarians, by Gary Hart, Simon and Schuster, 1996, pp 177-179.

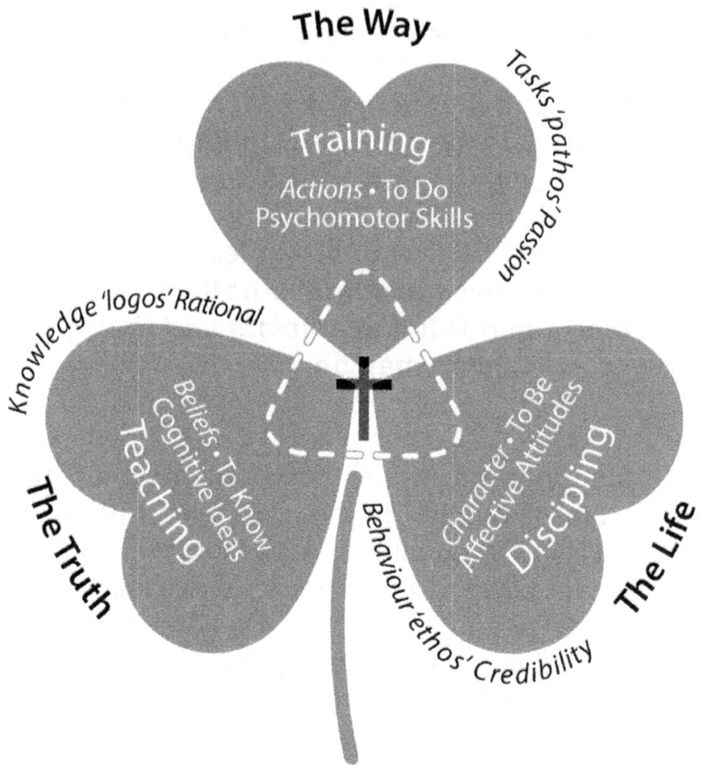

Educators talk about what they want the Learner "to know, to do, and to be" (knowledge, skill or character quality). But without the power of the Holy Spirit transforming the person's inner being this can produce a self-sufficient, arrogant lover of self—*"always learning but never coming to the knowledge of the truth…"*[190]

The primary aim of education for a Christian is to bring every person and all knowledge under the Lordship of Jesus Christ. *"You will know the Truth and the Truth will make you free."* [191]

---

190 2 Timothy 3:7

191 John 8:32

The Gift of Teaching [192] (adapted)

Pastor Jeff Carver writes: "The Greek word for those with the spiritual gift of teaching is *didaskalos.* From the root of this word we get our English word, 'didactic.' The word *didasko* means to teach, instruct, instill doctrine, explain, and expound...The Holy Spirit gives certain people the spiritual gift of teaching so that they would help the church fulfill her ministry as '*a pillar and buttress of the truth'* (1 Timothy 3:15). ... [They desire to follow in the footsteps of Jesus who taught in the synagogues and in the Temple as well as anywhere the people were gathered. They are called to demonstrate God's love while revealing His truth to the world without fear. The effect of their ministry is the upholding of God's Word and the growth and maturity of His Bride until the day of His return." [193]

How do we Improve Our Teaching?

Scripture says Jesus increased in *"wisdom and stature and in favor with God and men..."* [194] Each man must develop in the same four areas to fulfill his role as a Teacher.

- **Wisdom (Mental)**—a Teacher is a reader, a thinker, a lifelong learner with a clear mind that understands scriptural principles and knows how to apply them humbly.
- **Stature (Physical)**—a Teacher models good health principles. Nowhere is a Teacher excluded for being in any way disabled or limited but rather functions to the top capacity of his physical ability.
- **Favor with God (Spiritual)**—a Teacher first obeys and applies Scripture to his life. This gains God's approval before engaging with others to help them learn to apply Truth.

---

[192] http://www.spiritualgiftstest.com/spiritual-gift-of-teaching (accessed 18 January 2017)

[193] See also Ephesians 4:11; 1 Corinthians 12:28; Romans 12:7; James 3:1

[194] Luke 2:52

- **Favor with Men (Social)**—a Teacher loves people and shows it by the grace and kindness with which he shares life with them.

Teaching:

- **Involves knowledge (*to know*). Philosophy means *the love of wisdom* (*Philos:* love; *Sophia:* Wisdom), the process of thinking and believing the absolute biblical truth to know something correctly.** (See Exodus 18:20; Exodus 35:34; Deuteronomy 4:10; Deuteronomy 11:19; and 1 Samuel 12:23.)
- **Requires giving oneself to study/prepare** and to observe/do the Law of the LORD before communicating truth to others (Ezra 7:10; Psalm 51:13; Psalm 86:11).
- **Lays the foundation for building a disciple of Jesus Christ.** (Matthew 28:19-21). The authority to teach God's Word comes from the *source* of the message, the truth of God's Word, rather than the knowledge, personality, personal opinions or qualifications of the *messenger* (Luke 4:32; John 7:16).
- **Increases how a learner understands content or knowledge of the truth about a subject, fact or historical event.** (Hebrews 12:10-11; Revelation 3:19; Proverbs 15:32)

There are challenging verses in the Bible for teachers found in James 3:1-2: "Not many of you should presume to be teachers, my brothers, because you know that we who teach will be judged more strictly. We all stumble in many ways. If anyone is never at fault in what he says, he is a perfect man, able to keep his whole body in check."

Teaching requires:

- A readiness to learn (Mark 13:1);
- A teachable moment (John 8:2);
- A truth to share (Acts 5:42);
- A gentle relationship of trust (2 Timothy 2:24);

- A gifting by the Holy Spirit to understand and communicate (1 Corinthians 12:28);
- A commitment to truth (Titus 2:1-10); and
- Encouragement and correction mixed with knowledge and authority (Titus 2:15).

Can We Teach an "Old Dog" New Tricks?

- Some men who are failing spiritually at home are being asked to take spiritual leadership in their church because they have some financial skill or management expertise. Putting *New Life* in our Teaching requires willingness for Men, Husbands, and Teachers, in particular, to let the Holy Spirit speak to us – then through us.

TRAINING *THE WAY*	**TEACHING** *THE TRUTH*	**DISCIPLING** *THE LIFE*
to do Actions with Competency	***to know*** Beliefs with Knowledge	***to be*** Character with Wisdom
THE TRAINER Demonstrates Skills (Physical Facts) to Affect our Actions based on ***What we*** ***Say & Do*** ***to Master*** ***Skills***	THE TEACHER Shares Ideas (Mental Concepts) to Influence our Beliefs based on ***What we*** ***Think & Believe*** ***to Comprehend*** ***Ideas***	THE DISCIPLER Models Attitudes (Spiritual Disciplines) to Shape our Character based on ***How we*** ***Feel & Respond*** ***to Develop*** ***Attitudes***
TRAINEE has ***pathos***	LEARNER has ***logos***	DISCIPLE has ***ethos***
PASSION and **MOTIVATION**	**RATIONALITY** and **CURIOSITY**	**BEHAVIOR** and **CREDIBILITY**
to Perform Practical Tasks with a Mandate to Obey Specific Rules	to Acquire Specific Knowledge with Freedom to Apply New Truths	to Evidence Personal Attitudes with Authority to Show Wise Character

© 2017 Cunningham's Chart of TTD: Training-Teaching-Discipling

Sooner or later, every man will find himself trying to share an idea with another adult. It's a lifelong challenge to teach anyone when the learning requires a change of actions, beliefs or character. One's background, experiences, fears, beliefs, biases, and security are threatened by a change in thinking! Change may require owning up to a wrong or a misunderstanding. It may even cost money or a relationship to change one's behavior. Consider the smoker who has had a daily *smoke break* with a small group of fellow smokers. If he becomes convicted that smoking is not only unhealthy, but a waste of money and stinky, this change in thinking will eventually lead to a change in lifestyle, spending patterns, and friendships.

Teaching involves establishing a *Body of Truth* (Content); basing interaction on *Needs* of the Learner (Evaluation); and choosing the best/appropriate *Conditions for Communication* (Methodology). A Teacher attempts to control the appropriate *Content* needed by the Learners; individual and group *Learning Activities* and *Tasks; and* the overall *Conditions* for maximum learning. In reality, the Teacher (Facilitator) has *some Truth* but does not know everything. The Learner also has *some Truth* that is usually less than the Teacher has. And there is *some Truth* that both Teacher and Learner must discover together.

Many people who teach courses in Churches or Schools or Seminaries in a Christian context are Pastors, Speakers, and/or Faculty. God bless them all. But many of them are rational, linear learners, essentialists who like to control the teaching time believing they are to be *the source of knowledge*. Their attitude is: *"If you knew as much as I know, why would you be in my class?"*

A significant number of learners are kinetic (active) and visual learners. They need interaction (to apply knowledge), and they need visuals (to increase understanding). While we might say: "Thank God for PowerPoint," *PowerPoint is still basically a one-way lecture with visible words and a few pictures – Transmissive* Learning. We want to move to *Transformative* learning. Learning that changes lives. How we do it is not an easy task. It is ultimately the Holy Spirit's function. He uses each Teacher as His *agent of change*.

Competencies to Fulfill Role of TEACHER

Personal Checklist
Circle the best answer for each to determine score

Do I have…

1. Recognition of the extra responsibility and accountability placed upon those who teach? *"Let not many of you become teachers, my brethren, knowing that as such we shall incur a stricter judgment (*James 3:1).

1	2	3	4	5
Not at all	A little bit	Usually	Most of the time	Always

2. Knowledge of the skills, information or attitude that needs to be communicated to others?

1	2	3	4	5
Not at all	A little bit	Usually	Most of the time	Always

3. Training in the techniques of communication skills?

1	2	3	4	5
Not at all	A little bit	Usually	Most of the time	Always

4. Love for the people being taught? *"And we proclaim Him, admonishing every man and teaching every man with all wisdom, that we may present every man complete in Christ"* (Colossians 1:28).

1	2	3	4	5
Not at all	A little bit	Usually	Most of the time	Always

5. An evidence of wisdom in my own personal life?

1	2	3	4	5
Not at all	A little bit	Usually	Most of the time	Always

6. A knowledge of the Word of God? *"Let the word of Christ richly dwell within you, with all wisdom, teaching and admonishing one another…"* (Colossians 3:16).

1	2	3	4	5
Not at all	A little bit	Usually	Most of the time	Always

7. The 'gift of teaching'? (Romans 12:7)

1	2	3	4	5
Not at all	A little bit	Usually	Most of the time	Always

8. Respect for the needs of the learner, and gentleness in my approach to people? *"The Lord's bond-servant must not be quarrelsome, but be kind to all, able to teach, patient when wronged, with gentleness correcting those who are in opposition…and they may come to their senses and escape the snare of the devil, having been held captive by him to do his will"* (2 Timothy 2:24-26).

1	2	3	4	5
Not at all	A little bit	Usually	Most of the time	Always

Total divided by 8 =

Evidences Role of TEACHER Fulfilled

Personal Checklist
Circle the best answer for each to determine score

Is there…

1. Personal obedience to the command of scripture to teach my sons according to the description in Deuteronomy 6:4-9?

1	2	3	4	5
Not at all	A little bit	Usually	Most of the time	Always

2. Change seen in the lives of my *learners*? (i.e. personal growth plus increased self-satisfaction in the learners indicating that my teaching has had an impact on their lives!)

1	2	3	4	5
Not at all	A little bit	Usually	Most of the time	Always

3. A personal enjoyment in the fulfillment of the role, based on a sense of personal satisfaction at being able to see, 'light bulbs come on' in the mind and heart of a learner?

1	2	3	4	5
Not at all	A little bit	Usually	Most of the time	Always

4. Acknowledgement of this gift from those to whom I minister, or who observe my teaching?

1	2	3	4	5
Not at all	A little bit	Usually	Most of the time	Always

Total divided by 4 =

Role of TEACHER

Projects for Investigation and Discussion

[__] "Of 600 teens who attended a venereal disease clinic in New York City, only 21 percent said they had received any sex information from their parents" (Family Concern bulletin – quoted in Dads Only).

[__] "By age 16 the average child has watched TV for 12,000 to 15,000 hours, more time than he spends in school or with his parents" (Time magazine). What are the implications of TV for the role we have as men to be teachers of our children?

[__] Read Deuteronomy 6:4-9. List possibilities for how you could fulfill the nine assignments God have given to us.

[__] In Joshua 4:7, 21-24 we see a *memorial of stones* being set up as a visual teaching device. Study the passage and then suggest types of memorials that we as Teachers/ Fathers/ Grandfathers can set up in the lives of our family and children *"so that they may fear the Lord (our) God forever"* (v. 24).

[__] How can we teach our sons to become *"strong in spirit"*? (Luke 1:80).

[__] What could be done in your church to improve the quality of adult learning? Discuss.

Chapter 11

Leader • Relationship to His Followers

If any man desires the office of an overseer, it is a fine work he desires to do • 1 Timothy 3:1

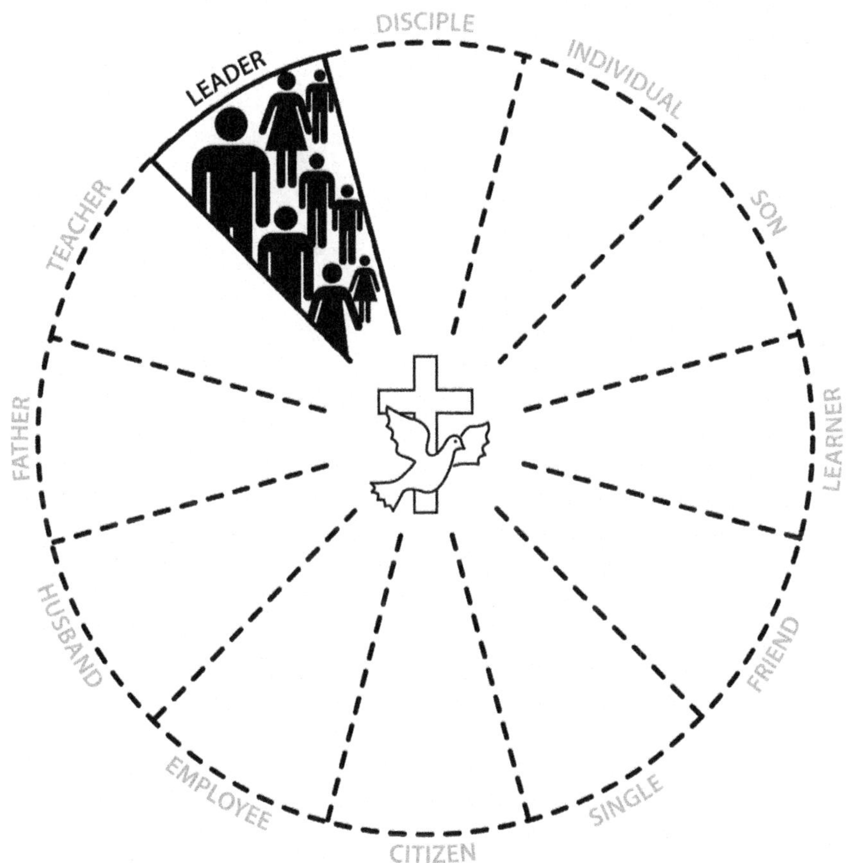

Who is The Greatest Leader?

Professional commentators and Christ's disciples had one character trait in common, they wanted to debate: *Who is or was the greatest*? Pick your sport. With some 4 billion followers, many would regard soccer as the most dominant sport in the world. 2.5 billion would say cricket. Even field hockey has over 2 billion. Sorry Canada, ice hockey has a small 75 million fan-base worldwide. It does not make it into the top ten. But every sport appears to have a debate over who is – or was – the greatest athlete in that sport.

So it was with Christ's disciples. They sensed a major assignment coming as ambassadors in Christ's new kingdom. As such, their pride began to swell. And *"there arose a dispute among them as to which one of them was regarded to be the greatest."* [195] This argument was significant between two brothers, James and John. Even their Jewish *Mamma* got involved with a request for one to sit on the right side and the other on the left side when Jesus established His Kingdom. [196]

Christ had only a few short hours left before He would be crucified and bring His earthly ministry to an end. He knew their hearts. Selfish ambition. So He gave His Philosophy of Christian Leadership in one final quick teaching. *"The Kings of the Gentiles lord it over them; and those who have authority over them are called 'Benefactors.'"* [197] Leaders of the Gentiles ruled the people. These leaders, in turn, served the Kings. The Kings provided what the people needed. For submitting and serving, the King would dispense favors to those who pleased him. The people existed to serve him – the leader. "But not so with you," said Jesus. "Let him who is the greatest among you become as the youngest and the leader *as the servant."* [198]

---

[195] Luke 22:24

[196] Matthew 20:20

[197] Luke 22:25

[198] Luke 22:26

Characteristics of the Youngest

At first glance, one would think (especially if one is the oldest child) that the first-born would be a better leader than the youngest! After all, are not most leaders first-born? The passage does not say the oldest cannot be a good leader. It says he will be a better leader if he exercises the qualities of the youngest:

- ***The youngest learns to submit to his elders.*** Older siblings have told him what, when and how to do most things in his early years!
- ***The youngest is sensitive to being put down.*** From his life experience, he has learned what it means to be *the runt of the litter*. He knows how to speak with sensitivity to his followers, the way he wanted older siblings to treat him.
- ***The youngest is often more relaxed and easygoing.*** An older brother or sister has claimed competitiveness and aggressive behavior in most cases. For the youngest remains the politicians' challenge of learning how to get along with contrary-minded people.
- ***The youngest tends to be protected by older siblings.*** Rather than physically *fighting for his rights* he learns that others will do that for him if he will be supportive of them.
- ***The youngest learns that protection comes from others who are stronger rather than one's own strength.*** A good lesson for learning dependency upon God in life's battles.
- ***The youngest can be the cause of jealousy from some siblings.*** Both Joseph and David were the youngest. Both were chosen by God to be leaders. And both received jealous responses from their siblings. The youngest is often sensitive to the feelings of jealousy that can emerge against a person in leadership.

Characteristics of the Servant

My younger sister Carolyn worked as a housekeeper in the home of a wealthy family while my brother-in-law went to a seminary in the same city. To her amazement, the life of a servant had some revealing aspects.

- ***The servant's obedience goes to the one he serves.*** There is no room for negotiation, compromise or correction.
- ***The servant's time belongs to those he serves.*** The needs of the master come ahead of personal comfort, priorities or goals. Carolyn felt like a slave to be kept up till 3:00 AM "to do the dishes after the party guests had left," and then told to be up "in time to prepare breakfast for the children."
- ***The servant's rights are surrendered to those he serves***. Even if the servant desires recourse for justice, this power is often given up, denied or taken away.
- ***The servant's attitude, loyalty, and submission is often more valuable than their actions***. Those in authority often change their attitude toward a servant whom they trust. They may even become more active and supportive of the servant's needs.

"Alpha Dog" Anyone? – "Yo Man, I'm the Leader!"

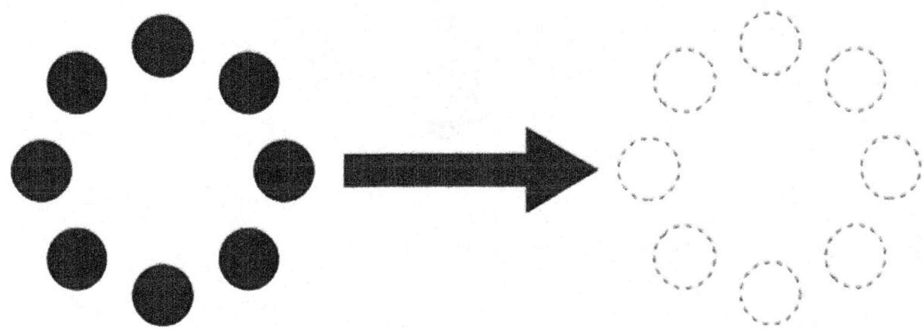

A leader is one who consciously or unconsciously influences a group or an individual towards a pre-determined goal.

Leadership: A Blend of Personality, Character and Style

I have worked with a variety of leaders. I have reported to different types of authorities. My conclusion moves towards saying that leadership is a blend of personality (character qualities) and style *(modus operandi).* One's style is the manner used to relate to subordinates, or those you are seeking to lead. I would say your *style* is a combination of your philosophical view of man, your theories of leadership and your personal behavior patterns.

Five styles of leadership in a visual manner

1. Guess Who?

"Guess Who?" Characteristics

- The leader becomes *one among equals* in the group.
- The leader may abdicate or withdraw from accepting responsibility for the team.
- The leader offers little direction or supervision of individuals or the group.
- Team members set their goals and work towards them
- The leader may serve as a resource person to the group.

2. Democratic

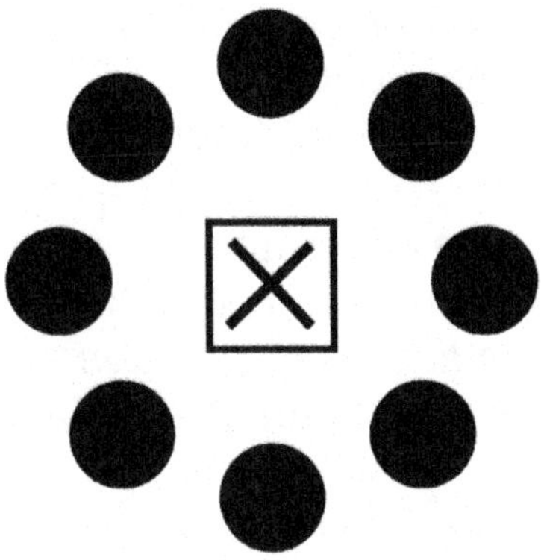

"Democratic" Characteristics

- The leader is usually very people-oriented, listens to their needs, stimulates them to action and offers positive encouragement.
- The leader permits the group to decide their course of action (usually through a majority vote).
- The leader commits to helping the team attain their chosen goal by encouraging members to participate.

3. Salesman

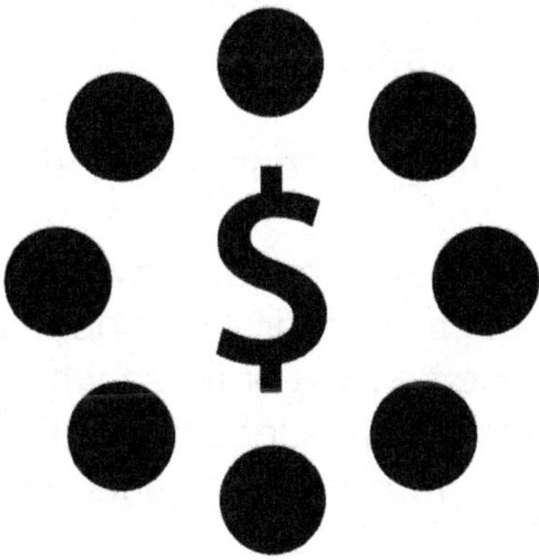

"Salesman" Characteristics

- The leader (or Management/Board) sets the goals and objectives for the group.
- The leader tries to sell the group on accepting and achieving the goals.
- Often there is little participation or involvement by the group in setting the goals. I worked with one authority that loved to talk about *participative management*. However, what he meant was the group participated by offering him suggestions, but not in making decisions. He made the decision and then *sold* his plan to us.

4. Big Daddy

"Big Daddy" Characteristics

- The leader is fully in charge but also wants everyone to like him.
- The leader may even reward loyalty above productivity, performance or competency, with bonuses, rewards or promotions to those he likes or those who show they like him.
- The leader may accept suggestions but supervises closely (a.k.a. *micro-managing*) all projects and progress towards *his* goals.

5. Dictator

"Dictator" Characteristics

Whether the leader has the title of Pastor, President or CEO, the Dictator leaders have the same desires: control, obedience, and loyalty.

- The leader is task-oriented. The job must be done at all costs.
- The leader permits no disagreements. Group members never ask a question related to the character or values of the leader.
- The leader rarely if ever accepts ideas from the group. *Psychic-numbing* sets in when the team gives up thinking and receives the security the leader attempts to provide.

Is there one style that is best?

No. Imagine a sports huddle in the middle of a game, and the Captain asks the team, "Ahhh, any thoughts on what we should do next? OK, that sounds good. Let's take a vote. OK, that one did not get a majority. Any other ideas?" The above scenario sounds ridiculous. At that moment the Team needs a Dictator, who makes the decision and moves the team towards their goal – literally.

But when the Church building committee meets to plan their new facility, they do not need *Mr. Money Bags* to walk in with the plans he paid his architect to draw and present it to the church as "Here's how the new building is going to look!" That is the time to let group members ask fundamental questions about the purpose of the building *before* drawing up the plans. The ideal is for a leader to adjust his style to the needs of the group, their skills, and time available to meet the goals, and extenuating circumstances affecting each member of the group.

Christ's Leadership Style in the Training of His Disciples

Christ shared every aspect of His life with those He trained. His was not *breakfast once a month* or *shared-air-space* for a fixed number of hours a week. He chose His disciples that they might be *"with Him."* Total immersion. They ate together. They traveled together and shared life together. Christ captured teachable moments from the routines of living to use for instruction, comfort, and exhortation. His actions, beliefs, and character were exhibited daily for public examination. The pressure of Pharisees constantly watching and the prejudices of individuals within the crowd failed to lessen the fragrance of His love for people. He set the example. His disciples duplicated His pattern.

Christ discipled "a few" while teaching "the masses." Visualize the King of Kings, Creator of the Universe, sitting around a Galilean campfire in *eyeball-to-eyeball* dialogue with fishermen and a tax collector! Individuals and their needs were the focus of Christ's ministry.

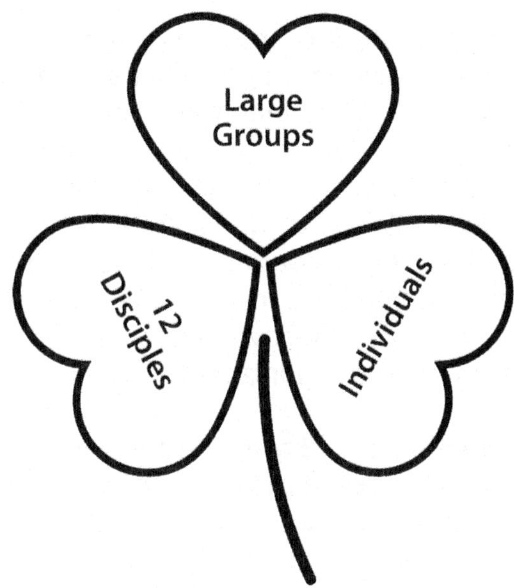

Jesus was teaching His Disciples to minister to the needs of Individuals even while *Feeding the 5000.*

Christ served the ones He was leading. *"The Son of Man"*—God in the flesh—***"...****did not come to be served, but to serve, and to give His life a ransom for many."* [199] Christ's leadership principles were modeled and exemplified while being taught. What He said, He did. Perfect Integrity! Jesus gained credibility for other teachings that *"were hard..."* [200] The loyalty of His followers is summed up in Peter's confession: *"Lord, to whom shall we go? You have words of eternal life. We have believed and have come to know that You are the Holy One of God."* [201] Their confidence in Him as a person led to their acceptance of His desires as a leader.

---

[199] Matthew 20:28

[200] John 6:53-69 So Jesus said to them, "Truly, truly, I say to you, unless you eat the flesh of the Son of Man and drink His blood, you have no life in yourselves.... 60 Therefore many of His disciples, when they heard this said, "This is a difficult statement; who can listen to it?" 61 But Jesus, conscious that His disciples grumbled at this, said to them, "Does this cause you to stumble? 62 What then if you see the Son of Man ascending to where He was before? 63 It is the Spirit who gives life; the flesh profits nothing; the words that I have spoken to you are spirit and are life."

[201] John 6:68-69

Christ permitted active participation by those He led. He gave His disciples clearly defined responsibilities. And He added the authority to do the task. They then went and *did it.* He prayed for them while they *did it.* Then, when they returned, He held them accountable for their actions and results! Opportunities arose to counsel those He led. Whether we view Christ's style as that of a Coach, Trainer, Teacher or Leader, the results are synonymous; He was *"Rabboni"* (Master). He made His disciples an integral part of His ministry. Personal objectives were welded together into a team ministry with shared organizational goals.

Christ (as Leader) was willing to be totally controlled by the Holy Spirit, not by personal glory or selfish ambition. *"Not as I will, but as Thou wilt..."* [202] was the motto of His earthly ministry. He gave total obedience to His Heavenly Father. Compare this to the attitude of Satan in his quest for the leadership of heaven. On five occasions in Isaiah 14 [203] the phrase *"I will"* is recorded (emphasis added):

- "*I will* ascend to heaven..." – desire for power.
- "*I will* raise my throne above the stars of God..." – the desire for acceptance – inflated estimation of his potential and abilities.
- "*I will* sit on the mount of assembly in the recesses of the north..." – the desire to be worshiped and approved.
- "*I will* ascend above the heights of the clouds..." – the desire to control the earth and its entire people.
- *"I will* make myself like the Most High." – the desire to be the supreme authority.

Not Jesus of Nazareth. As a result of His willingness to submit to the leadership of the Father, *"God highly exalted Him...that at the name of Jesus, every knee should bow, and every tongue confess that Jesus Christ is Lord..."* [204]

[202] Matthew 26:39

[203] Isaiah 14:13-14

[204] Philippians 2:9-11

Christ was *task-oriented* and *people-oriented* at the same time. While keeping His prime goal before Him (*"doing the will of Him who sent me..."*) [205] He showed love and respect for each person He met—regardless of age, sex or origin of birth. His kindest words were for those with the greatest human needs. His harshest words were for the hypocritical and legalistic Pharisees who were, in essence, the spiritual leaders of their day (see Appendix B).

Author Gary Collins called Jesus a *People-Helper.* [206] Jesus was able to encourage those he was leading; warned them of dangers they would be facing; told them what to do and say in times of stress or conflict; gave practical advice on how to apply what they were learning; and gave them a balance between working (doing) and relaxing (being). It is my theory there is more to be drawn from the leadership style of Jesus Christ than any other leader, living or dead!

God's Checklist for a Spiritual Leader

When an angel told Mary that she was to bear the child Jesus after the Holy Spirit had come upon her, her first response was classic. *"Nothing* (or "no word") *will be impossible with God."* [207] If God said it, Mary believed it. It was possible to do even if it sounded impossible.

The same applies to Leadership. God has clearly "said" what the qualifications are for a man seeking to give spiritual leadership. A helpful book on this subject is Gene Getz's classic, **The Measure of a Man.** His study caused me to dig into Scripture and find examples of men who met the stated qualifications. The following chart is a summary of my search.

I listed the qualifications alphabetically on the left side of the page. On the right is a reference (scripture text) to a man who evidenced

---

205 John 4:34

206 Gary Collins, How to be a People-Helper, Santa Ana: Vision House Publishers, 1976, pp.121-125

207 Luke 1:37

this character quality in his lifestyle. In the center is a five-part grid to give an arbitrary self-assessment for the degree to which you believe this quality is evident in your life.

For example, a "1" means you regard yourself as a *near-disaster* in this area. A "5" is evidence that you consider yourself as *mature* in this area (be careful ☺). Scores in between indicate where you feel you are in achieving this character quality.

When you finish the list, total the number of scores in each column. Take the overall total of all five columns and divide it by 22. This average shows your overall rating. Compare your score to the five ratings given for a Spiritual Leader.

CHECKLIST FOR A SPIRITUAL LEADER

CHECK ✓ 1 to 5 where 1 = "Never True for me" - to 5 Max = "Always True in my Life."

	CHARACTER QUALITY	1	2	3	4	5	BIBLICAL EXAMPLE
A	**Above Reproach**						**Nathanael** – John 1:47
	People give a good report of you in your daily lifestyle.	-	-	-	-	-	*"an Israelite indeed in whom is no guile…"*
B	**Blameless**						**Daniel** – Daniel 1:8
	Without cause for disgrace from secret unconfessed sin.	-	-	-	-	-	*"But Daniel made up his mind that he would not defile himself."*
C	**Convert: NOT a new Convert**						**Samuel** – 1 Samuel 2:26
	A basic knowledge of God through prayer, Bible Study and fellowship that stifles pride and temptation for personal glory.	-	-	-	-	-	*"Now the boy Samuel was growing in stature and favor with the Lord and with men."*
D	**Devout**						**Simeon** – Luke 2:25
	Given to worthy causes that bring glory to God.	-	-	-	-	-	*"…this man was righteous and devout."*
E	**Endurance**						**Paul** – 2 Timothy 4:1-8
	Able to appropriately reprove, rebuke, exhort, and encourage.	-	-	-	-	-	*"I have fought the good fight, I have finished the course, I have kept the faith;"*
F	**Fighter: NOT Pugnacious**						**Stephen** – Acts 7:59
	No gossip, slander or physical attacks on people	-	-	-	-	-	*"Lord Jesus, receive my spirit."*

	Trait	Example
G	**Gentle**	**Paul** – 1 Thessalonians 2:7
	Evidence the Galatians 5:22 "Fruit of the Spirit" in interpersonal relationships.	*"We proved to be gentle among you."*
H	**Hospitable**	**Lazarus** – John 12:2
	Home is open to help, share, love, and relate to both Christians and those of other beliefs. (Galatians 6:10)	*"Made Him a supper there…"*
I	**I – Ego – NOT self-willed**	**Boaz** – Ruth 3:13
	Freedom from stubbornness and selfish ambition that says: "I will" or "I am" or "My way."	*"If he will redeem you good…(if not) then I will redeem you."*
J	**Just**	**Ananias** – Acts 22:12
	Evidence of wisdom and understanding.	*"A man who was devout…and well spoken of…"*
K	**Knows how to Teach**	**Barnabas** – Acts 11:26
	Able to communicate life-changing principles through personal character development	*"…for an entire year they…taught…and the disciples were first called Christians at Antioch."*
L	**Loves what is good**	**Epaphras** – Colossians 4:12
	Thoughts are controlled by what is best for the development of others "to the image of Jesus Christ."	*"…laboring earnestly for you in his prayers that you may stand perfect."*
M	**Manages his household well**	**Cornelius** – Acts 10:2
	Has a oneness in spirit with "the wife of his youth" and children who live in obedience to Christ.	*"One who feared God with all his household, and gave many alms…and prayed to God continually."*

N	**Neighbors speak well of him**	**Philip** – Acts 6:3-5; 10:22
	Those outside the church community acknowledge that your reputation (outer image) is consistent with your beliefs (inner reality).	*"…select from among you…men of good reputation…and they chose…Philip."*
O	**One wife** – (Husband of)	**Noah** – Genesis 7:1 and 7
	Proven love and faithfulness in a redemptiverelationship with the "wife of your youth…" (1 Peter 3:7)	*"You alone have I seen to be righteous…then Noah and his sons and his wife…entered the ark."*
P	**Prudent**	**David** – 1 Samuel 16:18
	Humble behavior, disciplined, and appropriate to the situation.	*"…one prudent in speech…"*
Q	**Quick Tempered – NOT**	**Abel** – Hebrews 11:4
	Free from out-of-control anger	*"he obtained the testimony that he was righteous…though he is dead, he still speaks."*
R	**Respectable**	**Enoch** – Hebrews 11:5
	A well-behaved, orderly lifestyle	*"He was pleasing to God."*
S	**$ -- Free from the love of Money ($)**	**Moses** – Hebrews 11:26
	One recognizes the value and purpose of money without being in bondage to greed.	*"Considering the reproach of Christ greater riches than the treasures of Egypt."*
T	**Temperate**	**Paul** – 1 Corinthians 9:27
	One exercises a balanced, moderate, self-controlled pattern of living.	*"I buffet my body and make it my slave, lest possibly after I have preached to others I…be disqualified."*

U	**Uncontentious**						**Joseph** – Genesis 50:20-21
	One strives for unity without envy or jealousy or strife.	-	-	-	-	-	*"…God meant it for good…do not be afraid…so he comforted them and spoke kindly to them."*
W	**Wine – NOT addicted to**						**Lemuel** – Proverbs 31:4-7
	Freedom from personal addictions that have no value towards godly character development	-	-	-	-	-	*"It is not for Kings to drink wine, or for rulers to desire strong drink."*

	Add # in each column					
Total # of checks in each column	-	-	-	-	-	
Multiply	**X1**	**X2**	**X3**	**X4**	**X5**	
By						
Sub-Totals =	-	-	-	-	-	
TOTAL (add five sub-totals together)=			—			
Divided by 22 (Average) =			—			**= Your Score**

SUMMARY

1.0 — 1.5 = "Ye Must Be Born Again!" ☺

1.6 — 2.5 = Time For A Spiritual Overhaul

2.6 — 3.5 = Holy Spirit Has a Challenge

3.6 — 4.5 = Possible Candidate for Spiritual Leadership

4.6 — 5.0 = God's Measure of a Man

Competencies to Fulfill Role of LEADER

Personal Checklist
Circle the best answer for each to determine score

Do I have…

1. A personal commitment to being a 'servant' to those I am leading? (Mark 10:43-45)

1	2	3	4	5
Not at all	A little bit	Usually	Most of the time	Always

2. Recognition that any 'authority' I possess has been granted to me by God Himself? "[T]here is no authority except from God…" (Romans 13:1)

1	2	3	4	5
Not at all	A little bit	Usually	Most of the time	Always

3. Leadership skills related to planning, organizing, delegating, motivating, accountability, and evaluation? (Notice these skills in Christ's leadership with his disciples in Luke 9:1-10 and Luke 10:1-20.)

1	2	3	4	5
Not at all	A little bit	Usually	Most of the time	Always

4. The characteristics of being the *youngest/servant*? (Luke 22:25-30)

1	2	3	4	5
Not at all	A little bit	Usually	Most of the time	Always

5. Ability to use a variety of leadership styles based on an understanding of the needs and skills of the people, task to be done, and time available?

1	2	3	4	5
Not at all	A little bit	Usually	Most of the time	Always

6. Love for those being led and dedication to their personal development with the realization that my plans must be in accordance with those of God? *"A disciple is not above his teacher, nor a slave above his master."* (Matthew 10:24) **(How can a human leader have a goal or expect to exercise power that is beyond that of his creator? All leaders, to be effective, must be submissive to the ultimate goal and power and will of God.)**

1	2	3	4	5
Not at all	A little bit	Usually	Most of the time	Always

Total divided by 6 =

Evidences Role of LEADER Fulfilled

Personal Checklist
Circle the best answer for each to determine score

Have I demonstrated…

1. A group of people committed to supporting my leadership? (Watch the danger of this point as evidenced in Acts 5:35- 39. 'Followers' may prove the Role of Leader is being fulfilled but it does not indicate the quality or the effectiveness of the leader from a Biblical perspective. Both Theudas and Judas had 'followers.')

1	2	3	4	5
Not at all	A little bit	Usually	Most of the time	Always

2. Evidence that the members of the group are attaining their own goals to a level of personal satisfaction? (This is no reflection of the value of their goals.)

1	2	3	4	5
Not at all	A little bit	Usually	Most of the time	Always

3. Attainment of organizational goals and objectives? (Notice Joshua's decision as a leader in Joshua 24:15)

1	2	3	4	5
Not at all	A little bit	Usually	Most of the time	Always

4. Needs of group members being met along with the organization goals being attained? (Christ ministered to the needs of His disciples, while "doing the will of Him who sent me" (John 4:34).)

1	2	3	4	5
Not at all	A little bit	Usually	Most of the time	Always

5. Evidence of perseverance to accomplish the task? *"The end of a matter is better than its beginning."* (Ecclesiastes 7:8). **Notice the final words of Christ on the cross:** *"It is finished."* (John 19:30) **He had finished His purpose in coming to earth to do the will of His Father.**

Total divided by 5 =

Projects for Investigation and Discussion

[__] Locate Biblical evidence for occasions when Jesus Christ used each of the five Leadership Styles mentioned in this chapter.

[__] Prepare a definition of Leadership.

[__] Discuss: "Leadership is a Matter of Style." Do you agree or disagree?

[__] Interview three men in the role of a leader. Asks them to share with you their "Philosophy of Leadership." Share these findings with a group studying leadership.

[__] How do you account for the wide variety of personalities and abilities found among men who all claim to be pastor-teachers?

[__] Read a text on Leadership (i.e. *The Making of a Christian Leader* by Ted Engstrom.

Or *Servant Empowered Leadership* by Don Page). Discover principles of leadership to assist you in your role as leader.

[__] Who was the greatest Old Testament leader? Choose teams to work on a Leadership Case Study for each man suggested. Share ideas gained about the leadership qualities of each man. Note their strengths and their weaknesses.

[__] Consider the man who has been the greatest leader to you personally. Identify five character qualities in this man that caused you to recognize him. Why are they significant to you?

Chapter 12

Disciple • Relationship to His Lord

By this all men will know that you are My disciples, if you have love for one another" • John 13:35

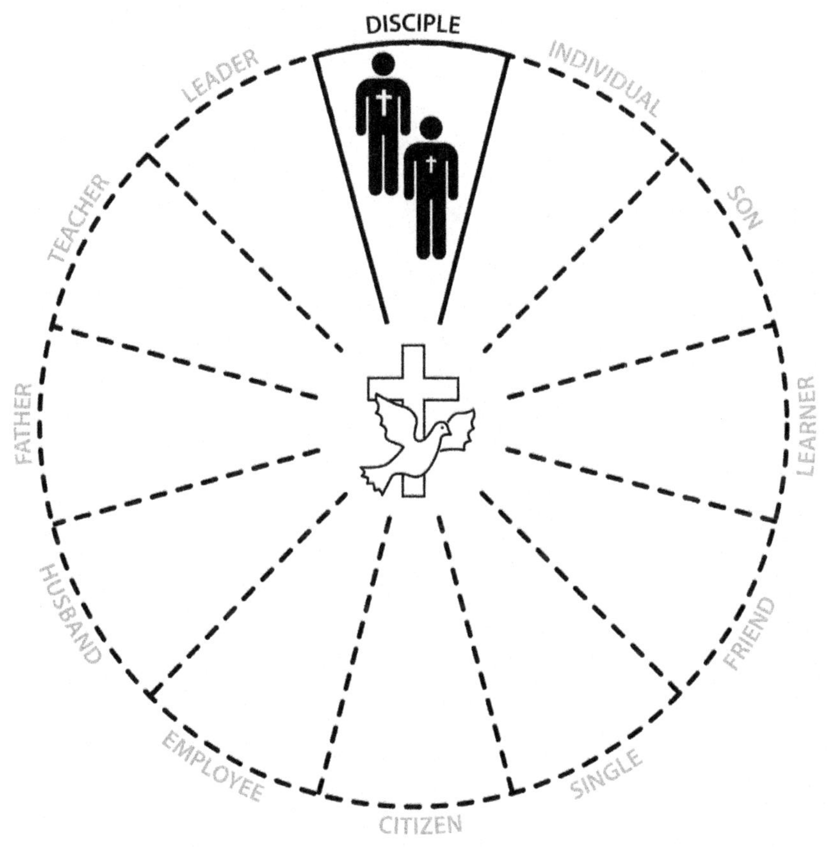

Forsake Not The Assembling of Yourselves Together

Story: In 1976 I had a vision to start a ministry for men called *Man Alive*. I had it all laid out, entailing a book, a monthly magazine, a weekly newspaper column for men, and conferences. The proposed goal was to equip (the word "empowering" was not as common in the 1970's) and enable men to be alive unto Christ. But with one phone call in 1979, it all came to an end. *"Cease and desist,"* was how the caller's lawyer worded it. The name I had chosen to register and the organization I was planning to create were deemed too closely identified with a woman's ministry called *Woman Alive.* They were planning to start a ministry to men using the name I had chosen! Like Moses running away after failing to free his fellow Hebrews in his own strength,[208] I ran away from the project. I went to Israel, finished my doctoral degree at the University of Toronto, moved to British Columbia, and taught at Trinity Western University. My "Men's Ministry" was buried in the sand, finished, so I thought. Now, here I am, some 40 years later, writing these thoughts with the Lord's help, for a new generation of men!

From my observation, some men appear to have greater fellowship and personal fulfillment outside their local Christian Church, than within their local assembly. So my brothers, let me make some observations for you as an older brother.

Observation #1 – Be an active participant and faithful supporter of your pastor and leaders in your local church.

I realize this can be a challenge. In my lifetime, I have experienced a variety of pastors in a diversity of denominations. Some pastors became strong personal friends. Some were good in the pulpit as a preacher, but weak in personal relationships. Either way, we continued to "go to church" as a family regardless of where we lived.

---

[208] See Exodus 2

Only once in 50 years did we ever choose to go to a new church because of theological differences. Virtually all the changes were due to moving or an internal change of pastors. No matter how hard it is, find and connect with a local group of believers. The scriptures are clear: *"not forsaking our own assembling together, as is the habit of some, but encouraging one another; and all the more as you see the day drawing near" (Hebrews 10:25).*

Men fulfilling their role as Disciples bring life to a local church. Show me a man who says, "I do not need a local church..." or "I don't attend church anymore..." and I will show you a man who is most likely ineffective in fulfilling his role as a Disciple.

I see three categories of Christian men in a local church. First are those in the "inner core." The heart of fellowship is to be as close to Jesus Christ, the Good Shepherd as possible. The closer you and I are to Jesus Christ, the closer we will be to one another as brothers in Christ (John 15).

The second category is the "middle majority." These brothers enjoy discussing their doctrinal distinctives. They like their method of worship so much so that they spend more time protecting their theological turf than drawing closer to the Master.

The third category is the "fanatical floaters." Like those spots that float on your eyeball, these men "float" in and out of churches. Now you see them, now they are gone. They always have an issue. The music is too loud. Need to sing more hymns and not repetitious choruses. Preaching is not good enough. People are not friendly enough. This group is a challenge for any disciple of Jesus Christ. Remember, churches are open to virtually everyone. The millionaire sits beside the welfare recipient. But, "fanatical floaters" are often narrow, legalistic separatists who are always right in their doctrinal distinctive and only fellowship with those who agree with them. Let's agree in advance—they are a challenge to love.

Story: We had one couple in one church who would faithfully come to church each week, stand up, raise their hands in worship, sing in a loud, monotone, out-of-tune voice, and then just before the pastor spoke they would walk out of the room and go home. One day, I had to satisfy my curiosity. I sat near them (enduring the "joyful noise" they made) and followed them when they left. "Why do you leave every week before the sermon?" I asked. "We do not agree with the teaching in this church," was the surprise answer. "But we have a variety of speakers. You never stay for any of them. Why do you come faithfully every week and loudly sing songs of worship out-of-tune?" I asked. "We were told to come and sing praises," was the answer. I often wondered who told them to come and to be disruptive. I once heard Pastor Chuck Swindoll say on a radio program: "When the Holy Spirit turns on the light of scripture, the light always seems to attract a few bugs!"

Observation #2 – Be Obedient and Walk Closely With Jesus.
"If we walk in the light as He is in the light we have fellowship with one another…"[209] And will walk together in the light. If two brothers are not able to fellowship, one of them is in the dark.

Story: In my years as a Christian, I have had some very close friendships with men. These I cherish. But I have also had some close friendships that drifted apart. The most obvious change in a friendship is when two brothers stop worshipping at the same church. One or both move geographically away from the other. The opportunities to be together diminish. That is only part of the reason. I have close friendships with men who live many miles, many hours away from my home. I have some friendships that have diminished with men just a walk away from my home. What makes the difference? As we said in the chapter on Friendship, a kindred-spirit relationship requires both brothers to be walking in the light of God's word.

[209] 1 John 1:9-10

I recently heard Pastor Tom Blackaby (son of renowned author Henry Blackaby) speak at an Iron Sharpens Iron Men's Conference. He made this statement: "I tell my church members, look at the person on both sides of you in church. Would you be willing to die for that person?" Tom bases this thinking on Romans 5:6-8. *"For while we were still weak, at the right time Christ died for the ungodly. For one will scarcely die for a righteous person—though perhaps for a good person one would dare even to die— but God shows his love for us in that while we were still sinners, Christ died for us."* Then Tom adds: "If you would not die for them, do you really love them?"

Observation #3 - Be Kind, Tenderhearted, Willing to Forgive.

Undeserved wounds come to each of us at some time in life. We cannot control the actions against us only our reactions to the event. We have the liberty to control how we respond to the hurt. Some respond with anger. Some try to escape, even resorting to substance abuse, anything to make the pain go away. Only the Holy Spirit can begin our recovery program and heal the wound by enabling us to forgive and eventually forget the pain. When you are able to forgive, you become a free person.

http://www.youtube.com/watch?v=czGP0klisdl

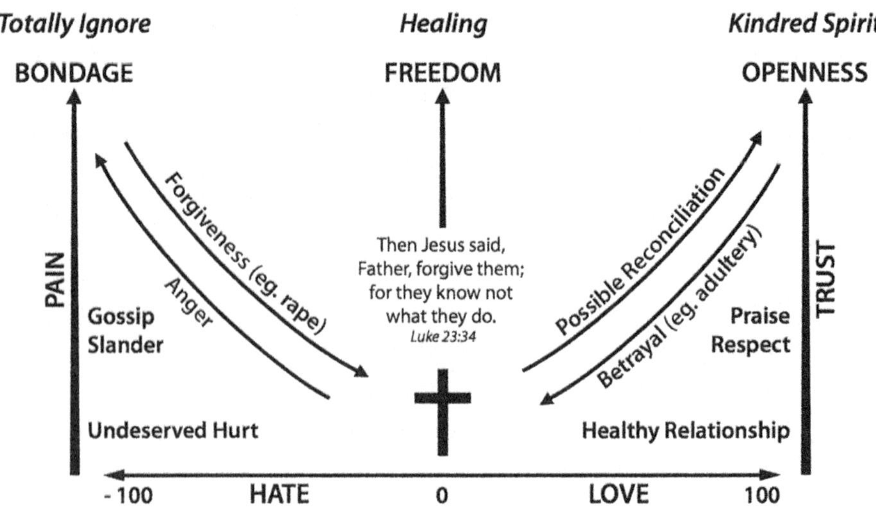

Observation #4 – Be a faithful disciple of Jesus Christ.

Our goal: To be conformed to the image of Jesus Christ. Our mandate: To *"preach the gospel"*[210] and do *"greater works"* [211] under the control of the Holy Spirit. Our methods: [212] To use biblically appropriate scriptures *"that I may know Him and the power of His resurrection and the fellowship of His sufferings, being conformed to His death; in order that I may attain to the resurrection from the dead."* [213]

For many men, the hardest time to be a Disciple of Jesus Christ is in times of solitude. In the Garden of Gethsemane before His betrayal, Jesus' disciples fell asleep. [214] He was alone. Then on the cross, as He took upon Himself the sins of the whole world, "*Jesus cried out with a loud voice, saying, 'Eli, Eli, lama sabachthani?' that is, 'My God, My God, why have You forsaken Me?'"* [215] Again He was alone.

Here is a quote etched on the wall of a German concentration camp in WW2 by a Jewish prisoner. It says:

---

[210] Matthew 28:18-20: "Jesus…said, 'All authority has been given to Me in heaven and on earth. Go therefore and make disciples of all the nations, baptizing them in the name of the Father and the Son and the Holy Spirit, teaching them to observe all that I commanded you; and lo, I am with you always, even to the end of the age.'"

[211] John 14:12-17: "Truly, truly, I say to you, he who believes in Me, the works that I do, he will do also; and greater works than these he will do; because I go to the Father. Whatever you ask in My name, that will I do, so that the Father may be glorified in the Son. If you ask Me anything in My name, I will do it. "If you love Me, you will keep My commandments. I will ask the Father, and He will give you another Helper, that He may be with you forever; that is the Spirit of truth, whom the world cannot receive, because it does not see Him or know Him, but you know Him because He abides with you and will be in you."

[212] Psalm 37:4 "Delight yourself also in the Lord, and He shall give you the desires of your heart" and 1 Timothy 4:7 "Discipline yourself for the purpose of godliness."

[213] Philippians 3:10-11.

[214] Matthew 26:40-41: "And He came to the disciples and found them sleeping, and said to Peter, 'So, you men could not keep watch with Me for one hour? Keep watching and praying that you may not enter into temptation; the spirit is willing, but the flesh is weak.'"

[215] Matthew 27:40

I believe in the sun,
even when it is not shining.
I believe in love,
even when I do not feel it.
I believe in God
even when He is silent.[216]

As we come near the end of this text, let me briefly offer what I see as spiritual disciplines that can be turned into spiritual delights.

DISCIPLINE #1 - THE BIBLE – ***God's Word is Authoritative*** **–** *"Your Word is a lamp to my feet..."* [217]

To approach God, we must believe that He exists and that He rewards those who diligently seek Him. God's Word is authoritative. God speaks to us as we read it. That's the amazing part of reading the Bible. We get to hear God speak, to hear His voice, and to choose to obey Him. Our greatest joy as a Disciple of Jesus Christ is to read, study, and obey God's Word. God's word speaks to us as we listen to it and read it.

DISCIPLINE #2 - WRITING – ***The Joy of Journaling*** – *"these things write..."*

Someone wrote every word in the Bible. They *"spoke from God, as they were carried along by the Holy Spirit."* [218] To write, as God reveals the thoughts, is a powerful way to recall what He is saying to us. Writing in a journal records God's words spoken to us from Scripture, nature, and conversations with friends. Words written today become our history when reading them tomorrow. One thought written can be retained longer than many thoughts unrecorded, no matter how well we retain thoughts. Journals become personal "history books" of how God works in our life. I re-read them periodically to try and learn from experiences and insights gained from my life adventures. The key is to begin writing...

---

[216] Source unknown

[217] Psalm 119:105

[218] 2 Peter 1:21b

Perhaps this is your first experience writing your thoughts. The first fear to overcome is that someone may read what you write today. True – they may, someday – but that is secondary to the value it has for you in writing it today. The second concern may be "What if I change my mind – or how I feel today? Will I be embarrassed by what I wrote or felt today?" Perhaps, but this is how you feel at this moment. Knowing how you think or feel today permits you to measure change or progress in the future and give God the glory for the improvement. Try it.

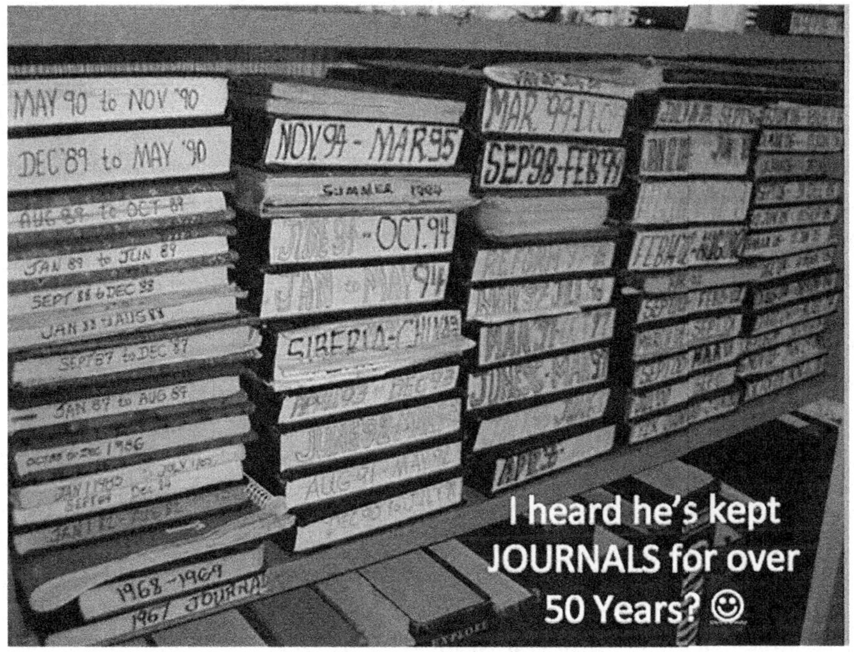

Author's Journals kept since 1967

DISCIPLINE #3 – STILLNESS/SILENCE/SOLITUDE

Quietness Precedes Knowledge – *"be still and know that I am God..."* [219]

Time Alone In Secret With The Lord – *"...could you not watch with me one hour?"*

Some men shudder to think of being alone to become a Disciple of Jesus Christ. But, it's in times of silence and solitude – to *be*

---

[219] Psalm 46:10

still and know [220] – that we hear that still, small voice of the Holy Spirit. Scriptures say that Heaven is *a prepared place.* (John 14). In essence, Heaven is a prepared place for prepared people. If we choose to spend eternity with God our Heavenly Father, we need to begin now (as His Disciples) to experience the joy of His presence and enjoy His fellowship. Psalm 23 says: *"He leads me beside the still waters."* As you walk beside still waters, you will notice the mirrored reflection of your image in the water. Calm water is required to see a clear reflection. The character image of Christ is reflected more clearly in our personality, for others to observe if we are still before the Lord. As the calmness of the water dissipates, so does the clarity of the reflection. Quietness and readiness in one's inner spirit precede knowing God. The God-centered life finds a balance between the severe isolated sacrifice of the ancient desert fathers and the hectic swamped service of the modern city saints. When God becomes the focus of our life, we lose any sense of fear and rush. Disciplined time with the Lord releases holy boldness for ministry.

It is a primary response for humans to fear:

* *Isolation - without amenities*
* *Being alone - without friends*
* *Hunger - without food*
* *Silence - without sounds*
* *The unknown - without control*

The Bible tells of many people the Lord used – after they spent a period alone with Him.

- **Jonah** – *The Ultimate Evangelist* – spent a three-day retreat in the belly of a whale – *alone with the Lord* (Book of Jonah).
- **Saul** – *The Exemplary Missionary* – spent a three-year study leave in the desert of Arabia, *alone with the Lord* (Galatians 1:11-2:1).

---

[220] Isaiah 30:15: "In repentance and rest you will be saved, In quietness and trust is your strength."

- **Joseph** – *The Gifted Administrator* – spent some time in prison *alone but "the Lord was with him,"* (He) showed him kindness and granted him favor ... the Lord was with Joseph and *"gave him success in what he did*" (Genesis 39:20-40:1).
- **Jeremiah** – *The Maligned Prophet* – spent time imprisoned in a vaulted cell in a dungeon, where he remained *a long time* (Jeremiah 37:16).
- **John** – *The Abandoned Apostle* – spent his remaining life *exiled on the Isle of Patmos "because of the Word of God and the testimony of Jesus*" (Revelation 1:9). It was here that the Lord spoke to him in a most compelling and unusual way to give us the Book of Revelation.

Inner Spiritual Practices teach us to be dependent on the living God and Father of our Lord Jesus Christ. The removal of physical distractions and our focused orientation to the truth of God's word permits one to experience first the presence of God and then grow to know the person of God.

Paul said: *"I want to know Christ and the power of His resurrection and the fellowship of sharing in His sufferings, becoming like Him in His death and so somehow to attain to the resurrection from the dead."*[221] Isaiah wrote: *"This is what the Sovereign Lord, the Holy one of Israel says: In repentance and rest is your salvation. In quietness and trust is your strength, but you would have none of it."* [222] When we confess our faults to God, we recognize our need to keep our relationships clear with God.

Jesus practiced Stillness, Silence and Solitude on a number of occasions.

- Matthew 4:1 – to establish the mandate given to him by God
- Matthew 14:13 – after a time of grief
- Matthew. 14:23 – for a time of communion with the Father
- Mark. 1:35 – to pray before a primary preaching assignment

---

[221] Philippians 3:10-11

[222] Isaiah 30:21

- Luke. 4:42 – after a spiritual victory / before changing locations for ministry
- Luke 6:12-19 – before choosing his 12 Apostles.

Stillness / Silence / Solitude is time *away*—away from people, cell phones, computers, TV!

Stillness / Silence / Solitude is time *alone*—to pray with time to listen

Stillness / Silence / Solitude is time *with God*—and He chooses to bless us *through it.*

DISCIPLINE #4 - LISTENING - ***The Necessity of Listening*** - *"speak Lord for your servant heareth"*

Listening may be the most important tool you can use in helping a person or hearing God speak from His Scriptures into your need at this moment. The listener needs to permit the speaker to talk at his or her own pace. Allow the speaker to share their story with full attention (not while looking out the window). Often people listen just long enough for the speaker to take a breath and then interrupt with "their story!"

DISCIPLINE #5 - EXAMINATION - ***Forgiveness, Freedom, and Possible Reconciliation*** - *"let a man examine himself..."* [See Discipline #3 earlier in this chapter]

"I tell you, whatever you ask for in prayer, believe that you have received it, and it will be yours. And when you stand praying if you hold anything against anyone, forgive him, so that your Father in heaven may forgive your sins" [223] Inner Spiritual Practices turn into Spiritual Delights when we have a clean heart. *"Create in me a clean heart O God, and renew a right spirit within me."* [224]

DISCIPLINE #6 - MEMORIZATION - ***The Delight of Scripture Memorization*** - *"this book...shall not depart"*

[223] Mark 11:24-25

[224] Psalm 51:10

Whitney, in his helpful book **Spiritual Disciplines for the Christian Life**, identifies proven benefits of memorization:

- Memorization Supplies Spiritual Power – Ps. 119:11
- Memorization Strengthens Your Faith – Pr. 22:17-19
- Memorization Supports Witnessing & Counseling – Acts 2:14-40
- Memorization Provides Spiritual Guidance – Ps. 119:24
- Memorization Stimulates Meditation – Ps. 119:97

DISCIPLINE #7 - MEDITATION - *The Means and Methods of Meditation* – "you shall meditate day and night."

"May the words of my mouth and the meditation of my heart be pleasing in your sight O Lord, my Rock and my Redeemer." [225] Unlike New Age / Eastern religious meditations where one clears the mind or relaxes or empties oneself, Christian meditation involves filling your mind with God and truth and good things.[226] Acts 9:17 says to *"be filled with the Holy Spirit..."* According to Philippians 4:8 we are to identify things to think about (meditate) that are: true, noble, just, pure, lovely, good report, have virtue, and are praiseworthy.

DISCIPLINE #8 - PRAYER - *When you Pray...The Master's Model* – *"teach us to pray."*

The astronomer Dr. Hugh Ross says: "Because we are spiritual beings, we humans can pray. Through prayer, we can cross the space-time manifold of the cosmos and converse with God in His extra-dimensional realm. Because prayer is extra dimensional in its reach, it must be considered the most powerful capacity God has made available to us in our current [four] dimensional context. [Length, Width, Height & Time]. Prayer is so powerful; it comes with special cautions and restrictions on its use." [227]

---

[225] Psalm 19:14

[226] Joshua 1:8 – Whitney, Spiritual Disciplines for the Christian Life, p.43

[227] Hugh Ross, Beyond The Cosmos – 1996 p.123

DISCIPLINE #9 - GIVING - When you Give...Give in Secret

In the SSTS [228] text compiled with my lifelong friend Paul Estabrooks we said: "Materialism is the attitude that says money, property, possessions, physical comforts, as well as worldly fame and honor, are the most important things in life. Not to say, 'There is no God,' but to say, 'We don't have any need for God!'"

Materialism is the subtlest trap of Satan. We can have all the Christian externals and yet be complete materialists in our hearts. For Christians, materialism is much like the frog in a pan of water that is slowly heated. He boils to death because he does not realize the danger quickly enough to jump out of the pot before it is too late.

In Matthew's Gospel (Chapter 6) Jesus teaches us to give to the needy. *"Beware of practicing your righteousness before other people to be seen by them, for then you will have no reward from your Father who is in heaven. Thus, when you give to the needy, sound no trumpet before you, as the hypocrites do in the synagogues and in the streets, that others may praise them. Truly, I say to you, they have received their reward. But when you give to the needy, do not let your left hand know what your right hand is doing, so that your giving may be in secret. And your Father who sees in secret will reward you"* – (Matthew 6:1-4 ESV).

There are two opposing masters on Earth: God and Money. You are a slave to the one you obey. [229]

[228] Standing Strong Through the Storm, Paul Estabrooks and Jim Cunningham, Open Doors International, 2nd ed. 2016.

[229] Matthew 6:24; Romans 6:16

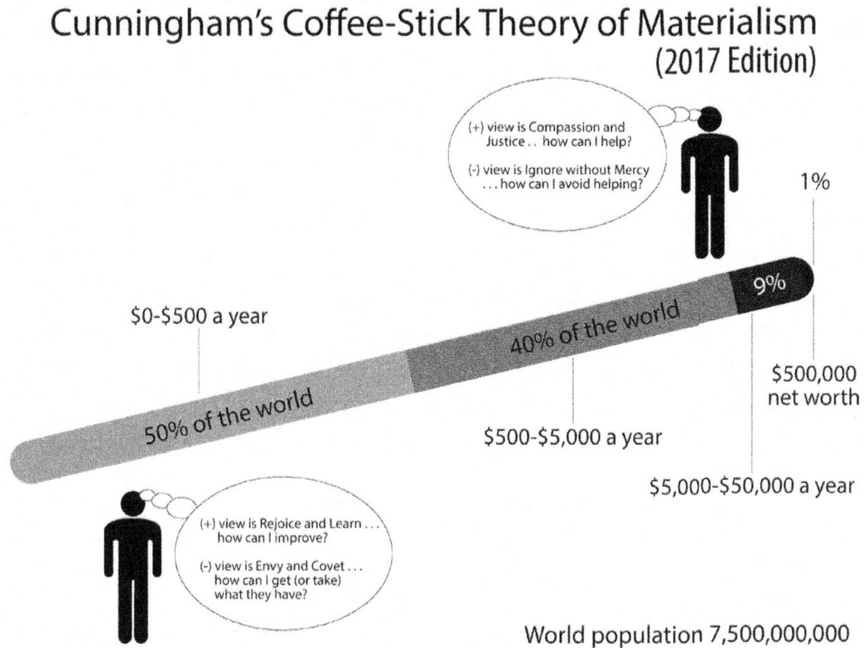

To compare down, with those who have less, creates one of two attitudes: The positive view is compassion and justice thinking: "How can I help?" The negative view is to ignore without mercy thinking: "How can I avoid helping?" The opposite of love is not always hate – it is also to ignore!

To compare up, with those who have more, generates one of two attitudes: The positive view is to rejoice and learn, thinking: "How can I improve? Teach me." The negative view is envy, thinking: "How can I get (or take) what they have?" And who of us has never envied?

This graphic gets an amazing variety of responses depending where I show it. It helps some who tend to think of themselves as poor to see that when they step off the plane in another country they are wearing eyeglasses worth more than some annual salaries. They may also have a laptop computer worth more than annual income for half the world! And some buy return airline tickets worth enough to identify themselves as part of the "upper-10%"! Many in North America are currently (may change soon) among the world's rich just by virtue of birth! Am I complaining? No. Am I rejoicing? Yes. Do I know what to do about it? Follow my own chart I guess!

"*When you give…when you pray…*(and) *when you fast…"* is the expectation of our Lord's teaching in Matthew 6. Not "if you give… if you pray…and if you fast." Giving, praying and fasting are among the most private, secret and personal of spiritual practices…and the most misunderstood. Those who fail to practice these delights in secret with a humble attitude can become like pharisaical sounding brass and legalistic tinkling cymbals.

DISCIPLINE #11 - FASTING - *When you Fast - The Purpose of Fasting*

Matthew 6:16-18 (ESV) *says: "And when you fast, do not look gloomy like the hypocrites, for they disfigure their faces that their fasting may be seen by others. Truly, I say to you; they have received their reward. But when you fast, anoint your head and wash your face, that your fasting may not be seen by others but by your Father who is in secret. And your Father who sees in secret will reward you."*

Fasting in our society is tough to do without spiritual superiority and pride creeping in with the hunger pangs! The very fact that 2 Chronicles leaves fasting out of the repentance equation is significant to me. Isaiah 58 identifies the kind of true fasting the Lord wants: with compassion and obedience against injustice and oppression—along with abstaining from food.

Psalm 16 takes on a whole new meaning during a fast especially verse 11: *"…In Your presence is fullness of joy…"* (NASV). Fasting is the total abstinence from all food for a definite period. (From the old English word *"faesten"* meaning firm or fixed: hold firm under fixed conditions.)

Physical Benefits of Fasting

- *Promotes weight discipline;*
- *Provides physiological rest (digestive, glandular, circulatory, respiratory systems);*
- *Allows elimination of wastes/toxins and purification of blood and lymph systems; and*
- *Overall revitalization.*

Spiritual Benefits of Fasting

- *Time to be alone with the Lord "in His presence."*
- *A humbling of oneself before the Lord in prayer.*
- *A heightened level of spiritual sensitivity, alertness, and discernment.*
- *A time of personal re-examination of one's motives, goals, and values*

Story: I am not a mystic. Neither am I the son of a mystic. But fasting remains an integral part of my spiritual journey. I recall my first "Day of Prayer & Fasting" back in my Bible College days. It proved to me that one could go more than eight hours without food—and not die! For the first 20 years or more of my marriage, I did not drink coffee so there was no caffeine withdrawal to cause headaches whenever I fasted. Most of my first fasts were for a particular purpose. To write my final doctoral dissertation at the University of Toronto, in 1981, I headed to the Crieff Hills Community Center near Puslich, Ontario for seven days of fasting and fast non-stop writing. During my sojourn at Cedar Springs (in USA) in 1990, I began drinking coffee again. Since then during each fast, whether three, seven, ten days, plus one 28-day fast in 1995 and eventually a 40-day fast in 1997, the first three days remain the hardest. The body has to get over the caffeine withdrawal, headaches, and tiredness that come with the first three days. From then on – Day 4 to Day 40 – the stomach gives up and ceases sending messages to the brain, so the hunger pangs disappear. My 40-day fast did include clear fruit juices. It helps if your water is bottled without chlorine and fluoride. Live with the bad breath. Chewing gum and sucking breath mints only send sugar and saliva to your stomach, creating a false expectation of food – and may create extra gas! Fasting permits time to focus on spiritual renewal; specific intercessory goals for family and country; solitude and silence before the Lord; and a time to listen to Him speak from His word. A highlight experience during the 40-Day Fast occurred three times: twice at Cedar Springs and once in my car between Cedar Springs and Lynden on the East Badger Road. I sensed the over-powering smell of "fresh bread." I can only suggest that Jesus Christ, the "Bread of Life," was there with me in a very significant manner. I cherish the time alone with Him.

DISCIPLINE #12 - SPIRITUAL FORCES - Spiritual Warfare - *"let this mind be in you."*

What is the relationship between Spiritual Practices and Spiritual Warfare? It appears that in post-Pentecost believers, there is no known example of a believer in Jesus Christ being possessed by a demon or by the devil. 1 John 4:4 says: *"You…are from God and have overcome them* [v.3 – every spirit that does not acknowledge Jesus is not from God…] *because the one who is in you* [the Holy Spirit – the Spirit of truth] *is greater than the one who is in the world"* [the devil – the spirit of falsehood]. Strengthening our Inner Spiritual Practices helps us deal with Anger (Ephesians 4:26-27), Selfishness and Greed (Jude 11-13), Temptation (James 1:14), and Pride (Proverbs 11:2).

DISCIPLINE #13 – HUMILITY - To Be and Become vs. To Do and Be Gone - *"He Humbled Himself…"*

"Do nothing out of selfish ambition or vain conceit, but in *humility* consider others better than yourselves. Each of you should look not only to your own interests, but also to the interests of others. Our attitude should be the same as that of Christ Jesus: who being in very nature God, did not consider equality with God something to be grasped, but made himself nothing, taking the very nature of a servant, being made in human likeness. *And being found in appearance as a man, he humbled himself and became obedient to death – even death on a cross. Therefore God exalted him to the highest place and gave him the name that is above every name, that at the name of Jesus every knee should bow, in heaven and on earth and under the earth, and every tongue confess that Jesus Christ is Lord, to the glory of God the Father"* (Philippians 2:1-11).

DISCIPLINE #14 - WORSHIP - *Enter His Gates With Thanksgiving in Your Heart*

Have you ever heard a Worship Leader say to a congregation usually just before a song: "Are you ready to worship?" What does he mean? Usually he means, "We are now going to clap our hands, raise our arms, and sing loudly. We are going to make a joyful noise unto the Lord…"

But is that what the Bible means by worship? Worship includes many of the previous topics considered.

- *Giving* is an act of Worship
- *Meditation* is an act of Worship
- *Praying* is an act of Worship
- *Fasting* is an act of Worship and
- *Reading Scripture* is an act of Worship as is Singing!
- *Even enjoying a beautiful Sunset* can become an act of worship.

DISCIPLINE #15 - REMEMBERING - *Encouraging Yourself in the Lord*

Have you ever noticed how many times in Scripture we are told to remember something? *Our greatest battles/calamities/tests often come just moments before our greatest blessings!* So be encouraged. We may not know how we will handle stressful situations with the pressures on us, but God is in control. He will, on His timeline, lift us out of the despair of Ziklag into the palace of His anointing. In the meantime, our goal is to *"find strength in the Lord our God"* (1 Samuel 30:6b).

As we conclude the role of a man as a Disciple of Jesus Christ, we come to the hardest part of being an active practitioner of the role. Scripture says: *"Clothe yourselves with humility."* We must become what God allows us to become and let others observe the progress. A weightlifter rarely talks about "how much" he lifts. He wears a T-shirt that shows the results!

Those who practice these Spiritual Disciplines the most effectively will over a period of time be seen as humble saints on earth, knowing that everything they are and everything they have achieved is a gift from God. They understand adversity and suffering. They understand pain and sorrow. And they exhibit grace and humility. Humility may well be the hardest of all character qualities to obtain. Pride dies slowly. Ego loves the attention. And others always have plans for your giftedness.

Two Proverbs encourage us to serve Christ until we see Him face-to-face:

- *"He who ignores discipline* (Spiritual Practices) *despises himself, but whoever heeds correction gains understanding. The fear of the Lord teaches a man wisdom, and humility comes before honor"* (Proverbs 15:32-33).

- *"Humility and the fear of the Lord bring wealth and honor and life"* (Proverbs 22:4).

All Men Will Know

John 13:35 can become a powerful life verse. *"By this all men will know that you are My disciples, if you have love for one another…"* Notice what is ***not*** included to be a Disciple.

Academic Intelligence – Nowhere does scripture suggest you must have a Doctorate degree from a University to become a Disciple of Jesus Christ or be an academic genius to teach others. The early Disciples were *"ignorant and unlearned men"* who had been with Jesus. When a man genuinely loves people it shows each time he meets another person. They find him easy to like.

Some may regard him as easy-going, naïve, even *earthy,* but this man loves people. He has no fear of them for his perfect love has cast out fear. Some of the highest academics live in fear! They are afraid of people, afraid of failure, afraid of communicating incorrectly. Ultimately they are afraid of themselves.

Personal Wealth – While many men mentioned in Scripture were wealthy (Abraham, Job, Solomon) the more typical men used by God included shepherds, farmers, and fishermen. The famous John D. Rockefeller found himself wasting away with an unhealthy body, unable to be cured by doctors. One day, he decided "If I am going to die, I might as well give away my money while I am alive to the people I want to help." So he began giving away his money. The story goes that by the time he had set up the Rockefeller Foundation his health had improved. His mind was off himself and on helping others.

> Story: In my lifetime, I have been blessed to stay overnight in hundreds of homes. Some were luxurious homes owned by millionaires equipped with servants and multiple toilets. Others were simple homes owned by people of modest means living in Northern Canada. Personal wealth, or lack thereof, is one of the least criteria in selecting or assessing a Disciple of Jesus Christ. I pray we remember that when appointing Elders in our churches.

Public Fame – *"Isn't that ?" (Insert name).* While it is always exciting to meet someone who is famous, it's more common to meet genuine saints who are plain, ordinary, and unknown. The great shock in Heaven will be the number of ordinary little men who are there. The Bible records names of unknown men like Aquilla, Epaphras, Tychius, and Rufus, whose primary recognition is based on their faithfulness as Disciples of Jesus Christ.

The greatest *thorn-in-the-flesh* to the Apostle John (the Disciple whom Jesus loved and who is recording the phrase we are studying) was a man named Diotrephes. Diotrephes was one of the leaders in an assembly to which John was writing. He had one major disqualifying character quality. He *"loved to be first among them."* Diatrophes disqualified himself as a Disciple of Jesus Christ by seeking fame for himself rather than love for those he served. It takes a wise man to handle fame and humility.

Dr. Gary Collins[230] offers ten items he believes a man needs to be "great" as a Disciple of Jesus Christ:

- Strive for excellence. Do the best you can with the abilities you have.
- Be dissatisfied with injustice, lack of growth, and no change.
- Be a visionary. Where there is no vision you will perish.
- Be action-oriented. Stick your neck out for what needs to be done.
- Be a communicator – of truth, feeling, warmth, and love.
- Be self-disciplined in studying, reading, writing, eating, sleeping, and working.
- Be persistent. Stick to a task.
- Be balanced. In family, work, social activities, mental growth.
- Be under the control of the Holy Spirit.
- Be humble. God resists the proud but gives grace to the humble.

It's a continual amazement to see what God can do in the life of one person who seeks to be fully surrendered to Him. Let me tell you about the changes that took place in one man!

He is a public speaker today. Yet during his first public speech in Grade Nine English Class, he took one look at his classmates, began to cry, looked out the window, and told a tree *The History of the Newspaper* for five minutes. Needless to say, the tree received the message with mixed emotions. The young man was embarrassed and thought he would never speak in public again.

[230] Author's personal notes from an address entitled: "The Essence of Greatness," given by Dr. Gary Collins at the Wheaton Scholastic Honor Society, Wheaton College, Wheaton IL, November 1976.

He is a writer. Yet he had to repeat a year of High School English Composition to graduate. He could *dangle a participle* so far over the edge of a *split infinitive* that he usually changed tenses in the middle of his run-on sentences. The only thing he knew about a preposition and a pronoun was that one of them was the wrong word to end a sentence with!

He is a lifelong learner. Yet he was not admissible to University immediately after High School because his grades were too low. He was able to enroll in Teacher's College and become an Elementary Teacher back in the 1960's because there were so many children and so few teachers!

He is an avid outdoorsman. Yet in High School he was barely able to run 100 yards (pre-metric) in less than 17 seconds! *Flash* was not his High School nickname. Yet he completed the Sea of Galilee Marathon, Outward Bound, and a two-week canoe trip in Tweedsmuir Wilderness. He backpacked ten days through the Northern Cascade Mountains, canoed five days down the Columbia River and another five days on Murtle Lake in British Columbia.

He is an International Consultant in Adult Education. Yet up to age 21 he had never been more than a few hundred miles from his home. Now he has taught adults and visited over 45 countries.

He is an avid follower of politics and ran for public office. He views running to be a Federal Member of Parliament (in Canada) as *the-Olympics-of-politics* and to compete a high honor and evidence of trust even through he lost by a narrow margin.

He is happily married for 50 years to the same wife, with two sons and five grandchildren. Yet as a single man he always feared he would not find *Mrs. Right.*

He is spiritually alive. Yet for many years he was out of fellowship with his Heavenly Father – and many people.

What caused all these changes? One day this man knelt down and said to Jesus Christ: "Lord, I give up. My life is going nowhere under my control. I surrender to You as my Lord and Savior. Please forgive me of my disobedient and selfish ways. I ask You to live inside me and make me the kind of man You want me to be. You rule me, Lord. Fill me with Your Holy Spirit and use me to Your Glory – anyway You choose! Amen."

How do I know all of this?
Simple.
I am that man!
Jesus Christ is my Lord.

With His help, all men will know that He is able to change anyone into the kind of man he was intended to be by the *Master-Plan and Power* of His Holy Spirit.

"Iron sharpens iron, so one man sharpens another." [231]

I appreciate the men who have discipled me in my lifetime. Sure there were days when I wondered what was going on. Or times when I was discouraged and ready to pack up and move to Dubai! But let me assure you, now that I am older, God's way is *"good, acceptable and perfect..."* and a lot more exciting. I can show you a list of jobs I applied for and never obtained. And I can tell you of jobs I never formally applied for, but obtained, enjoyed, and grew by doing them. Here are some of my "Discipling" brothers who invested heavily as mentors in my life.

- **Norman Mills** – Maternal Grandpa Mills mentored me until I was 21. He embedded my love for the outdoors and all the joys of hunting, fishing, camping, gardening—and honey!
- **Harold Cunningham** – Dad taught me faith *without* his eyesight. To persevere and keep faith in Christ without always understanding why things happen the way they do.
- **Andy Kozakavich** – Administrator friend at Green Meadows Elementary School, Etobicoke, ON. The classiest, most

[231] Proverbs 27:17

gifted, hardworking eventual Superintendent of Schools you'd ever want to meet who encouraged me to "follow my passion for teaching."

- **Mel Johnson** – Toronto Pastor and later Host of Young World Radio, Minneapolis, MN. Mel first led me to the Lord at age 9 and later turned my life around spiritually at age 21. He sent me a hand-written letter every October 24 until the year he died, reminding me of my decision to serve Jesus Christ on October 24, 1964.
- **Paul "Pablo" Estabrooks** – Lifetime friend, brother, peer mentor, and "Best Man" at my wedding. We've been everywhere in over 30 countries together, teaching, serving, laughing, and loving life together as kindred spirits.
- **David Bell** – Favorite Education Faculty at London College of Bible and Missions, London, ON. Dave taught me to keep viewing life through the lens of scripture.
- **Don Merrett** – Met when I was 21. He became my Western Divisional Director with Christian Service Brigade, Winnipeg, MB, and eventually my lifelong mentor till he passed at age 92! Don shared his diplomatic passion for loving people, gently sharing his faith, and praying without ceasing till God gave the answer.
- **Herb Brandt** – Pastor at Richmond Bethel MB Church, Richmond, BC. Herb became more than a pastor. He became a friend, a business partner, and a wise counselor.
- **Eitan Israeli** – Adult Education dissertation advisor at the Hebrew University, Rehovot, Israel. Eitan and I share a mutual respect and kindred spirit for each other's faith journey.
- **Harro VanBrummelen** – Dean of Education at Trinity Western University, Langley, BC. Harro was a brother, an encourager, and an exceptionally gifted mentor.
- **John Bargen** – Founder of Cedar Springs Christian Retreat Center, Sumas, WA. I've watched John model his spirit of generosity from 1970 to the writing of this book.
- **Brother Andrew** – Founder of Open Doors International, Harderjik, Holland. A treat to read Andrew's books, visit his home, and have "iron-sharpens-iron" dialogues related to

serving our Lord Jesus Christ during his visits in Canada. A remarkable model of vision.

To each of you – and a host of other men, too numerous to name – I say: "THANKS!"

May the thoughts shared in this chapter and the full book move both of us in the direction of becoming a Disciple of Jesus Christ – Men Alive Unto God – until we see Him *"face-to-face."* [232]

[232] The CSB Watchword at the close of each meeting said: "Now we trust in God to keep us, bright and keen for Christ, because we love Him, because we want to serve Him, until we see Him face-to-face." Amen.

Competencies to Fulfill Role of DISCIPLE

Personal Check List
Circle the best answer for each to determine score

Do I have…

1. **A personal acceptance by faith of Jesus Christ as the Son of God who died for my sins and rose to live in me?** (Romans 10:9-10)

1	2	3	4	5
Not at all	A little bit	Usually	Most of the time	Always

2. **Commitment to the Scripture as being the inspired Word of God, my final authority in faith and practice?** (2 Timothy 3:16-17)

1	2	3	4	5
Not at all	A little bit	Usually	Most of the time	Always

3. **My personal life goals and desires of my heart conforming to that *"good and acceptable and perfect will of God"*?** (Romans 12:1-2; Matthew 7:21)

1	2	3	4	5
Not at all	A little bit	Usually	Most of the time	Always

4. **An attitude of humility and a pure heart?** (James 4:8-10)

1	2	3	4	5
Not at all	A little bit	Usually	Most of the time	Always

5. A desire to obey the commandments of Jesus Christ, especially that of "loving one another"? (1 John 3:24, and John 14:35)

1	2	3	4	5
Not at all	A little bit	Usually	Most of the time	Always

Total divided by 5 =

Evidences Role of DISCIPLE Fulfilled

Personal Check List
Circle the best answer for each to determine score

Have I demonstrated…

1. A willingness to forgive others? (Matthew 6:14-15)

1	2	3	4	5
Not at all	A little bit	Usually	Most of the time	Always

2. Freedom from guilt and forgiveness from God for past evidences of personal disobedience and rebellion? (1 John 1:5-10)

1	2	3	4	5
Not at all	A little bit	Usually	Most of the time	Always

3. Improved relationships with people through healed conflicts and restoration for wrongs committed (Colossians 3:12-17)

1	2	3	4	5
Not at all	A little bit	Usually	Most of the time	Always

4. An observable reduction in my life of:

* anger (__) * wrath (__) * malice (__)

* slander (__) * bitterness (__) * envy ( )

* hypocrisy (__) * guile (__) * lying (__)

1	2	3	4	5
Not at all	A little bit	Usually	Most of the time	Always

5. A greater measure of:

* love (__) * joy (__) * peace (__)

* kindness (__) * goodness (__) * patience (__)

* gentleness (__) * self-control (__) * faithfulness (__)

* humility (__) * compassion (__)

(Galatians 5:22-23; and Colossians 3:12)

1	2	3	4	5
Not at all	A little bit	Usually	Most of the time	Always

6. An increasing fulfilment of the "Universal Responsibilities Towards All Men" (see Appendix A)?

1	2	3	4	5
Not at all	A little bit	Usually	Most of the time	Always

7. Boldness and courage to stand for principles and lifestyle values that are in accordance with God's Word? (1 Thessalonians 5:21-22)

1	2	3	4	5
Not at all	A little bit	Usually	Most of the time	Always

8. Practical evidences of the qualities of Spiritual Leadership developed within me as I mature in Christ? (See Chapter 11 on God's Criteria for Spiritual Leaders; 1 Timothy 3:1-7; and Titus 1:6-9.)

1	2	3	4	5
Not at all	A little bit	Usually	Most of the time	Always

9. A desire, backed by appropriate action, to bring about restored relationships with those who are in spiritual error? (Matthew 18:12-35)

1	2	3	4	5
Not at all	A little bit	Usually	Most of the time	Always

10. Recognition of the Holy Spirit working through the gifts He has given me to enable me to be more effective in my witness for Christ and ministry to the body of Christ? (1 Peter 4:10-11)

1	2	3	4	5
Not at all	A little bit	Usually	Most of the time	Always

11. Practical opportunities for me to share with "those of the household of faith": helping widows, and fatherless through hospitality, financial assistance, and visits? (Galatians 6:10 and James 1:27).

1	2	3	4	5
Not at all	A little bit	Usually	Most of the time	Always

Total divided by 11 =

Role of DISCIPLE

Projects for Investigation and Discussion

[__] Complete Appendix A on *The Universal Responsibilities Toward All Men.* Fill in the spaces with the names of individuals that will make the exercise personal and appropriate.

[__] Romans 8:28 says: *"we know that God causes all things to work together for good to those who love God, to those who are called according to His purposes."* Share an experience from your life where you can now look back on an apparent tragedy and see how God has subsequently worked out His good and acceptable and perfect will.

[__] Discover examples of God's dealing with disobedience in the Old and New Testament. Why is disobedience of such a major concern to God and us as His disciples? (Notice 1 Samuel 15:22-23).

[__] Identify attitudes, relationships and priorities that a man should have towards 1) his local church and 2) the ministries of para-church organizations.

[__] "Fellowship with believers of 'other churches' is necessary and valid for personal Christian growth as a disciple." Debate the benefits and dangers of the above statement.

[__] Study Romans 6:1-11. Verse 11 says, *"Even so consider yourselves to be dead to sin, but alive to God in Christ Jesus."* Identify how we can be men who are *"alive unto God in Christ Jesus."*

APPENDIX A

Responsibilities to all Men

The **BIBLE** is *God's Owner Manual* giving us ***B**asic **I**nstructions **B**efore **L**eaving **E**arth*.

The Bible is a *Spirit-Directed Guide* on how a man is to function. When a relationship is not running smoothly or when an attitude is bent the wrong way or when an ill feeling is plugging the tubes, it's time to Check the Owner's Manual – REBOOT – and begin again!

The Holy Spirit is like our internal technician, our IT specialist. He practices preventive maintenance with our attitudes and actions to become conformed to the image of Jesus Christ.

Consider the steps for how we learn a skill, any skill:

Step 1 – **Observe** someone else doing it.
Step 2 – **Decide** (internally) that we want to learn that skill.
Step 3 – **Attempt** the skill on our own and fail to be as successful as we would like to be.
Step 4 – **Seek** advice and guidance from a respected person who has mastered the skill.
Step 5 – **Listen** to the Master's instructions of what to do and how to do it.
Step 6 – **Watch** how he does it.
Step 7 – **Practice** under his guidance, supervision, and control.
Step 8 – **Listen** to the evaluation or assessment of our effort.
Step 9 – **Repeat** until satisfied you can do it on our own.
Step 10 – **Do** the skill subconsciously.
Step 11 – **Gain** self-confidence and lose embarrassment.
Step 12 – **Discover** ways to improve your skill.
Step 13 – **Help** others learn the skill.

From the Core Responsibilities listed in the 12 Primary Roles there emerged a list of Internal Attitudes and External Actions that appear to apply to all Christian men, in any country, in any culture, at any time in history. Romans 12:18 says: "*If possible, so far as it depends on you, be at peace with all men.*" But, I know, as the author of this text, that there are men out there who are tough hombres to live with and even harder – seemingly impossible – to love. They have an ideology, belief, attitude, mannerism, appearance or just a cynical sneer that turns us off.

What are we to do with these guys? How are we to respond to them? Do we:

- **Avoid them?** The opposite of Love is NOT Hate. The opposite of Love is to ignore. To hate someone, we must admit they exist. To ignore them is to say, "They have gone behind the sun. I do not see them. They do not exist."
- **Slander them?** Nearly every person on Earth has one friend, or in some cases hundreds of friends who think different to my assessment of this guy. They like him. All we can hope to do is slander his name or reputation so they will take up our reproach and maybe not like him.
- **Judge them?** This only reveals our inner anger and insensitivity to the trained observer.
- **Criticize them?** They usually have some redeeming virtues beyond whatever we do not like about them.
- **Hate them?** That just burns out our innards and destroys us, not them.
- **Plan against them?** No, we are God's children. He will look after the vengeance part!
- **Kill them?** The consequences of this are considerably worse than any current difficulty!

Look at the following list of *Responses and Responsibilities* found in the Bible. The word *response* comes from the Latin *"spondere"* meaning, *"to promise."* A response is *a way to act* in fulfillment of a pledge. Responsibility is an obligation or a promise that a person has to fulfill that in turn makes him accountable to someone for his action, behavior or assigned task.

Jesus said: *"If you love me, you will keep my commandments"* (John 14:15). We are responsible to God our Heavenly Father and our Creator! We are to show God that we know how to live with one another as He planned. He gave us the Holy Spirit to help us have the grace and wisdom and love to "do it!" (See Isaiah 55:11.) It's possible!

Assignment

The following list of *Responsibilities* is numbered from 1 to 22. The first few are innate responses related to our attitudes towards people. The next items are external responses related to our actions towards other people. Jesus called the Pharisees hypocrites because they were applying action without the proper attitude of the heart.

1. Read each response and the scripture that gives evidence for our responsibility.

2. Think of a person with whom you feel the least amount of this kind of a response. Let's call him your *LLP (Least Liked Person)*.

3. Write the person's name in the space beside the response.

4. Pray and ask God to forgive you for any previous wrong response to this person in this area. (Matthew 6:14-15 and 1 John 1:9).

5. Ask God to give you the grace to fulfill a particular action that would positively alter your relationship to this LLP.

Notice that the attitudes and actions are somewhat parallel to the characteristics of an Elder! In essence, all Christian men are to develop (aspire to attain) the godly character of an Elder.

Ready?

Internal Responses of Attitude

1. Love Them

"By this, all men will know that you are my disciples if you have love for one another..." (John 13:35). See also Romans 13:8, 1 Peter 1:22, 1 Peter 4:8, and John 4:12.

With your help Lord, I will show love to

_______________ by ________________________________

____

2. Pray for Them

"First, I urge that entreaties and prayers and petitions and thanksgivings be made on behalf of all men..."- (1 Timothy 2:1). See also James 5:16.

Father, I pray for ______________________________ that

____.

3. Desire the Best for Them

"See to it that no one repays another with evil for evil, but always seek after that which is good for one another and for all men"- (1 Thessalonians 5:15).

The best thing I could desire for _________________ would be

____.

4. Praise God for Them (and not like the Pharisees did in Luke 18:11!)

"*...always giving thanks for all things* (and all people made in the image of God) *in the name of our Lord Jesus Christ to God, even the Father...*" (Ephesians 5:20).

Father, I thank you for ____________________ and praise you

in Jesus name for ______________________________________

5. Do not Judge Them

"Therefore let us not judge one another anymore, but rather determine this—not to put an obstacle or a stumbling block in a brother's way" (Romans 14:13). See also Matthew 7:1 and Romans 12:19.

Father, I admit I judged ___________ about _______________

________________________________. Help him to be willing to

forgive me when I confess it to him.

6. Be at Peace with Them

"...Pursue peace with all men, and the sanctification without which no one will see the Lord" (Hebrews 12:14). See also Romans 12:18 and Romans 14:19.

I can now show that I am at peace with ________________ by

____

____.

7. Forgive Them

"So, as those who have been chosen of God, holy and beloved, put on a heart of compassion, kindness, humility, gentleness and patience; bearing with one another, and forgiving each other, whoever has a complaint against anyone; just as the Lord forgave you, so also should you" (Colossians 3:12-13). See also Ephesians 4:32.

Father, I forgive ______________________________

for ______________________________________

8. Accept Them

"Therefore, accept one another, just as Christ also accepted us to the glory of God" (Romans 15:7).

Father, I know that I do not accept ____________________.

But, with your help, I am going to prove that I accept ________

by ______________________________________.

External Responsibilities of Action

9. Avoid Offending Them

"It is good not to eat meat or to drink wine, or to do anything by which your brother stumbles" (Romans 14:21).

Lord, I will no longer ______________________ so that I

do not offend ________________________________.

10. Show Respect to Them

"Never pay back evil for evil to anyone. Respect what is right in the sight of all men" (Romans 12:17).

I will show respect to ______________________________

by____.

11. Honor Them

"Honor all men..." (1 Peter 2:17). See also Romans 12:10 and 13:7.

Lord, I could honor ______________________________ by

____.

12. Be Humble with Them

"...all of you clothe yourself with humility towards one another" (1 Peter 5:5).

Heavenly Father, you hate pride. I have been proud in my relations with ______________________________.

By Your grace and with Your help, I will humble myself, go to ______________________________ and ask

him____

____.

13. Speak Positively about Them

"Do not speak against one another..." (James 4:11). See also James 5:9.

The most positive things I can say about _________ are that he

____.

14. Be Kind/Gentle with Them

"The Lord's servant must not be quarrelsome but *__be kind to all__*, *able to teach...patient when wronged, with gentleness, correcting those who are in opposition"* (2 Timothy 2:24). See also Ephesians 4:32.

"Lord, I will be kind/gentle to ____________________________ by

____

____.

15. Do Good for Them

"So then while we have opportunity, let us *__do good to all men__* *and especially to those who are of the household of faith"* (Galatians 6:10).

If I were to ____ for

______________________________ I know it would be an example

of 'doing good for them.'

16. Serve Them

"...through love *__serve one another__*" (Galatians 5:13). See Ephesians 5:21.

I could put my love in action with ___________ and serve him by

____

17. Encourage Them

"But encourage one another day after day as long as it is called Today – lest any one of you be hardened by the deceitfulness of sin" (Hebrews 3:13).

With God's help I will encourage ____________________ by

____

____

18. Show Hospitality to Them

"Be hospitable to one another without complaint" (1 Peter 4:9).

Lord, arrange for __________________ to accept my invitation

to my home for ______________________________.

19. Be Honest With Them

"Do not lie to one another since you laid aside the old self" (Colossians 3:9). See also Ephesians 4:15; James 5:16.

Lord, help me to be honest with ________________________

by telling him __________________________________ in love.

20. Comfort Them

"Therefore comfort one another with these words" (1 Thessalonians 4:18). See Galatians 6:2.

By Your grace, Lord, help me comfort ____________________

by____

____

21. Counsel Them

"If a man is caught in any (sin) you who are spiritual restore such a one in a spirit of gentleness; looking to yourselves lest you too be tempted" (Galatians 6:1).

Lord, I believe You are asking me to try, with Your help and grace

to counsel ____ by

____

22. Teach Them

"...with all wisdom teaching and admonishing <u>one another</u>..." – (Colossians 3:16). See Romans 15:14.

Heavenly Father, with your grace I would like to teach __________

the following truths from Your Word, the Holy Bible: __________

____

APPENDIX B

Who Are the Pharisees Today?

The primary and constant external threat to the earthly ministry of Jesus Christ was a small group of men called the Pharisees. These *separated ones* were a small but highly visible minority group. Sources suggest perhaps 6,000 in total during the years Christ taught His disciples.

To the Pharisee, the Torah (Law) was not only the law but also the instruction for daily life. They believed the Babylonian exile was due to the Jewish people failing to keep the Torah. These men were the teachers of the Law. They met, studied and interpreted situations not mentioned in scripture. Their majority decision was binding on the people. Hence their need to shadow Jesus constantly to make certain He was not teaching the people false views. The Pharisees' position of authority and respect as *Torah scholars* would be threatened by anyone who *spoke with authority*[233] but was not one of them!

Luke vividly describes the Pharisees (who were called "*Teacher*"). [234] They loved to...

...walk around
[*visibility*];
...in flowing robes
[*ego-status*];
...be greeted in the marketplace
[*prestige*];
...have the most important seats at meetings
[*power*];
...and the places of honor at banquets
[*honor*].

[233] Mark 1:27; Luke 4:32; and Luke 4:36

[234] Luke 20:45-47

John the Baptist scraped the Pharisee's theological scales by calling them a *"brood of vipers"* [235]" They were a little *miffed* to say the least. *"We have Abraham as our Father…"* [236] was their pious reply. John warns the Pharisees that *"out of these stones God can raise children of Abraham,"* so beware Pharisees. He then reminds them "*every tree that does not bear good fruit is cut down and thrown into the fire."* [237]

Let's *take a walk* through the Book of Matthew, written to the Jews, to meet this mysterious group of men and see what we can learn to improve our service for Jesus Christ.

Characteristics of the *Separated Ones (aka Pharisees)*

1. Pharisees are Strict. Pharisees observed every Old Testament law. Before his conversion, the Apostle Paul was Saul of Tarsus. He shared his family background by saying, *"I lived as a Pharisee, according to the strictest sect of our religion."* [238]

2. Pharisees are Legalistic. Little joy. Life was Law. Law was Life. There were some 613 laws in the Torah. The Pharisees added *"the traditions of the elders…"* (e.g. washing hands before eating). [239] To them, one's actions were more important than one's relationships. Compare this with what the prophet Micah writes: "*And what does the Lord require of you but to do justice, to love kindness, and to walk humbly with your God?"* [240]

Even after accepting salvation by grace through faith in Jesus of Nazareth as their personal Messiah, some Pharisees had a long, hard struggle to be free of past legalism. Some (in Acts 15:5)

---

[235] Matthew 3:7 -- But when he saw many of the Pharisees and Sadducees coming for baptism, he said to them, "You brood of vipers, who warned you to flee from the wrath to come?

[236] John 8:39

[237] Matthew 3:10

[238] Acts 26:5

[239] Mark 7:3 and 5

[240] Micah 6:8

argued at the Jerusalem Council *"it is necessary to circumcise* [new Gentile converts] *and to direct them to observe the Law of Moses."* This view generated an exhaustive debate over what additional requirements should be put on Gentile Christians after they received Christ by faith as their Savior. Fortunately for all Gentile men, "legalism" was overruled by "liberty." Peter (himself a Jew) helped the Pharisees see that they should lay no greater burden than a few agreed essentials, e.g. *"abstain from fornication."* [241] A leader today who wants to add anything to your faith in Jesus Christ (according to Ephesians 2:8 and 9) is in all likelihood a Pharisee.

But, you ask, "How can anyone add anything to faith to become a follower of Jesus Christ?" Let's consider this question: "Could Jesus join my church? I know the requirements for joining a Church are often stronger – and stricter – than the requirements for salvation. That is why we ask:

- **Could Christ join your Church if He was a different color or race, or spoke with an accent?** The truth is that Jesus was brown-skinned according to the color of His family descendants in Israel at the time
- **Could Christ join your Church if He drank wine?** The accusation that he was *"a gluttonous man and a drunkard"* did not come from him eating oatmeal cookies and drinking warm goat's milk in the homes of "*tax-gatherers and sinners."*
- **Could Christ join your Church if He had no steady income? Home? Money?** He said, *"The foxes have holes, and the birds of the air have nests, but the Son of Man has nowhere to lay His head."* [242] How could someone with His "instability" and limited income help pay off the church mortgage?
- **Could Christ join your Church if He studied from His Aramaic Bible instead of your approved English translation?** Some churches would deny membership to anyone

[241] Acts 15:28-29

[242] Matthew 8:20

who did not read from their approved version or accepted their favorite additional referenced authors.

- **Could Christ join your Church if He was *"filled with the Holy Spirit"* but did NOT speak in tongues?** Some churches pride themselves on having the power of the Holy Spirit, whom Jesus sent to Earth as *"the Comforter,"* but claim "speaking in tongues" is the *prima facie* evidence for "being saved" and as a shibboleth for Church membership! At no time did Jesus ever "speak in tongues" even though He was "baptized by the Holy Spirit" at the Jordan River. [243]
- **Could Christ join your Church if He showed His emotions?** Would you want a man in your membership who knew how to weep at the funeral of a friend; cry over the lost condition of a city of people who were refusing Him as their Savior; got so angry He cleaned out all secondary activities from His "House of Prayer." Would you desire to have this Man in your church?
- **Could Christ join your Church if He didn't worship Mary?** Scripture never records Mary as anything more than an earthly parent of Jesus. Jesus never worshiped Mary. In fact, when His disciples told Him, "Behold, Your mother and Your brothers are standing outside seeking to speak to You…" He answered, "Who is My mother and who are My brothers?" Then He adds, "…whoever shall do the will of My Father who is in heaven; he is My brother and sister and mother." Hardly the kind of response to gain acceptance into many churches today!
- **Could Christ join your Church if He helped meet the *social needs* of people?** Christ was a constant doer of "good works." He related to people and their needs. He ate in their homes. He attended their weddings. He cried at their funerals. He shared in their joy and their sorrow. He ministered to their poor health. He fed those who were hungry.
- **Could Christ join your Church if He missed Sunday Services to help people?** Would Christ dutifully attend every meeting? Where would He be if He had to choose between "the work of His Father" and "the work of the

[243] Matthew 3:16

church"? What's the "Pharisaical-Barometrical-Reading" in your church?

3. Pharisees are Self-Righteous. Jesus knew this fact when He told the people: *"unless your righteousness surpasses that of the scribes and Pharisees, you will not enter the kingdom of heaven."* [244] And Luke records a quick insight into the lifestyle of the Pharisees:

- **They are proud.** *"The Pharisee stood and was praying thus to himself, 'God, I thank Thee that I am not like other people: swindlers, unjust, adulterers…'"* In their mind, they were super-spiritual in their actions and behavior. Spiritual, but arrogant!
- **They are devout.** *"I fast twice a week; I pay tithes of all that I get."* Wow. They dressed righteously. They looked righteous. They acted righteously. They talked righteously. They prayed righteously. How much better could a man get than all this evidence of true spirituality? Some pastor's dream of a church filled with men who "tithe-fast-pray"!

4. Pharisees are Outwardly Moral. The Apostle Paul admits that his life as a Pharisee was "blameless." He was *"circumcised the eighth day, of the nation of Israel, of the tribe of Benjamin, a Hebrew of Hebrews, as to the law a Pharisee; as to zeal, a persecutor of the church; as to the righteousness which is in the Law, found blameless."* [245] What a man. What a life. But he admits that compared to *"knowing Jesus Christ my Lord…"* [246] all of these outwardly moral actions were "rubbish" (or whatever word your culture may choose to use!). Anyone who seeks to gain salvation and get to Heaven on their good works apart from accepting the shed blood of Jesus Christ as the payment for their sins is at best deceived and at worst a Pharisee.

[244] Matthew 5:20

[245] Philippians 3:5-6

[246] Philippians 3:8

5. Pharisees are Very Critical. Whenever the Holy Spirit is at work, there will be some criticism. After Jesus had cast out a demon, the Pharisees were quick to criticize and say: *"He casts out demons by the ruler of demons..."* [247] Whoa. Hold on. Let God be the Judge. Let God take the vengeance. God will defend His Church, His Body, and His Bride. Even today we can experience attacks of hostility just by mentioning a person's name that others do not like. Hold on. Let's let God be the Judge.

6. Pharisees are Sign-Seekers. "*Teacher, we want to see a sign from You...*" [248] The Pharisees heard what Jesus said. They witnessed His abilities to do miracles. But, just to be certain that He was the Messiah they wanted *a sign.* It does not say what would have satisfied them as a sign but think about today. We do the same thing. We have the Bible. We have the Church. We have the power of the Holy Spirit living within us upon salvation. But still, some say: "Give us a sign, and then we will believe." Graciously tell these sign-seeking Pharisee friends: God is at work. Jesus is alive. The Bible is real. We have the gift of the Holy Spirit. Jesus has given us all power and all authority to go and make disciples. Let's stop demanding God to do something our way to prove something we already by faith believe!

7. Pharisees are Tradition Worshippers. They worry about tradition and rituals and regulations more than people, relationships, and growth. A potentially divisive issue in many churches could be called "worship styles" especially as it relates to music. While music is but one aspect of worship, it has transitioned in many churches from *soft a cappella harmony* to pump organs to electric organs to guitars to drums to electric guitars to *harsh amplified rhythm.* New songs are sometimes a challenge for those who worship their traditional hymns. Christ warned us to *"beware the leaven of the Pharisees."* [249] One *puffed-up* Pharisee in a church can affect an entire congregation by their teaching.

---

[247] Matthew 9:34

[248] Matthew 12:38

[249] Matthew 16:5

8. Pharisees are Manipulative. They play what could be called theological gymnastics and ask diversionary questions. Goal: to keep the heat of God's word from penetrating their thin, self-righteous skin. Jesus penetrated their mind, heart and spirit with His gracious responses to their trick questions on a series of sensitive topics like divorce: *"Is it lawful for a man to divorce his wife for any cause at all?"*; taxes: *"Is it lawful to give a poll-tax to Caesar, or not?* And: *"which is the great commandment in the Law?"* [250] Notice the repetition of the phrase *"Is it lawful?"* Pharisees betray their legalistic and manipulative spirit in the questions they ask.

Pharisees are beginning to sound like *Spiritual Sociopaths*. Psychopaths tend to be violent. Sociopaths tend to be manipulative. Most sociopaths display some of the following characteristics:

- ***Egocentric***: They are in love with themselves. People begin to whisper: "I don't feel comfortable around him" or "I do not trust her." A number sort of puff under their breath and say things like: "I know things about this person, but no one would ever believe me..."
- ***Do not follow the counsel of others***: They ask for and then ignore the advice. Sociopath A would constantly ask his friends, "What do you think I should do/say?" – listen to their counsel and do something entirely different.
- ***Have no or low self-esteem*** causing them to manipulate anyone who may expose them. They have the selfish belief that everything must revolve around their gratification - events, schedules and free time.
- ***Deceive themselves*** into thinking they are OK. One community was shocked to have a public official arrested and charged with owning and producing child pornography. His peers rated him as an exemplary professional. However, he had three lives:

  A public life as a professional
  A private life as a member of the gay community
  A secret life as a child-abusing pornographic photographer.

[250] Matthew 19:3; 22:15 and 22:36

- ***Do not think of the consequences of their actions,*** only how they can make themselves look good.
- ***Have superficial charm*** with a trail of exploited, used and discarded people in their past.
- ***Think they are poor, innocent, rejected, and lonely.***
- ***Confess if caught only if it helps their 'image.'*** Rarely or never say: "I have sinned" or "I was wrong" or "Forgive me" or experience any "broken spirit...or a broken and contrite heart" (Psalm 51:17). Sociopath B did not stop having extramarital affairs until one of the women involved went public with her story. This man's wife and others had heard his deceptive cover up story over and over: "I have confessed, God has forgiven, it will never happen again," but it did – many more times! They show little remorse.
- ***Always right in their own eyes and constantly rationalize***: "You misunderstood" or "It was a mistake." Sociopath C never dealt with his years of adultery because he deceived himself by saying, "I always wore a condom, so it was not true adultery." After being photographed with a prostitute he publicly confessed his sin – and did it again.
- ***Make completely contradictory statements*** to protect themselves regardless of the outcome.
- ***Jealous: Tend to be jealous and insecure*** around those they perceive as "better" than themselves.
- ***Create confusion*** as a double-minded person. Like to say: "Oh, *you* must have misunderstood me…I didn't mean that…"
- ***Aggressive: Extremely competitive and must win.*** Must have their way or remove the opposition.
- ***Lack discernment:*** Show partiality. Have an unapproachable "blind spot."
- ***Seek Loyalty: Reward loyalty above performance. Like weak "yes men"*** while shredding relationships with people, they perceive to be "strong people."
- ***Break Relationships: Lack the ability to resolve conflict or restore relationships with people they have offended*** – it is easier to write them off, move on, and start over.
- ***Condescending: Male sociopaths have an inappropriate condescending attitude towards women.*** Sociopath D

had had an affair with his secretary that had been covered up for years.

- ***Flatter: Excessive flattery of others*** is a form of hatred, e.g. when men look at women with contempt and arrogance and make them feel like clothes racks, sex objects or used toys. Such men are very plastic and artificial in their relationships – some women call them "sleazy."
- ***Controllers: Love to control, dominate and belittle people,*** and are masters of one-upmanship, verbal put-downs, and abuse.
- ***Abusive: Take the offensive verbally – or spiritually. Sociopaths harm people perceived to be threats.*** They accuse them of "being ambitious"; "not being a team player"; "lacking loyalty to them"; "showing a lack of good judgment and deference." They will say you are: "not trusted"; "not focused"; "not being effective"; "not a compatible fit"; "being black or white" and "lacking flexibility."
- ***Controllers: Sociopaths must be in control.*** They dominate a conversation by controlling the topic, by standing to gain superiority, by inappropriate interruptions, humor, or merely staring at the speaker to intimidate.
- ***Manipulative: Use humor and personal charm to manipulate.*** They turn their greatest personal assets into major weaknesses.
- ***Unaccountable: Are virtually unaccountable for their time, money or actions***
- ***Psychic Numbing: Guilty of psychic numbing.*** "Everything is under control, and I am in control, 'Trust me'..." – to question them is to lack trust. How do you photograph a Sociopath sneaking into hotel rooms with envy or ego, selfish ambition, image, self-glorification, empire building, partiality, unapproachability, hypocrisy or earthly wisdom? The answer is we can't. Therein lies a factor in the Sociopath's continued survival and success – until he is discovered.

9. Pharisees are Lovers of Money [251] *"Now the Pharisees, who were lovers of money, were listening…and scoffing at Him."* Christ must have known there were Pharisees within earshot when He said, *"No man can serve two masters…You cannot serve God and mammon* (riches)." Since Scripture says, *"The love of money is the root of all sorts of evil"* [252] the Pharisees were, in essence, evil men. Their hatred of Jesus came from a fear of what He was seeing in them.

Jesus reveals some further insights into their character. [253]

- **They are hypocrites** – *"They say things and do not do them."*
- **They are legalists** – *"They put heavy loads (laws) on men's back's backs, yet do not help them…"*
- **They are proud** – *"They do all their deeds to be noticed by men…"*

Jesus then pronounced eight "woes" or curses against the Pharisees. Ouch. Does this sound familiar today?

Woe #1 – (v.13) *"hypocrites…you shut off the kingdom of heaven from men."*
Do we call ourselves Christians and cause others to want nothing to do with Christianity?

Woe #2 – (v.14) *"you devour widows' houses…and make long prayers."*
Do we take money from widows, but neglect to visit them and minister to their needs?

Woe #3 – (v.15) *"you travel…to make one proselyte (and) make him…a son of hell…"*
Do we burden new converts with our legalistic "heavies" to make them like us?

Woe #4 – (v.16) (You say) *"Whoever swears by the temple, that is nothing; but whoever swears by the gold of the temple, he is obligated."*

[251] Luke 16:14

[252] 1 Timothy 6:10

[253] Matthew 23 – entire chapter

Do we stay away from movies – yet watch pornography at home? Do we avoid committing adultery – but undress every woman we meet with our eyes?

Woe #5 – (v.23) *"...you tithe on mint and dill...and have neglected... justice and mercy and faithfulness."*
Do we "pick" at small things, yet ignore important matters? Jesus said the Pharisees *"strain at a gnat, and swallow a camel"* – (v.24).

Woe #6 – (v.25) *"...you clean the outside of the cup...but inside... are full of self-indulgence."*
Do we have an attitude of entitlement, thinking we deserve a reward because we work so hard for Jesus?

Woe #7 – (v.27) *"...you are like whitewashed tombs...appear beautiful...full of dead men's bones and uncleanness."*
Do we appear righteous but in reality are full of hypocrisy and lawlessness?

Woe #8 – (v.29) *"...you build the tombs of the prophets...and say, 'If we had been living...we would not have been partners with them in shedding the blood of the prophets.'"*
Do we judge others – even historical figures – and end up being the victim of our own judgment?

All Jesus can say after proclaiming eight woes is to condemn the Pharisees: *"You serpents, you brood of vipers (snakes), how shall you escape the sentence of hell?"* (v. 33). Could this be why Jesus told His disciples to be *"wise as a serpent"* [like the Pharisees] but be *"harmless as a dove"* [as His disciples]?[254]

Let me suggest this is a most appropriate time to examine Pharisees at the end of a study of the *Roles of Men*. Pharisees were members of a very strict "MEN ONLY" religious club. But instead of encouraging one another to *"love and good deeds"* [255] they became a legalistic, self-righteous group who imposed their views on everyone else without grace, mercy or justice.

---

[254] Matthew 10:16

[255] Hebrews 10:24

Scripture tells us how to deal with these Pharisees in our life. Do not gossip about them. Do not slander them in public. Do not rebuke them. Instead, go to the individual alone. Tell him his biblical error as Matthew 18:15 says to do. If he hears you, you have won a brother. If he does not hear you, take two or three others as witnesses, so every word is established. If he does not hear them, tell it to the church. And if he refuses to hear the church, let him be to you as a heathen and a publican.

At all times we must love Pharisees and pray for them. One of the boldest, most zealous Christians in Church history was at one time a Pharisee – Saul of Tarsus, who became the Apostle Paul.

Appendix C

SPIRITUAL-ISSUES-QUADRANT DO WE DISCUSS-DEFER-DEBATE-DIE?	
DISCUSS ***OPEN-MINDED POSITION*** • Does Christ return before, during or after a "Tribulation"? (Sure hoping before but ☺) • Which English Bible is most accurate? • Inter-racial Marriages? • Imbibing? • Clapping? • Raising Hands in Worship? • Mode of Baptism (Favor Immersion) • Elder Leadership (Elders: *"husband of one wife"*)	**DIE** ***INFLEXIBILE*** ***NEVER CHANGE MY VIEW*** • Jesus Christ is Risen from the dead. • Jesus is ALIVE! • Salvation is by Grace through Faith in Jesus Christ. Period! • The Bible is the Infallible Word of God.
DEFER ***FLEXIBILE VIEW*** ***MAY CHANGE MY VIEW*** • What day do we worship? (Sat? Sun?) • Will there be dogs in Heaven? (I am not "dogmatic" on this one ☺)	**DEBATE** ***CLOSED-MINDED POSITION*** • Baptism = Sign of Obedience • Abortion = Murder • Divorce = Hardness of Heart • Gambling = Wasted Resources • Gay lifestyle = Abomination to God's Creation of Male and Female

At the risk of being misunderstood, God is pro-choice. God allows us to make choices. He began with two trees in the Garden of Eden and permitted Adam and Eve to **choose** whether they would obey. Joshua told the Children of Israel, "***choose** for yourselves today whom you will serve: whether the gods which your fathers served which were beyond the River, or the gods of the Amorites in whose land you are living; but as for **me and my house**, we will serve the Lord."* I do not want to fight issues and then change my mind 10 years later. Let's agree to choose our issues based on lifelong scriptural principles.

With God's help, we can win men to Christ, and encourage them, by our lifestyle, to ***choose*** to become *"Men Alive Unto God"* through faith in Jesus Christ. Amen.

Thanks

The scariest moment of my writing career is to watch a file leave my computer knowing it will soon return as a book with my name on it as the author. Why scary? A book is somewhat permanent. The words typed, like dollars spent, cannot be retrieved. Sure, there can be addendums and 2nd Editions, but from this moment forward, I'm accountable for each word – and any errors – in this book. That's a wee bit scary!

So, let me thank some people who have helped me over the years to get this to the point where I finally hit "send the file."

- Rita. Most wise husbands, who write books, thank their wife. But this is more than being wise! Saying thanks to Rita is a sheer delight after 50 years of receiving her grace, forgiveness, and insights with understanding. Rita's wit, wisdom, and worldview are beyond the norm. She's my lifelong Angel! Thanks m'love.
- Tze Lin for letting his wife May Ong invest the extra time to graciously and efficiently edit the text! Thanks, May!
- Laird Salkeld, who took sketches from me and turned them into visuals for you! Thanks Laird.
- Craig Murdoch, Chairman of Go Teach Global. More than a Scottish-beard with a dry-sense of humor, Craig is a first-rate advisor and trusted friend. Thanks, Craig!

Epilogue

Rev. Paul Johnson, a longstanding friend, was Executive-Director of Open Doors Canada. He began his ministry with ODC in 1988. On Sep 16, 2016, at 6:29 PM, I sent an email to Paul (and our mutual "kindred spirit" OD brother Paul Estabrooks) outlining what had recently happened in my world. On Sep 17, 2016, at 5:18 AM, Paul (PJ) Johnson wrote a response to me (below). The next week, on the afternoon of Sep 24, 2016, PJ was riding a friend's motorcycle in the foothills of the Rocky Mountains outside Calgary, Alberta with a group of brothers from the CMA (Christian Motorcycle Association). The sky was blue. The road was dry. On a slow turn on the paved highway, PJ had a major heart attack, went onto the grass, over the handlebars, and into Heaven! The following email is the longest, most passionate and final email from my brother just days before he met our Lord. With permission from his family, I share portions with you for your encouragement: the last words from a faithful Disciple of Jesus Christ,

---

Jim,

Is anyone seeing the terror of these days? Is there even a genuine care or are we like the children of Israel? We are the sons of Abraham, Isaac, and Jacob but we have forgotten our Heavenly Father's calling, purposes and most of all our guardianship to steward our lives in a manner as to fulfill doing the will of the Father.

I believe the front line of our Enemy has been turned up as an attempt to disallow continued growth, harmony, and effectiveness. He has succeeded in altering our vision from steadfastly being on Him to being focused on us and the things of this world.

The systematic attack is now far too evident on far too many fronts in too many churches, ministries and families bringing disunity, infighting, separation, and dishonor. The fight for "earthly" control has become an epidemic.

Father help us to draw our spiritual line in the sand. Help us gain our strength afresh from the living water. Help us to seek your face, to see, hear and know you and your ways. Assist us Lord as watchmen to not only see the danger but also give us the ability to have a clarion call to those you have entrusted for us to stand watch.

Lord steady our hearts, clear our minds and empower us to seek and do your will. Father our protector our strength our all in all we surrender to who is was and always will be. Father, we bow down and say the battle is the Lord's and Father we pray you will assist us to stand in the gap.

Father open our eyes to see, our ears to hear and our mouths to speak. Make our crooked ways straight, our mountains laid low and our valleys an experience of still waters and green pasture. Be still my heart, be still my spirit, be refreshed, my soul. Bind the broken heart and pour out your Alabaster upon wounds. Renew a right spirit within me oh Lord.

Father in the name of Jesus Christ of Nazareth, son of the living God we ask for this spirit of division, destruction, and scattering of the sheep be broken and replaced with the heartbeat of our living Father. Get behind us Satan in the name of the Lord. Spirit of division, destruction, and deception be broken. Lead us not into temptation but deliver us from evil.

Jim, blow the trumpet, sound the alarm. Watchman, cry out in the name of God and warn the people. Bind up the broken hearted. See the massive Alabaster box God has given us for the healing of a nation and for nations to be blessed as it is restored and renewed.

I know my plans for you, says the Lord to do good and not evil, to enlarge your influence and your impact to have the later days to be even greater than the former.

Oh God have your way with us. Shine brightly through these earthen vessels oh Lord. Grant us a Godly heart and assist us to fulfill the warrior commission you have issued.

Jim, you are loved, honored and have been given some incredible skills by your Heavenly Father. You are one called to stand in the gap. Thank you for sharing this pain, this incredible broken heart, for the insight of the battle and for seeing this thing for what it is. Thank you that in the midst of being led by God you have spoken life into the heart of a larger issue-taking place in the body of Christ in our nation.

Father help us to hear and respond. Create in us a clean heart oh God but even more so may we be used to intercede and be drawn closer to you. I trust you will receive this as not just a rambling of Paul Johnson but see here a beginning of healing on more fronts then we can imagine. See here inside of this oil being poured out on hearts and the beginning of a solution.

Bless you, my brother. Terrorism may attempt to bring us down, but an everlasting Heavenly Father has an antidote. Thank you for bringing a place of healing to this heart, a greater hope, a resolve to receive from the Father a heavenly touch. Shall we be bold enough to ask God to bring us into a three-strand cord, which cannot be broken? Can we believe together that seeking is a solution and that in the answer God will be glorified?

Bless you, brothers,

Paul

One week later, PJ met our Lord, face-to-face – a Man Alive Unto God!